ADMINISTRATIVE TRIBUNALS

A Legal Handbook

Lisa Braverman

CANADA LAW BOOK INC.
240 Edward St., Aurora, Ontario, L4G 3S9

The paper used in this publication meets the minimum requirements of American National Standards for Information Sciences – Permanence of Paper for Printed Library Materials, ANSI Z39.48-1992.

National Library of Canada Cataloguing in Publication Data

Braverman, Lisa, 1968-
    Administrative tribunals : a legal handbook

Includes bibliographical references and index.
ISBN 0-88804-355-4

    1. Administrative courts—Canada. 2. Administrative law --
Canada. I. Title.

KE5029.B73 2001   342.71'0664   C2001-903506-3

Foreword

A dministrative tribunals are called upon to make decisions in areas of the law as diverse as copyright and social assistance, securities and land use planning, and immigration and the environment. More significantly, their decisions impact countless citizens in fundamental ways in their daily lives. Administrative law contains the legal principles and precepts within which all administrative tribunals operate.

In this book, Lisa Braverman has sought to empower tribunal members who must make critical decisions daily. She provides them not only with a comprehensive and accessible introduction to the law, but also with numerous practical tips for writing decisions, conducting hearings and making determinations as to credibility.

Perhaps, the most important contribution of this book is that it provides decision-makers both with a broader understanding of their role and that of administrative tribunals generally in the Canadian legal system, and with a set of practical tools to enable them to play their role well. Thus, while the author provides her readers with a much needed introduction to legal vocabulary, the legal history of some fundamental concepts, such as procedural fairness, she also offers techniques for simple and effective writing tailored to the administrative context.

Ms. Braverman has succeeded in creating in one volume a powerful and instructive guide for decision-makers. I have no doubt that agencies will find this book to be an enormously rich resource. Members of the administrative justice community are in her debt. I am delighted to be able to recommend the book with enthusiasm.

November, 2001   The Honourable John Maxwell Evans
                                            Federal Court of Canada

Preface

Administrative tribunals[1] are a very important part of Canadian government because of the variety of functions they perform, which include providing advice, developing policy and making decisions. Moreover, in performing all of these functions, but particularly the decision-making function, these tribunals have a profound impact on the lives of all Canadians. Given the fact that very large numbers of people are affected, some administrative tribunals which act as decision-makers have had a greater influence on Canadians than the courts.

Staff and members of administrative tribunals come from many different backgrounds with different education and work experience. As a result, it is very important to ensure that they are aware of and understand the legal principles for conducting the day-to-day work of the administrative tribunals and for making their decisions in a fair manner. For example, how can a member of an administrative tribunal conduct or even take part in a hearing if he or she does not even know the reason why a hearing is required in the first place.

Many administrative tribunals conduct training for their new members. For the training to be effective, consistency in the quality, content and length of the training is important, and the training should be provided by a variety of different individuals including lawyers and senior members of the administrative tribunal. In addition, preparing appropriate introductory or background written materials for staff and new members of administrative tribunals ensures that consistent, basic and universal training is being provided. The information in this handbook has been developed to address this by beginning with an introduction to law in general and providing background material on such things as the development of administrative law and the reasons for creating administrative tribunals.

The main purpose of this handbook is to provide staff and members of administrative tribunals with a simplified but comprehensive introduction to administrative law so that you are able to know your responsibilities and perform your

---

[1] I use the word "tribunal" or "tribunals" throughout this handbook; however, this information also applies to agencies, boards and commissions.

required tasks correctly and effectively. Interestingly, a study was conducted on the training for administrative tribunal members in Canada and it discovered that administrative law, considered essential by 58% and quite important by 33% of the respondents to the study, was provided as part of the training only 60% of the time.[2]

---

[2] D. Labelle, "Report on the Study on Training for Administrative Tribunal Members in Canada" (1992-1993), 6 C.J.A.L.P. 251, at pp. 255-6.

Acknowledgments

I want to thank the current and past partners and staff of Steinecke Maciura LeBlanc for their advice, support and encouragement in writing this book. I want to especially thank Richard Steinecke for inspiring me to write this book and for his insightful comments in the course of reviewing the manuscript. I also want to thank Elizabeth Ackney for editing and formatting the manuscript.

It is also extremely important that I thank my family and friends. Without their advice, support and encouragement, I would never have been able to write and ultimately finish this book. My parents Bill and Marilyn, my brother Ian, and my sisters Jenn and Hayley, require a very special thank you for their patience and understanding especially regarding the time that I needed to devote to writing this book.

Lisa Braverman
August, 2001

Table of Contents

1

Introduction to Law

(1) What is Law?

"What is Law?" appears to be a straightforward question, yet, it does not have a clear and simple answer. Through the years, many different answers have been given:

> "Law presents itself primarily and essentially as a system of rigid rules."
>
> Sir John Salmond
> 19th century English legal scholar

> "Law is the highest reason, implanted in Nature, which commands what ought to be done and forbids the opposite."
>
> Cicero
> ancient Roman politician

> "Law is a form of order, and good law must necessarily mean good order."
>
> Aristotle
> ancient Greek philosopher

> "Law is the crystallization of the habit and thought of society."
>
> Woodrow Wilson
> 20th century American President

To begin to find out what law is, the main components that make up a legal system need to be reviewed. It is also useful to identify the basic functions of a legal system. Finally, it is important to examine the theories that have been developed to explain the nature of law.

(2) Components of Law

When people think about the legal system, they think about the two most commonly known components of law — a system of rules or laws *and* the legal officials and institutions that create, enforce and interpret those rules. There is also a third component — the legal values that are regarded as important by society.

(a) Legal rules

It is generally accepted that the law consists of a system of rules, which establish a person's rights and duties. Baseball is another example of a system of rules. However, if a player did not follow all of these rules during the course of a baseball game, he or she would not be charged with a criminal offence and face a possible jail sentence. In fact, there may be no punishment for breaking any of the rules of the game. This example illustrates that there is an important difference between laws and other types of rules because the state will only enforce the rules and impose punishment for breaking rules when a legally authorized body passes these rules. The *Highway Traffic Act*,[1] the *Young Offenders Act*[2] and the *Canadian Charter of Rights and Freedoms*[3] are examples of legal rules.

A common but false view of laws is that they only restrict a person's freedom. While all legal rules direct or guide a person's behaviour, it is wrong to regard them solely as limits placed on a person's life. In fact, many laws allow people to do things that could not be done without these laws. For example, laws create and maintain institutions to provide public services such as schools, universities, hospitals and airports.

Given the fact that the law is not only a series of restrictions or limits but also offers benefits or rights, laws can be looked at according to a cost/benefit analysis. This means that every restriction or limit on an activity may mean a corresponding benefit or right. As a result, people prefer laws where the costs of the restrictions or limits are small compared to the benefits that the laws provide.

(b) Legal institutions

Legal institutions and the officials who work in these institutions are a very important component of the law. This is because legal rules must come from somewhere and they will not be able to function effectively on their own. To function effectively and efficiently, any system of laws requires three elements: procedures to make rules, methods of implementing and enforcing those rules, and ways for deciding what these rules require in specific situations. These three features can also be referred to as the legislative, executive and judicial functions of a legal system.

The legislative function refers to the procedures for making rules. The Latin root of the word "legislation" means "the bringing or proposing of a law". The federal Parliament and the provincial legislatures are the main lawmaking authorities of the Canadian legal system.

---

[1] R.S.O. 1990, c. H.8.
[2] R.S.C. 1985, c. Y-1.
[3] Part I of the *Constitution Act, 1982*, being Schedule B of the *Canada Act 1982* (U.K.), 1982, c. 11.

The executive function involves putting the law into effect. The word "executive" comes from the verb "to execute" which means "to carry out" or "to implement". The federal and provincial Cabinets, Ministers, civil servants working in the government ministries, many administrative tribunals and Crown corporations are responsible for implementing the law. The law enforcement officials such as the Royal Canadian Mounted Police, the provincial or municipal police and prison guards are also an important part of the executive branch of the Canadian legal system.

The judicial function involves making decisions about how the law applies in specific situations. The Latin root of the word "judge" means "to declare the law". The courts and administrative tribunals have the main responsibility for interpreting and applying the law in specific situations.

Even though it is useful to divide legal institutions into these three categories, there is a lot of overlap in the functions of specific institutions. For example, the same institution often performs more than one function such as an administrative tribunal (*i.e.*, the Canadian Radio-television and Telecommunications Commission) and sometimes there is only a small difference between making, implementing and applying the law.

(c) Legal values

Every law promotes certain values and the legal system in general represents the set of values that are regarded as important by society. For example, the value that society puts on complying with agreements is reflected in the law of contracts or the importance of individual rights and freedoms is reflected in the *Canadian Charter of Rights and Freedoms* (the "Charter").

There are two main reasons why it is important to have an understanding of the values reflected by the laws. First, a person's understanding of law is incomplete unless he or she can see the purpose of the laws and the implications of promoting them. Second, as citizens, individuals should try to develop informed opinions about what laws we should have in place. Weighing the costs and the benefits of the different laws helps an individual develop an informed opinion. The benefits are the values that the law protects or promotes and the costs are the values that the law restricts.

(3) Functions of Law

In general, people are able to solve most of their problems without relying on rules or laws. However, as these problems become more complicated or when many people are involved, laws become necessary or even vital. Laws are necessary because they establish the rules governing human behaviour and interaction that are used by society to ensure it operates in a systematic and fair manner. A common misconception is that the only function of law, or the main function, is to prevent people from doing certain things. In reality the law has many other functions, regulating conduct in many different ways.

(a) Protects the public

One of the functions of the law is to protect members of the public. For example, criminal law prevents or prohibits certain criminal acts such as murder, assault, kidnapping, break and enter, fraud and theft. It also describes the penalties or punishments for breaking the law, such as fines or prison sentences.

(b) Establishes rights and duties

Another function of the law is to establish the rights and duties among individuals and between individuals and government. A right is something that a person is entitled to, while a duty is something that must be done. For example, labour law, also known as employment law, establishes the rights and duties between employers and employees, such as the right of employees to strike and the duty of employers to provide a safe working environment.

(c) Prevents or resolves disputes

An important function of the law is to provide a basis for preventing or resolving disputes. For example, contract law establishes the requirements for making legally binding agreements or contracts. When a person buys a new house, the terms are set out in the agreement of purchase and sale. This agreement will contain standard wording relying on the experience of the real estate agent in knowing what the courts will consider valid and enforceable. As a result, the real estate agent uses his or her knowledge and experience to prevent disputes. However, a dispute over the terms of the agreement may still occur. If the dispute cannot be resolved through discussion and negotiation, it may be necessary to go to court to get a judge to interpret the agreement. Consequently, the judge resolves the dispute.

(d) Gives remedies

The law also gives people remedies if their rights or freedoms have been breached or violated. A remedy is a legal measure for removing or correcting a wrong that has occurred. For example, human rights law protects people from many different kinds of discrimination and harassment. If an employer has sexually harassed an employee, the law lets the employee know what remedies are available and how to get them.

(e) Establishes government

The law establishes the structure of Canada's governments, distributes duties and powers to the three branches of government,[4] and describes the division of lawmaking authority between the federal and provincial governments.

---

[4] The three branches of government are: legislative, executive and judicial.

(f) Provides a guide for making laws

Finally, the law provides a guide for making new laws or changing existing laws. The federal Parliament and the provincial legislatures must comply with the rules that have been established to make new laws or change existing laws. This process will be discussed in more detail later in this chapter, under the heading "Creating and Changing the Law".

(4) Theories of Law

The major philosophies or theories to explain the nature of law are divided into three schools of thought. These are legal positivism, natural law and legal realism. Within each school of thought, there are different versions (there are also many others in addition to the ones mentioned here).

(a) Legal positivism

Positive law refers to laws that have been expressly laid down by a legally recognized authority. This is contrasted with natural law which consists of law not expressed by any legally recognized authority.

Legal positivism originated with English philosophers such as Thomas Hobbes, Jeremy Bentham and John Austin. Herbert Hart, an Oxford University philosopher, has developed the leading modern explanation of this theory of law.

The main characteristic of legal positivism is the rejection of any connection between law and morality. Instead, law can be explained by referring to the pre-existing rules expressed by legal authorities. This is often described by using the phrase "law as it is" which can be contrasted with the phrase "law as it should be". This means that a law may be unjust or have undesirable effects on society, but, this does not mean that the law is not legal. This has substantial implications for judges when they interpret and apply the law because legal positivism requires judges to determine whether the law has been applied impartially and not to consider the justice or fairness of their decision. Sir Thomas Taylor, former Chief Justice of Manitoba, applied this approach when he stated: "I am not here to dispense justice, I am here to dispose of this case according to the law. Whether this is or is not justice is a question for the legislature to determine."[5]

There are two versions of legal positivism, the "letter of the law" and the "spirit of the law". The "letter of the law" version is the more traditional approach and it means that the law should be applied according to the literal meaning of the words in the legislation. This version requires judges to assume that the legislators or lawmakers expressed exactly what they meant in the words used in the specific law. In contrast, the "spirit of the law" version requires that the purposes and values of the law must be considered when deciding the mean-

---

[5] Quoted in R. Case and D.J. Baum, *Thinking About Law: An Issues Approach*, 2nd ed. (Toronto: IPI Publishing Ltd., 1995), at p. 20. Sir Thomas Taylor was the Chief Justice of Manitoba from 1887 to 1899.

ing of the law. This version requires judges to focus on the intentions of the law-makers rather than on the literal meaning of the words used in the specific law.

(b) Natural law

Under natural law, morality regulates the way human beings are required to function. Natural law is considered by its supporters to be a "higher" law which is superior to all laws made by legally recognized authorities. In contrast to legal positivism, the main characteristic of natural law is the recognition that there is an essential connection between law and morality. However, this creates a big problem of identifying the content and scope of natural law since there is no clear set of moral principles to guide the determination of what is law.

Aristotle and his mentor, Plato, were considered to be the earliest natural law philosophers. Aristotle and Plato heavily influenced St. Thomas Aquinas, another early supporter of natural law. Similar to Aristotle, St. Thomas Aquinas strongly believed in the connection between law and reason. He stated: "an unjust and unreasonable law . . . is not law but a perversion of law".[6]

There are two versions of natural law, "popular morality" and "critical morality". "Popular morality" means that judges make decisions about what the law is by determining what is considered to be just by most people in the community. In other words, judges could review the results of public opinion surveys when making decisions about how the law should be applied. In contrast, the "critical morality" version means that judges make decisions about what the law is by determining what would be just, given the most reasonable view of the moral standards that is in use within the community. This version is different from the popular morality version because the morally reasonable decision may be critical of popular opinion and it also goes a step further by allowing for the fact that the majority of people in the community may be wrong.

(c) Legal realism

Legal realism criticizes the idea that the legal system is based on legal rules because its supporters believe that legal rules cannot determine the outcome of disputes. Legal realists do not believe that judges decide cases by applying the legal rules to the facts. Instead, legal realists stress the importance of the political, economic and social reality in understanding law and in making decisions. Realists are primarily concerned with "law in reality" because they believe that legal rules cannot and do not control the decisions of judges since many factors influence the decisions of judges including a judge's individual discretion.

In opposition to legal positivism and natural law, legal realism began in the United States at the end of the 19th century. Jerome Frank, a former United States Federal Court judge, is a well-known legal realist. He emphasized that judges make decisions based on hunches and intuition.

---

[6] *Ibid.*, at p. 21.

There are two distinct branches of legal realism, "sociological jurisprudence" and "legal realist". Supporters of the "sociological jurisprudence" branch believe that decisions by judges should be made based on realistic expectations about the effects of law on society. Supporters of this approach also believe that law can achieve its intended goals if judges are concerned about the social consequences of their decisions. For example, if women are going to receive employment equity, judges must look at the actual work environment to determine what kinds of decisions would lead to equality. Sociological jurisprudence developed as a result of the concern about the inadequacy of the "letter of the law" approach.

On the other hand, the "legal realist" branch looks at the effects of political and social factors on legal decisions. It looks at how the legal system actually operates in reality not how it is expected to operate. Legal realists believe that it is wrong to regard law as only a system of rules because they consider law to be what the judge decides to enforce based on an evaluation of a variety of factors. They believe judges make decisions based on their personalities and abilities, their political views, and their own views of their legal and moral obligations.

(5) Origins of Canadian Law

Originally, the Europeans, made up predominantly of English and French, were the largest group of settlers in Canada. The English settlers brought their laws, customs and traditions while the French settlers did the same thing. However, the English and French legal systems were very different — the French legal system was based on the Civil Code while the English legal system was based on the common law and equity.

(a) Civil Code

The Civil Code has its origins in Roman law in the 5th century. Roman laws were constantly being developed to meet the increasing and complex needs of the Roman Empire. Eventually, starting in 528 A.D., the Roman Emperor Justinian decided to codify or systematize the law that had developed during the Roman Empire which became known as Justinian's Code or the Civil Code. Subsequently, all legal disagreements in the Roman Empire had to be resolved by examining and relying on this Code.

After the fall of the Roman Empire, the Justinian Code was forgotten for a period of time. However, it became important once again starting in the 1100s. Consequently, legal scholars began to review and study the Code and it had a major impact on their thoughts relating to the law. Over time, the European countries developed and adopted codes whose basic principles were taken from the Justinian Code. For example, in the early 19th century, Napoléon Bonaparte revised French law by arranging for and supervising the writing of the Napoleonic Code. The Napoleonic Code, also known as the French Civil Code, was mostly based on French law but also on Roman law as set out in the Justinian Code. Eventually, when the French settled in Quebec, they brought with them the

French law in the form of the Napoleonic Code. As a result, the law in Quebec is found in Codes. Quebec has two Codes of law: the *Civil Code of Quebec*[7] which sets out the substantive law and the *Code of Civil Procedure*[8] which contains the procedural law. Substantive law describes our rights and duties while procedural law sets out the methods to protect and enforce these rights and duties.

Today, Quebec is the only Canadian province that is based on civil law. However, before Confederation, Canada was exclusively a civil law jurisdiction. This occurred because the British Parliament enacted the *Quebec Act, 1774*,[9] which made the French Civil Code the law all across Canada. The Act created one exception — English criminal law was to be used across Canada because it was not as harsh as the French law.

The English settlers did not like the French Civil Code. As a result, the British Parliament enacted the *Constitutional Act, 1791*,[10] which created two provinces, Upper Canada (now Ontario) and Lower Canada (now Quebec). In 1792, the first Act that was introduced by the Legislature of Upper Canada was to adopt English common law in Upper Canada. The maritime provinces inherited the English common law while the western provinces adopted the English common law.

(b) Common law

The common law originated in England in the 11th century. After the Romans left England, many different tribes from Northern Europe including the Anglo-Saxons, each of which had its own unique customs and traditions, occupied and controlled England. Subsequently, in 1066, the control of the Anglo-Saxons came to an end when the Normans invaded and conquered England and their leader William of Normandy became the King of England. This represented the beginning of the development of the common law in England.

The Norman conquerors did not bring a new legal system with them to England, but, they did bring the concept of a strong central government which was a major change from the decentralized and fragmented government that existed before the Norman conquest. They also brought a new court system which replaced local courts with, for the most part, royal courts. These royal courts, which were under the authority of the King, had two main components — central courts at Westminster and traveling judges who heard cases through all of England. The King would choose judges from his court and these judges would travel to different towns all over England to hear cases and resolve disagreements.

Initially, the traveling judges applied local customs and traditions or even common sense to resolve a particular dispute. When these judges came back to

---

[7] S.Q. 1991, c. 64.
[8] R.S.Q. c. C-25.
[9] (U.K.), 14 Geo. 3, c. 20.
[10] (U.K.), 31 Geo. 3, c. 31.

the King's court, they reviewed and compared their cases and the resulting decisions. At some point, they began following either their own previous decisions or the past decisions of other judges, instead of relying on local customs or common sense to resolve disputes. If a particular case had similar facts to a case that was previously decided, the judge would make the same decision as in the earlier case. As a result, a uniform body of law, based on the past decisions of judges, developed which was common all over England. It was known as the common law. Over time, the practice of following previous decisions or precedents became a strict rule called *stare decisis*, a Latin phrase meaning "to stand by things decided".

The common law is used in all of the Canadian provinces and territories, except Quebec, and by the federal government.

(c) Equity

Many different bodies of law were being introduced in the courts in England at the same time as the common law was developing in the royal courts. The most significant body of law was the law of equity because the common law became too rigid and inflexible. The common law courts did not recognize that some of the precedents were unfair and no longer applicable because society was changing and there was a need for the law to keep developing. As a result, the common law courts became restricted in terms of the kinds of cases they could hear and the types of remedies they would give.

Many people were becoming upset, disappointed and unsatisfied with the decisions made by the common law courts and went directly to the King for justice. The King passed on the responsibility of hearing and resolving these complaints to his Chancellor. The Chancellor was required to make decisions according to the King's conscience and do what was just or equitable in the circumstances of the case. When the volume of complaints became high, the Chancellor directed his staff to hear the complaints. Eventually, a Court of Chancery or Court of Equity was established with the Chancellor's staff becoming Chancery judges and it was not bound by the common law. Ultimately, similar to the common law courts, the Court of Chancery began following its own precedents and developed the body of law called equity. People could choose to go to either a common law court or the Court of Chancery. In the 19th century, common law and equity were combined — this meant that a person could no longer choose whether to use the common law or equity.

(6) Sources of Canadian Law

How does a particular society obtain the laws that regulate the conduct of its citizens? Just as law has many different interpretations, it also has many different sources. There are legal and non-legal sources of law. The term "non-legal sources of law" refers to historical records, non-legal documents, books on subjects not directly related to law, and bibliographies. These materials are non-legal because they only refer to the law indirectly, are not authoritative sources of the law, and they do not provide a review of the constant development of the law. In contrast, the "legal sources of law" make a direct reference to the law, are authoritative, and provide a way of reviewing the development of the law.

There are two major legal sources of law: primary sources and secondary sources. The primary sources of law, also called "primary legal materials", are the authoritative sources of the law. They are the documentation of the law that is laid down by the lawmaking authorities. The major primary sources of law are statutes, cases and the Constitution. The secondary sources of law, also called "secondary legal materials", are not the authoritative sources of the law but they consist of all of the publications that pertain to the law. The function of secondary sources of law is to summarize the law and direct the reader to the authoritative source such as a case or a statute. The secondary sources include legal textbooks, encyclopedias, dictionaries, digests and journals.

(a) Primary sources of law

(i) *Constitution*

The Constitution is the most important primary source of law. The British Parliament enacted the *British North America Act, 1867*[11] (the "BNA") which created the Dominion of Canada and divided the lawmaking authority between the federal government and the provinces. The federal government has authority or jurisdiction over national matters such as banking, trade and commerce, defence, and postal service. In comparison, the provinces have authority or jurisdiction over local matters such as municipal institutions and property and civil rights.[12]

The federal government cannot make laws that are within the authority of the provinces and the provinces cannot make laws that are within the authority of the federal government. If the federal government or any of the provinces makes a law dealing with subject matter that is outside its authority, the law will be *ultra vires* or "beyond the scope of power". This means the law is invalid and has no legal force or effect. If a law is within the scope of authority, it is considered to be *intra vires*. The courts are responsible for deciding whether a federal or provincial government has exceeded its jurisdiction when making laws.

When the BNA was initially enacted, the British Parliament maintained the authority to make laws applying to Canada. In 1931, the British Parliament gave up the right to make laws for Canada. Since 1931, Canadian politicians struggled to get complete Canadian independence because the BNA was the Canadian Constitution, yet, it could only be changed by the British Parliament. In 1981, the federal government and nine out of the ten provinces (except Quebec) agreed on

---

[11]   1867 (U.K.), c. 3.

[12]   The provinces' authority over property and civil rights includes the regulation of professions.

a formula for amending the Constitution in Canada. The federal government and these nine provinces also agreed that the Constitution would include a Charter of Rights and Freedoms.

Consequently, in 1982, the British Parliament enacted the *Canada Act, 1982*,[13] which terminated its authority over the Canadian Constitution, changed the name of the BNA to the *Constitution Act, 1867*, added the Charter[14] and added the formula for amending the Constitution.

(ii) *Statutes*

Statutes are a very important primary source of law. Under the written component of the Constitution, there are 11 legislative bodies in Canada.[15] One is the federal Parliament and the others are the 10 provincial legislatures.[16] The Constitution grants each of these bodies legislative authority to enact statutes, but, their legislative authority is specifically limited to certain subject matters. This kind of legislation is referred to as primary legislation because it is passed by the legislative body itself.

There is also another kind of legislation in Canada and this is referred to as subordinate legislation. It is called subordinate legislation because a person or a tribunal that is subordinate to a legislative body enacts it. Subordinate legislation is as valid and effective as if the federal Parliament or one of the 10 provincial legislatures had enacted it. Subordinate legislation exists in many different forms such as: by-laws, ordinances, orders in council, codes, rules and regulations. Subordinate legislation usually contains most of the detail that was omitted from the primary legislation.

Primary and subordinate legislation are interconnected because a legislative body enacts the primary legislation and then the primary legislation grants authority to a subordinate body or a delegate (*i.e.*, an administrative tribunal) to pass by-laws, ordinances, orders in council, codes, rules and regulations. When an administrative tribunal enacts subordinate legislation such as regulations, it must enact these regulations according to the authority set out in the primary legislation. If an administrative tribunal enacts regulations that go beyond the authority granted to it by the primary legislation, those regulations will be invalid.

Primary and subordinate legislation need to be differentiated from policies and guidelines, which are the instructions prepared by government departments and administrative tribunals about how to interpret and apply legislation. Policies or

---

[13] (U.K), 1982, c. 11.

[14] A copy of the Charter can be found in Appendix H.

[15] The Northwest Territories, Nunavut and the Yukon Territory are considered territories, not provinces. Therefore, their governments are not considered to be legislative bodies with the authority to enact statutes. Nevertheless, the laws of these territories are valid and have official legal authority because they have been authorized by the legislative authority of the federal Parliament.

[16] The provincial legislatures are also called provincial Parliaments.

guidelines are usually placed in administrative manuals, but, they have no official legal authority. Nevertheless, they must be compatible with the primary and subordinate legislation.

(iii) *Cases*

Another primary source of law is the decisions of courts. However, a statute overrules all the inconsistent case law dealing with the subject matter of that particular statute. If a statute applies to your situation, it will be applied rather than the particular case if there is an inconsistency between the statute and the case.

In deciding cases, judges usually set out in writing the material facts of the case, the legal and factual issues, the decision and the reasons for decision. The reasons for decision, also known as *ratio decidendi*, act as a guide for courts in the future to follow if a similar fact situation is to be decided again. As mentioned previously, the courts are required to follow previous decisions because of the doctrine of *stare decisis*. As a result of the doctrine of *stare decisis*, a body of case law has developed which serves as a guide for judges in deciding cases in the future. This body of case law is known as the common law.

Basically, the common law is considered to be a series of principles expressed through the decisions of courts over the years. This means that as new fact situations develop and as judges decide new cases, the existing principles are broadened, exceptions are created, and the body of case law is expanded. In summary, all the case law including all the principles and exceptions that have been expressed in the cases form the basis of the common law.

(b) Secondary sources of law

Secondary sources of law summarize the law and direct the reader to the authoritative sources. They are also sources of discussion, commentaries, analysis and critiques of the law. An example of a secondary source of law is the *Canadian Encyclopedic Digest*,[17] a loose-leaf encyclopedia which provides comprehensive essays on broad areas of the law. Another example is the *Index to Canadian Legal Literature*,[18] a journals index which provides a subject and author index for legal articles and case reviews published in Canadian law journals.

(7) Classification of Canadian Law

Law can be classified into two basic categories: substantive law and procedural law. Substantive law sets out the rights and duties of each person in society. An example of substantive law is the right to enter into a legally binding contract. In contrast, procedural law sets out the steps and procedures involved

---

[17] (Toronto: Carswell, 2001).
[18] *The Canadian Abridgement: Index to Canadian Legal Literature* (Toronto: Carswell, 2001).

in protecting and enforcing these rights and duties. An example of procedural law is the procedures for enforcing a legally binding contract.

(a) Public law

Substantive law is then divided into public and private law. Public law deals with the relationship between individuals and the state and also the relationship between the different levels of government. The major types of public law are criminal law, administrative law and constitutional law.

(i) *Criminal law*

Canada's criminal law is a set of rules made by the federal government that prevent or prohibit certain criminal acts such as murder, assault, kidnapping, break and enter, fraud and theft. Most of Canada's criminal law is contained in the *Criminal Code*[19] where criminal actions and their penalties or punishments are set out. In addition to the *Criminal Code*, there is also the *Controlled Drugs and Substances Act*[20] and the *Young Offenders Act*. Criminal law is probably the one area of public law with which a person is most likely to come into contact, either as a witness, a juror, a victim or an accused.

(ii) *Administrative law*

Administrative law, one of the fastest growing areas of law, governs the relationship between individuals and government and administrative tribunals. For example, legal disputes over various issues such as employment insurance, labour relations, immigration, telephone rates, cable television service, transportation, sale and consumption of alcohol, and competition are resolved by specialized administrative tribunals that have been created. These administrative tribunals make decisions on behalf of government because the federal and provincial governments have delegated or passed on the right to make decisions to them. Administrative law will be examined in greater detail in the next chapter.

(iii) *Constitutional law*

Constitutional law sets out the structure of the federal government and describes the division of lawmaking authority between the federal and provincial governments. Provincial governments have authority over local matters whereas the federal government has authority over national matters. Since the Charter was added in 1982 to the Constitution, constitutional law also protects the rights and freedoms of individuals from being violated by the government.

---

[19] R.S.C. 1985, c. C-46.
[20] S.C. 1996, c. 19.

(b) Private law

In comparison to public law, private law[21] deals with the personal relationships between two or more persons or between persons and organizations. The major types of private law are family law, contract law, tort law, property law and labour law.

(i) *Family law*

Family law governs the relationships between individuals living together even if they are not married and between parents and children. This area of law deals with things such as marriage, separation, divorce, adoption, child custody, spousal and child support, division of property and child protection.

(ii) *Contract law*

Contract law sets out the requirements for legally binding agreements or contracts and the rights and duties that are imposed on the parties involved in these contracts. Contract law also gives parties the right to go to court to get remedies if the terms of contracts are broken.

(iii) *Tort law*

A tort is considered a private wrong committed by one person against another person. When a person intentionally or carelessly causes harm, injury or loss to another person or his or her property, the conduct is considered to be wrongful because it falls below the standard of acceptable behaviour required by society. Tort law gives the person the right to go to court to get compensated for the harm, injury or the loss that was caused by the other person.

(iv) *Property law*

Property law deals with the relationships between individuals regarding various property issues such as the buying, selling and renting of land or buildings. Many of the laws affecting property were established a long time ago by the English courts. Most of the case law dealing with property has been put into statutes.

(v) *Labour law*

Labour law, also known as employment law, deals with the relationships between employers and employees. Labour law deals with things such as hours of work, minimum wages, pay equity, working conditions, workers' compensation and termination.

---

[21] Private law is also called civil law.

(8) Creating and Changing the Law

The procedures for creating or changing a law depend on the source of law. Case law can be created or changed by a court giving a different decision from earlier cases in that area of law.

Constitutional law can be changed in a couple of different ways. First, the *Constitution Act, 1982* provides a formula for amending the Constitution. Amendments can be made if agreed to by the federal government and two-thirds of the provinces that have at least 50% of the population of Canada. Second, constitutional law can be changed by the courts in the same way that case law can be changed. Given the fact that it is difficult to amend the Constitution, constitutional law is usually changed through the decisions of courts.

Statutes are created or changed by a specific process. Changing a statute is done in the same way as creating a new statute. New law or changes in the current law start off as proposed legislation or bills. There are two kinds of bills: public bills and private bills. Public bills are introduced by cabinet ministers (government bill) or by any other member of the Parliament[22] (private member's public bill) and usually affect the entire province or country. A private member's public bill is rarely passed and is usually only proposed to influence government decisions or draw attention to a specific problem. In comparison, a government bill is usually passed because it is proposed as part of the government's programs and it has the support of the relevant government. In contrast to public bills, private bills are normally introduced by a member of Parliament (not a cabinet minister) for a specific purpose and usually affect a particular individual, a small group of individuals, or a corporation.

A bill must go through several stages before it becomes law. The process starts with the sponsoring member who presents a motion in the House for the introduction and first reading of the bill and explains the objectives of the bill. There is no discussion or debate at this stage. Then, a decision is made on whether to accept the bill for future debate. If the decision is yes, the bill is assigned a number, printed and scheduled for second reading. Each member receives a copy of the bill and it is available to the public.

Second reading usually takes place several days later to give members time to study the proposed bill. During second reading, the members discuss the principle of the bill and its broad purposes. Members are allowed to only speak-once during the debate. After the debate, members vote on whether to let the bill go to the next step.

A bill often goes to a standing or select committee to be studied in detail and to make recommendations for amendments.[23] The committee may hold public hearings where people affected by the bill have a chance to express their opin-

---

[22] The word Parliament refers to the federal Parliament and the provincial legislatures.

[23] In the federal process, a bill may be sent to a committee for study directly after first reading if it was introduced in the House of Commons.

ion. In some cases, a bill may go directly to third reading without going to a committee first. If it does go to a committee, each section of the bill is discussed, amendments are proposed, and a vote is taken on each section including the proposed amendments. Depending on the bill, the committee stage may last from a few days to several months.

After the bill has been examined in detail, the committee will report back to the House. The bill may go to the Committee of the Whole House for further consideration or directly into third reading for final debate on the amendments made by the committee. After a bill is given third reading, a final vote is taken.

The federal process is very similar to the process followed in the provincial legislatures. The biggest difference is that the bill must go through the House of Commons and Senate before it becomes law. After third reading and final vote in the House of Commons, the bill would go through the same process in the Senate. Senate consideration is usually a routine matter. Similarly, if a bill was introduced first in the Senate, after third reading and final vote in the Senate, it would go through the same process in the House of Commons.

After third reading, the bill goes to the Lieutenant Governor of the province or Governor General of Canada for royal assent. The phrase royal assent is used because the Lieutenant Governor or Governor General assents or agrees to the bill on behalf of the Queen by his or her signature. A bill only becomes a statute after royal assent occurs and it is now called an Act. This means that the bill is now law.

However, a law does not always come into effect with royal assent. In some cases, another date is specified when the law comes into effect. In other cases, it indicates that the effective date will be decided later by the Cabinet. Once a date is chosen, it must be approved by the Lieutenant Governor or Governor General and fixed by proclamation. Proclamation is considered to be a public announcement that the law has come into effect. Proclamation is often delayed to allow government departments time to adapt. On occasion, there are some laws that are never proclaimed, and thus, they never take effect. Therefore, a bill takes effect on one of three dates: when it is given royal assent, on a specified date, or on a date to be set by proclamation.

(9) Canadian Court System

The federal and the provincial governments establish the courts in Canada. The federal government has established the Supreme Court of Canada and the Federal Court of Canada and it appoints judges to both of these courts. The federal government has also created a system of courts for the Northwest Territories, Nunavut and the Yukon Territory.[24] In contrast, the provinces have established

---

[24] The system of courts in the Northwest Territories and the Yukon Territory is similar to the system of courts in the provinces: Court of Appeal, Supreme Court, and lower trial court. In Nunavut, there is a single level trial court — the Nunavut Court of Justice — and a Court of Appeal.

their own courts. Even though the names of the courts are different, the structure of the courts in each province is almost the same. Each province has a Court of Appeal which is responsible for hearing appeals from the trial courts in that province. All the provinces also have a Supreme Court or Superior Court which is a trial court that has unlimited jurisdiction. While the provinces establish these courts, the federal government appoints the judges. All the provinces also have junior or lower courts which deal with criminal cases, family disputes and small claims. Many of the provinces have consolidated these individual lower courts into one overall Provincial Court with separate divisions. The provinces establish these courts and appoint judges or justices of the peace to them.

(a) Supreme Court of Canada

The Supreme Court of Canada is considered to be an appeal court, the highest appeal court in Canada. This means that the court hears appeals only and does not conduct trials. It hears appeals from the Courts of Appeal of the provinces and territories and from the Federal Court of Appeal. In addition, it does not agree to hear all appeals but generally only appeals that are important in order to interpret the law in a complex and confusing area. It also hears matters that are referred to it by the federal government, especially constitutional questions. A panel of Supreme Court judges hears arguments presented by lawyers and it then gives a written or oral decision. For very important cases, the entire nine members of the Supreme Court hear the case. The members of the panel who hear a particular case may not agree about whether the appeal should be dismissed or allowed but the final decision will be made by a simple majority. The majority decision is a precedent for all the Canadian courts to follow when they are confronted with cases with similar facts.

(b) Federal Court of Canada

The Federal Court of Canada hears cases dealing with disputes between the provinces and the federal government and also disputes among the provinces. It also hears cases relating to claims against or even by the federal government and other federal matters such as taxation, copyrights, trademarks and patents. The Federal Court of Canada has a trial and an appeal division. The Federal Court – Appeal Division, also known as the Federal Court of Appeal, hears applications for judicial review from federal administrative tribunals such as the Canadian Radio-television and Telecommunications Commission and appeals from its own Trial Division.

(c) Courts within the provinces

Generally, within each province, there are three levels of courts: the Court of Appeal, the Superior or Supreme Court of the province, and the Provincial Court.

Each province has a Court of Appeal which hears appeals from the trial courts within that province. A panel of three or five judges hears appeals and the appeal is determined according to the decision of the majority of judges. The decision of a Court of Appeal in a particular province is binding on all other courts in that province but it is only persuasive on any of the courts in other provinces.

Each province also has a Superior or Supreme Court.[25] It has jurisdiction in criminal and civil matters to hear cases that are beyond the jurisdiction of the Provincial Courts. The names of this court are not uniform across the provinces — four of the provinces are called "Court of Queen's Bench"[26] while the others are either called Supreme Court or Superior Court. The decision of a Superior or Supreme Court in a province is binding on the lower levels of court within that province but it is only persuasive on other judges of the Superior or Supreme Court in that province.

In the past, provinces such as Ontario, British Columbia and Nova Scotia had an intermediate trial court, known as the County or District Court. Currently, none of the provinces have this level of court.

Each province also has a Provincial Court which is the lowest level of court. The Provincial Court is further divided into various subdivisions such as the Criminal Division, Family Division, Youth Division, and Civil Division or Small Claims Court. The decision of a Provincial Court is not binding on any other Court but it is persuasive on other judges or justices of the peace of the Provincial Court in that province.

(d) Specialty courts

There are also courts that fulfill special or unique functions. One example is the Surrogate or Probate Court which hears cases dealing with matters that relate to the estates or property of dead persons. This may include the probate of wills (the official process of proving a will as authentic) and the administration or settling of estates of persons who died without leaving a will. In some provinces, the function of the Surrogate Court is given to the Superior or Supreme Court.

[25] In Ontario, there is a special Divisional Court which hears applications for judicial review, unless they are urgent, and some types of appeals from administrative tribunals.

[26] The four provinces are Alberta, Manitoba, New Brunswick and Saskatchewan.

2

What is Administrative Law?

(1) Introduction

Administrative law is the name given to an area of law which is very difficult to define. It is commonly thought that administrative law is made up only of the principles that govern the actions of administrative tribunals.

In reality, administrative law is made up of three components:

1. The actual by-laws, rules and regulations and other forms of subordinate legislation made by administrative tribunals.
2. The principles of law governing the actions of administrative tribunals and their decisions.
3. The legal remedies available to those affected by unlawful administrative action or improper decisions of administrative tribunals.

(2) How and Why did Administrative Law Develop?

The major function of the provincial legislatures and the federal Parliament was to make new laws or change existing laws. As a result, Ministers became responsible to the provincial legislatures and the federal Parliament for implementing these laws with the assistance of civil servants who worked in the various government ministries. The role of the courts was to interpret and apply these laws and ensure that the intentions of the provincial legislatures and the federal Parliament were followed. Until the 20th century, there were very few administrative tribunals.

World War I led to a significant increase in government involvement in the economy. This resulted in the establishment of many administrative tribunals such as the Board of Grain Commissioners, the Food Control Board, and the Wage Trade Board. In addition, Labour Relations Boards and Workers' Compensation Boards were also established.

Between the end of World War I and the Great Depression, government involvement in the economy was fairly insignificant. In the 1930s, government involvement increased again to deal with the economic and social problems that resulted from the Great Depression. During World War II, government involvement was extremely high because the federal government took very tight control over the economy. After World War II, large numbers of the administrative tribunals that were established during World War II were maintained and many more administrative tribunals were established.

One of the main reasons for the large increase in the number of the administrative tribunals and the resulting expansion and growth of administrative law was that the provincial legislatures and the federal Parliament did not have the time and expertise to make laws in all the required areas. For example, the provincial legislatures and the federal Parliament were not able to include enough detail in these new laws to allow for effective regulation. In addition, the courts were not able to deal with the large increase in disputes because the court process was slow and expensive and the judges did not have the specialized knowledge and experience which is required to resolve administrative disputes.

Robert Macaulay and James Sprague in their book entitled *Practice and Procedure Before Administrative Tribunals*[1] provide 15 reasons to explain the growth of administrative law. These reasons include:

1. the sheer volume of government interaction/intervention in the private and public sector;
2. the opportunity to implement creative government strategies through innovation and experimentation, rather than through the cumbersome legislative process;
3. the complexity of government programs and initiatives;
4. the necessity of delegating statutory obligations to qualified persons;
5. the need to place legal limitations on the actions and powers of government officials;
6. the need to ensure flexibility in the daily administration of government operations;
7. the occasion for greater discretion and freedom from political interference;
8. the chance to provide a specialized, highly detailed, technical response on a case-by-case basis;
9. the efficiency of dealing with recurring problems of a certain kind;
10. the impracticality of adding routine administrative matters to the heavy caseload of the courts;
11. the prohibitive costs of gaining broad access to the courts to enforce rights that fall within the administrative arena;
12. the ability to relieve ministers of sensitive political decisions by placing issues in a non-political setting;
13. the major advantage of policy development. It is far better for a minister to make commitments at the latest possible moment and upon political testing, rather than acting at the earliest possible moment;

---

[1] R.W. Macaulay and J.L.H. Sprague, *Practice and Procedure Before Administrative Tribunals* (Scarborough: Carswell Thomson Professional Publishing, 1997), pp. 1-2 to 1-2.1 (1992, release 1). Excerpts printed by permission of Carswell, a division of Thomson Canada Ltd.

14. the advantage of a supervisory judicial review of administrative decisions to ensure adherence to principles of procedural fairness and natural justice;[2] and
15. the need to create a readily accessible, informal public hearing forum.

As a result, there is probably no other area of law that has grown as extensively as administrative law. In fact, administrative law has profoundly affected the lives of all Canadians because many aspects of a person's life are regulated today by administrative tribunals in many different areas. These include things such as: communications, consumer protection, energy, environment, food and agriculture, forestry, health, housing, human rights, immigration, labour relations, professions and occupations, recreation, transportation and workers' compensation.

The Supreme Court of Canada[3] affirmed this viewpoint when it stated the following:

> Administrative boards play an increasingly important role in our society. They regulate many aspects of our life, from beginning to end. Hospital and medical boards regulate the methods and practice of the doctors that bring us into this world. Boards regulate the licensing and the operation of morticians who are concerned with our mortal remains. Marketing boards regulate the farm products we eat; transport boards regulate the means and flow of our travel; energy boards control the price and distribution of the forms of energy we use; planning boards and city councils regulate the location and types of buildings in which we live and work. In Canada, boards are a way of life. Boards and the functions they fulfil are legion.

(3) What are Administrative Tribunals?

Developing an acceptable but also a comprehensive definition of the term "administrative tribunal" is very difficult. Many people have a traditional concept of what a typical administrative tribunal looks like. They believe it is a permanent body consisting of at least two or more members external to the provincial or federal governments who decide matters dealing with individual and group rights usually after a hearing has taken place. The problem with this traditional concept is to decide what variations from the typical administrative tribunal are acceptable without it becoming something other than an administrative tribunal. For example, it is important not to exclude from the definition those bodies which have either sole decision-makers or decision-makers who work in a particular government department. Also, bodies that do not make decisions in a final manner but only provide advice or make recommendations and bodies that use decision-making techniques other than a hearing such as mediation and negotiation, should also be included. In addition, the activities of many bodies

---

[2] The principles of natural justice and fairness will be discussed in more detail in the next chapter.
[3] *Newfoundland Telephone Co. v. Newfoundland (Board of Commissioners of Public Utilities)* (1992), 89 D.L.R. (4th) 289, [1992] 1 S.C.R. 623 at pp. 634-5, 95 Nfld. & P.E.I.R. 271, 4 Admin. L.R. (2d) 121, 134 N.R. 241.

involve determining matters other than those dealing with individual and group rights such as setting policy or establishing general standards that must be followed and these bodies should also not be excluded.

(4) Why were Administrative Tribunals Created?

There are a large number of reasons why administrative tribunals have been created by the provincial and federal governments. All of these reasons originate from the fact that the activities of government have become very complex and difficult to regulate by government employees who lack specialized skills and knowledge and an awareness of the larger social implications of their decisions. It is interesting to note that many of these reasons are either the same or similar to the reasons which were discussed earlier for the growth of administrative law. Macaulay and Sprague[4] summarize the reasons for creating administrative tribunals:

1. the immense workload of the Legislature requires some delegation of the decision-making to others, particularly agencies;
2. it is easier, quicker and less expensive to implement innovative government strategies through agencies than through the cumbersome process of legislation or amendment;
3. many kinds of policy and decision-making needs are better delegated to specialists within agencies rather than the generalists within the civil service;
4. it is easier for the Legislature and far less risky to the government to place legal limitations on an agency than the civil service, where the government is the employer and therefore, directly responsible;
5. with its immense size, the government can be more flexible working through a small number of agencies than through 85,000 civil servants;
6. agencies allow the government to operate with greater freedom from political pressure;
7. agencies permit a lower unit cost of response to recurring problems;
8. agencies offer an inexpensive alternative to the very high cost of gaining access to the courts in order to enforce rights that fall within the administrative area;
9. agencies relieve ministers from sensitive political decisions by placing issues in a non-political setting;
10. agencies are an excellent arena in which to test administrative policy before being adopted or rejected by a ministry;
11. agency decisions are more easily reviewed by the courts than ministerial decisions;
12. an agency is a very manageable forum for public participation, one of the cornerstones of open government;
13. agencies are the only real forum where adjudicative, legislative, and administrative skills can be exercised by the same body;
14. it is easier for government to overturn or deal otherwise with a wayward decision of an agency than it is to overturn a ministerial decision; and
15. agencies are an inexpensive and experienced forum within which one can search out solutions to report to Cabinet without Cabinet becoming immediately involved.

---

[4] *Op. cit.*, footnote 1, at pp. 2-30 to 2-31 (1990, release 1).

(5) Types and Functions of Administrative Tribunals

Traditionally, administrative tribunals had to be distinguished in relation to their function because courts reviewed administrative action and gave remedies only when it involved one type of administrative tribunal: an administrative tribunal which exercised a judicial or quasi-judicial function. However, over time, the need for a classification of administrative tribunals has been reduced especially with the introduction of the principles of fairness, which applied to all administrative tribunals.[5] Nevertheless, an awareness of the traditional classification is important in order to have a full understanding of administrative law.

There are four major types of administrative tribunals. The first type of administrative tribunal exercises a "legislative" function. This kind of administrative tribunal sets policy and makes rules, regulations, by-laws and other forms of subordinate legislation. This type of administrative tribunal generally has a very wide discretion.

The second type of administrative tribunal exercises an "administrative" function. An administrative tribunal exercises an administrative function when it makes decisions based on the general policy that is set out in the governing statute which establishes the administrative tribunal. In making these decisions, it has substantial discretion to set policy.

The third type of administrative tribunal exercises a "ministerial" or "executive" function which involves no discretion. For example, an administrative tribunal that issues licences has no authority not to issue a licence when an applicant meets all the requirements, such as paying the appropriate fee and filling out the appropriate documents. These administrative tribunals do not set policy or make any kind of subordinate legislation.

The fourth type of administrative tribunal exercises a "judicial" or "quasi-judicial" function. These administrative tribunals also do not set policy, and thus, make decisions that are solely based on pre-existing policy. This kind of administrative tribunal has very little discretion because they must make their decisions according to the pre-existing policy that is contained in their governing statutes.

It is important to note there are administrative tribunals that perform a combination of one or more of these functions and there are also some administrative tribunals that perform all four of these functions.

---

[5] There have been some cases where the courts have stated that the principles of fairness do not apply to administrative tribunals exercising a legislative function. There have also been other cases where the courts have stated that the principles of fairness do apply to administrative tribunals exercising a legislative function. Therefore, the law is not entirely clear. In a fairly recent decision of the Supreme Court of Canada, the court in *Wells v. Newfoundland* (1994), 177 D.L.R. (4th) 73, [1999] 3 S.C.R. 199, 180 Nfld. & P.E.I.R. 269, 15 Admin. L.R. (3d) 274, 46 C.C.E.L. (2d) 165, 99 C.L.L.C. ¶210-047, 245 N.R. 275, commented that the principles of fairness do not apply to legislative decision-making. Unfortunately, this does not end the debate because this was only a comment made by the court and was not a necessary part of their decision.

As a result, Macaulay and Sprague[6] have chosen to move away from the traditional classification of administrative tribunals and instead have divided the administrative tribunals in Canada into eight general categories according to their purpose or role:

1. *Agencies which investigate, report and advise.* These are also referred to as review agencies. Examples include: the Federal Environment Assessment Review Office, the Canadian Employment and Immigration Advisory Council, the Cultural Property Export Review Board, the Conservation Review Board and the Agricultural Licensing and Registration Review Board.

2. *Agencies which deal with appeals and mediation.* These adjudicate and get involved in personal rights protected by legislation and the *Canadian Charter of Rights and Freedoms.*[7] Examples include: the National Parole Board, provincial Parole Boards, the Patent Appeal Board, the Agriculture, Food and Rural Affairs Tribunal[8] and the Public Service Grievance Board.

3. *Agencies which deal with the individual.* These are also referred to as human rights and freedom agencies. Examples include: the Ombudsman, Human Rights Tribunals, Workers' Compensation Boards, Criminal Injuries Compensation Boards and the Privacy Commissioner.

4. *Agencies which are regulatory, adversarial and deal with large sectors of the federal and provincial economies.* These are also referred to as economic regulatory agencies. Examples include: Security Commissions, Public Utilities Boards, the Canadian Radio-television and Telecommunications Commission, the Competition Tribunal and Energy Boards.

5. *Agencies which deal with land planning, property values, assessment and land compensation.* These deal with the local government. Examples include: Municipal Boards, Housing Commissions, Land Value Appraisal Commissions, Expropriations Compensation Boards and Planning Boards.

6. *Agencies which deal with employment, wages, social assistance benefits and pensions.* These are also referred to as socio-economic agencies. Examples include: Labour Relations Boards, Public Service Commissions, Minimum Wage Boards, Industrial Relations Boards and Social Affairs Commissions.

7. *Agencies which set material standards and implement regulation or control certain aspects of product/commodity marketing.* Examples include: Marketing Boards, Building Standards Boards, the Atomic Energy Control Board, Grain Boards and the Trademark Opposition Board.

8. *Agencies which deal primarily with natural resources and their preservation or conservation.* Examples include: Mining Boards, the Niagara

---

6 *Op. cit.*, footnote 1, at pp. 2-7 to 2-11 (1988 and 1992, release 1). Adapted by permission of Carswell, a division of Thomson Canada Ltd.

7 Part I of the *Constitution Act, 1982,* being Schedule B of the *Canada Act 1982* (U.K.), 1982, c. 11.

8 This administrative tribunal was previously called the Farm Products Appeal Tribunal.

Escarpment Commission, the Conservation Review Board, the National Energy Board and Environmental Assessment Boards.

(6) Administrative Tribunals and the Courts

Administrative tribunals are often considered to be the same as courts even though they are very different from one another and have been created to fulfill distinct functions.[9] Macaulay and Sprague[10] describe some of these differences as follows:

1. Perhaps the most important characteristic of the administrative arena is that issues are consistently resolved in the public interest. Notwithstanding that an issue is raised by one party with a particular interest in the outcome, when the merits of that issue come before the administrative decision-makers the final decision should accord with the statutory mandate to pursue the public interest. By contrast, while courts may consider public policy in their proceedings, their role is exclusively limited to adjudicating in accordance with legal rules and adversarial proceedings in which there are winners and losers.
2. Courts have a duty to interpret and apply the law; they do not legislate. Administrative entities, while creatures of statute, may formulate policy which is very close to a law-making function.
3. Courts are bound by precedent: the principle of *stare decisis*. Boards, commissions and tribunals are not. These administrative bodies have an interest in maintaining a pattern of consistent and perhaps predictable rulings, but they are not bound to follow previous decisions. They are therefore more flexible. Power to vary agency decisions to reflect current facts is, indeed, a flexible power not possessed by courts.
4. Courts function on the basis of formal rules. The administrative setting is generally informal; sometimes with rules and sometimes without. That degree of informality may be determined from the enabling legislation and the applicable discretionary code of practice and procedure.
5. Courts are bound to adhere to rules of natural justice[11] in proceedings before them. Recent trends in administrative law show a shift from the strict application of natural justice rules to a wider, more flexible standard of "procedural fairness" for boards.
6. Courts entertain adversarial proceedings, reach decisions, and may never see the parties again. This is not the case with administrative entities, particularly those which are regulatory in nature. They have an organic, ongoing relationship with a relatively small number of regulated entities.
7. Courts have no duty to an industry or its relationship with other factors in the economy. Agencies, boards and commissions interact regularly with an industry and develop an expertise and sensitivity for its problems.

---

[9] The Supreme Court of Canada in *Ocean Port Hotel Ltd. v. British Columbia (Liquor Control, General Manager)* (2001), 108 A.C.W.S. (3d) 3, 2001 SCC 52, very recently acknowledged that there is a fundamental distinction between administrative tribunals and courts.

[10] *Op. cit.*, footnote 1, at pp. 1-6 to 1-8 (1991, release 2 and 1994, release 1). Footnotes omitted from the original.

[11] An example of this is the formal rules of procedure.

8. Courts entertain an original hearing and have no inherent power to review a decision. However on appeal, another court may review and base a decision on facts gathered at that original hearing. Appearances before administrative bodies are also original hearings, and in many cases, the panel has statutory jurisdiction to review or rehear its own decisions on its own motion.

. . . . .

9. Administrative bodies may have staff, counsel and periodically employ consultants who prepare and present briefings before hearings. Courts usually have no technical staff.
10. Administrative procedure often includes a review of pre-filing evidence, an interrogatory process, and the advantage of a daily transcript. courts may only review a limited amount of pre-filing material and often have no daily transcript.
11. Boards, commissions, and tribunals usually sit collectively as panels in the conduct of a hearing. With the exception of review or appeal proceedings, courts sit with only one member presiding.
12. It is often possible to settle a court case. Indeed, most actions filed are settled rather than litigated. A regulatory issue such as a rate increase for a utility must be decided by the board and cannot be worked out by settlement by the parties.[12]

These differences illustrate an important point. Administrative tribunals may sometimes look like or appear to be similar to courts on the surface but, in reality, they fulfil very distinct and different functions in society compared to courts. As a result, an administrative tribunal should never be thought of as a lesser or lower court. An administrative tribunal's impact or influence can be just as significant as a court.

---

[12] This is beginning to change in many areas that pursue alternative dispute resolution techniques.

3

The Principles of Administrative Law

(1) Procedural Principles: Natural Justice and Fairness

Generally, administrative tribunals must ensure that they follow proper procedures when making decisions. In each situation, what is considered "proper" depends on many things, including the particular facts and surrounding circumstances of each case. Usually, a statute, regulation, by-law or rules will establish the basic procedures that control the process of making decisions by an administrative tribunal. These basic procedures include: adequate notice, the right to counsel, and the right to present evidence and to cross-examine witnesses. These are commonly found in the governing legislation of the administrative tribunal.

In addition to the governing legislation of the administrative tribunal, there are also general procedural statutes in some provinces. In Ontario, the *Statutory Powers Procedure Act*[1] (the "SPPA") outlines the general procedures for certain administrative tribunals. Similarly, in Alberta, the *Administrative Procedures Act*[2] (the "APA") also sets out the general procedures. Both of these Acts will be discussed later on in this chapter. For the most part, these Acts codify the common law regarding procedures for administrative tribunals.[3]

However, the law regarding the procedures of administrative tribunals is not contained only in the governing legislation.[4] For example, when the governing legislation does not establish basic procedures, there are certain common law

---

[1] R.S.O. 1990, c. S.22. A copy of the Act can be found in Appendix B.

[2] R.S.A. 1980, c. A-2. A copy of the Act can be found in Appendix C.

[3] Since the SPPA has been amended several times since it was first introduced in 1971, the common law requirements regarding procedures for administrative tribunals have been codified in the legislation. In contrast, the APA has been mostly unchanged since it was first introduced in 1966. Therefore, many of the common law requirements regarding procedures for administrative tribunals have not been codified in the legislation.

[4] The *Canadian Charter of Rights and Freedoms*, Part I of the *Constitution Act, 1982*, being Schedule B of the *Canada Act 1982* (U.K.), 1982, c. 11, is also relevant when

principles regarding procedures which will be applicable to ensure that all individuals who are affected by the actions or decisions of government including administrative tribunals are treated fairly. These procedural principles are the principles of natural justice and, more recently, the principles of fairness.

(2) Natural Justice

(a) Application of natural justice

Traditionally, the principles of natural justice were only applied to administrative tribunals that were classified as "judicial" or "quasi-judicial". Administrative tribunals, which carried out "legislative", "administrative" or "executive" functions, were not required to comply with the principles of natural justice. As a result, in the past, an initial decision had to be made about whether an administrative tribunal's function was "judicial" or "quasi-judicial" as opposed to "legislative", "administrative" or "executive". Once the function had been determined to be "judicial" or "quasi-judicial", the principles of natural justice would apply to the actions of the administrative tribunal and its decisions. The procedural protections imposed in those cases were usually trial-like procedures.

However, in the legendary decision by the British House of Lords in *Ridge v. Baldwin*,[5] the court moved away from a strict classification of the function of the administrative tribunal in determining what procedural protections would be given to individuals whose rights were to be affected by the actions or decisions of the administrative tribunal. Instead, the requirement of natural justice was to be inferred from the nature of the power that is being exercised by the administrative tribunal. This meant that the court looked at the nature of the power that the administrative tribunal is exercising instead of strictly classifying an administrative tribunal. As a result, the type of procedural protections available to a party appearing before an administrative tribunal varied according to the nature of the power of the administrative tribunal.

Despite this movement by the English courts away from a strict classification of the function of the administrative tribunal, the Canadian courts still continued to make a determination of whether an administrative tribunal was exercising a judicial or quasi-judicial function in order to determine whether the principles of natural justice applied. For example, in the case of *M.N.R. v. Coopers & Lybrand*,[6] the Supreme Court of Canada set out the factors which should be considered in determining whether a decision by an administrative tribunal was a

---

discussing the law regarding the procedures of administrative tribunals. It will be discussed in more detail in Chapter 6.

5 [1964] A.C. 40 (H.L.).

6 [1979] 1 S.C.R. 495 at p. 504, [1978] C.T.C. 829, 78 D.T.C. 6528, 24 N.R. 163.

"judicial" or "quasi-judicial" one to which the principles of natural justice would apply:

1. Is there anything in the language in which the function is conferred or in the general context in which it is exercised which suggests that a hearing is contemplated before a decision is reached?
2. Does the decision or order directly or indirectly affect the rights and obligations of persons?
3. Is the adversary process involved?
4. Is there an obligation to apply substantive rules to many individual cases rather than, for example, the obligation to implement social and economic policy in a broad sense?

The Supreme Court of Canada also indicated that this list of factors was not exhaustive. The Supreme Court concluded: "In more general terms, one must have regard to the subject matter of the power, the nature of the issue to be decided, and the importance of the determination upon those directly or indirectly affected thereby."[7]

Therefore, after considering these three general factors, a determination can be made as to whether a particular administrative tribunal is making a "judicial" or "quasi-judicial" decision. If it is determined that the administrative tribunal is in fact making a "judicial" or "quasi-judicial" decision, the principles of natural justice will apply.

An example of a decision, which would be considered "judicial" or "quasi-judicial", would be the determination by the Discipline Committee of an administrative tribunal that a professional had committed an act of professional misconduct or unprofessional conduct. Once a Discipline Committee makes a finding of professional misconduct or unprofessional conduct, the Discipline Committee has the power to impose various penalties. As a result, that type of decision would be considered "judicial" or "quasi-judicial" and would require procedural protections that would make the hearing before the Discipline Committee look very much like a trial.

(b) Content of natural justice

Once a determination is made that the principles of natural justice apply to the decision-making process of an administrative tribunal, the next question is what does natural justice include? Natural justice includes two basic components: the right to be heard and the right to an unbiased decision-maker.

(i) *The right to be heard*

The right to be heard includes many general procedural requirements. Generally, a person directly affected by a decision of an administrative tribunal must be given adequate notice of the allegations or charges being made against him or her and the proposed action. Notice will be adequate if it informs all of

---

[7] *Ibid.*

the persons who will be directly affected. Notice must also give sufficient information to those persons to allow them to have a reasonable idea of the conduct that will be examined, what decision(s) may be made, and the consequences or effect that this decision may have on them. A person needs to have adequate notice to enable that person to decide if he or she will attend any hearing that may take place and make any submissions. Adequate notice is also important once a person decides to attend the hearing in order to help that person prepare for the hearing and defend himself or herself at that hearing.

In addition to the requirement of providing adequate notice, a person must be given all relevant information about the case.[8] This is particularly important where negative allegations are being made against a particular person or where that person may be at risk of a penalty or restriction of his or her rights. This is usually referred to as disclosure. Providing disclosure is very important because administrative tribunals cannot rely on evidence given to them by one person or obtained on their own without disclosure and the chance to explain or respond to this evidence. Otherwise, administrative tribunals run the risk of having their decisions set aside or quashed by a court.

In many cases, the governing statute for the particular administrative tribunal sets out who the parties to the hearing are, who is to get notice, the timing and manner of that notice, the contents of the notice, and the obligations relating to disclosure of evidence.

Once it has been determined that adequate notice and disclosure has been given, the form of the hearing must also be considered such as whether there will be an oral hearing or only written submissions.[9] The right to be heard does not always mean that a person will have the right to appear and make submissions in person for all decisions. In some cases, a decision may be made after the administrative tribunal considers only written submissions from the parties rather than hearing from them in person.

If there is an oral hearing, the conduct of the actual hearing also leads to questions about procedural matters. This includes things such as the right to counsel or other representative, the right to present evidence and cross-examine witnesses, and whether the hearing is to be open to the public or is to be held in private. All of these procedural matters must be considered even though they may vary among different administrative tribunals. The procedural protections that are provided should be appropriate to the type of hearing that is taking place.

---

[8] In some cases, the courts have indicated that certain administrative tribunals are not required to disclose all relevant information about the case.

[9] The general procedural statute in Ontario, the SPPA, provides for three different types of hearings: oral, written and electronic.

As mentioned in the earlier section, many of these procedural matters have been incorporated in the SPPA or the APA, the general procedural statutes which are applicable to certain administrative tribunals in Ontario and Alberta.

(ii) *The right to an unbiased decision-maker*

The second basic component of natural justice is the right of a person who will be affected by a decision of an administrative tribunal to have an impartial and unbiased hearing. A person is entitled to have his or her submissions heard by a decision-maker who is impartial and unbiased. Any decision that is made by an administrative tribunal should be based on the evidence and the submissions made by the parties that appear before it and should not be influenced by outside or external factors.

A clear example of bias occurs when a member of the administrative tribunal has a direct financial interest in the outcome of the case which is before the administrative tribunal. Another clear example is when an administrative tribunal hears an appeal from its own previous decision. In addition, personal, professional or business relationships between a party or key witness and a member of the administrative tribunal who heard the case would likely be enough to establish a case of bias.

Because it is impossible to determine the state of mind of a decision-maker, the courts have taken the position that actual bias does not need to be shown but, instead, an unbiased appearance is adequate. The test that the courts have developed is whether a reasonably informed bystander could reasonably perceive bias on the part of the decision-maker. This test is often referred to as a "reasonable apprehension of bias". Therefore, the focus is not on a court's or administrative tribunal's opinion of what is bias, but, on the opinion of a reasonable person.

However, bias is usually quite difficult to prove and something more than general unsubstantiated claims of bias will be necessary. The case of *Newfoundland Telephone Co. v. Newfoundland (Board of Commissioners of Public Utilities)*[10] is an example of a case where the courts have found that there was bias. In this case, the Supreme Court of Canada decided that a member of the Board of Commissioners of Public Utilities had created a reasonable apprehension of bias by publicly expressing strong opinions about a case that was before him. His public comments indicated to a reasonable person that he had made up his mind even before the Board had heard all of the evidence.

In this case, the member had made public comments about the proposed expenses for the top executives such as salary and pension benefits that were the subject matter of the hearing. He said things such as: "I think that's an incredi-

---

[10] (1992), 89 D.L.R. (4th) 289, [1992] 1 S.C.R. 623, 95 Nfld. & P.E.I.R. 271, 4 Admin. L.R. (2d) 121, 134 N.R. 241.

ble sum of money to be paid for to manage a small telephone company . . . and I just think that it is unfair to expect ratepayers, the consumers, you and I to pay for this kind of extravagance".[11] The Supreme Court of Canada found that these comments created a reasonable apprehension or appearance that the member could not make an unbiased decision. As a result, the Supreme Court concluded that the decision of the Board was void and had no legal force or effect.

It is interesting to note that the Supreme Court of Canada also stated that if the member's comments had been made during the investigative stage, they would not have been able to conclude that there was bias because the test at the investigative stage was whether the comments demonstrated a closed mind. However, because the member had made these comments after a date for the hearing was scheduled and during the actual hearing, the test was whether there was a reasonable apprehension of bias and this test had been met. Therefore, the scrutiny that will be given to the conduct and statements of decision-makers may vary depending on things such as the timing in relation to the hearing.

If a member of an administrative tribunal expresses a strong opinion about an issue in general but not in relation to the facts of a particular case, courts are reluctant to disqualify that member before a hearing begins or to declare the decision of the administrative tribunal to be void. This occurs even if the administrative tribunal is faced with the same issue. Without some proof that the member will not be able to listen fairly and openly to the evidence and submissions of the parties, holding an opinion about an issue will not usually be considered as bias.

It should also be noted that the Supreme Court of Canada had determined that the Board exercised a "legislative function". Interestingly, the Supreme Court stated that more latitude should be given to administrative tribunals exercising "legislative" functions rather than adjudicative functions. As a result, the bias test will be applied differently depending on the nature and function of the administrative tribunal. The traditional reasonable apprehension of bias test will still apply to administrative tribunals who exercise a "judicial" or "quasi-judicial" function. A lower standard such as whether the decision-maker has a closed mind or is incapable of being persuaded will apply to administrative tribunals who exercise "legislative" functions or set policy.[12]

---

[11] *Supra*, at p. 629.

[12] In the same year, the Supreme Court of Canada in *Idziak v. Canada (Minister of Justice)* (1992), 97 D.L.R. (4th) 577, [1992] 3 S.C.R. 631, 59 O.A.C. 241, 9 Admin. L.R. (2d) 1 at pp. 33-4, 77 C.C.C. (3d) 65, 17 C.R. (4th) 161, 12 C.R.R. (2d) 77, 144 N.R. 327, indicated that the bias test would be applied differently depending on the nature and function of the administrative tribunal. If the administrative tribunal is performing an adjudicative function, the test is reasonable apprehension of bias: could a reasonably informed bystander reasonably perceive bias on the part of the decision-maker? If the administrative tribunal is performing a legislative function, the test is a closed mind: has the decision-maker prejudged the matter to such an extent that any representations to the contrary would be futile?

(3) Fairness

(a) Application of fairness

The principles of natural justice became less effective over time. A broad range of administrative tribunals was affecting individuals and the functions of these administrative tribunals could not always be classified as "judicial" or "quasi-judicial". In cases when the administrative tribunals were not being classified as "judicial" or "quasi-judicial" but, instead, as "legislative" or "administrative" or "executive", individuals were being denied any procedural protections. Also, when the principles of natural justice were applied, trial-like procedures were imposed that were sometimes not suitable for dealing with a particular situation.

As a result, the principles of fairness began to develop and be applied. The principles of fairness established a lower threshold for providing procedural protections and required less trial-like procedures than those established by the principles of natural justice.

The turning point occurred in the case of *Nicholson v. Haldimand-Norfolk Regional Board of Commissioners of Police.*[13] The Supreme Court of Canada recognized that a person's procedural rights did not depend on a determination that the function of a particular administrative tribunal was "judicial" or "quasi-judicial".

In this case, a probationary constable was dismissed from the police force after being a police officer for 15 months without being given notice of the grounds of his dismissal or an opportunity to make submissions to the Board of Commissioners of Police regarding its decision. A regulation made under the governing statute, the *Police Act,*[14] gave procedural protections to police officers when disciplinary charges were brought against them. However, this regulation also indicated that the power of the Board of Commissioners of Police to dismiss a probationary constable during the 18-month probationary period was not affected by these procedural protections.

The Supreme Court of Canada decided that the regulation excluded the requirement of a full hearing for probationary constables but it did not exclude Nicholson from all procedural protections. The Supreme Court of Canada recognized that a duty of fairness applied despite the fact that the Board of Commissioners of Police was exercising an administrative function. The Supreme Court of Canada stated that the duty of fairness required the Board of

---

[13] (1978), 88 D.L.R. (3d) 671, [1979] 1 S.C.R. 311, 78 C.L.L.C. ¶14,181, 23 N.R. 410. This case was the turning point because the Supreme Court of Canada for the first time followed the approach of the British House of Lords in *Ridge v. Baldwin, supra,* footnote 5.

[14] The name of the *Police Act* has been changed to the *Police Services Act,* R.S.O. 1990, c. P.14.

Commissioners of Police to inform Nicholson why he was being dismissed from the police force and to give him an opportunity, orally or in writing, to make submissions.

(b) Content of fairness

The *Nicholson* case and cases that were decided subsequently focused less on whether any procedural requirements are to be imposed on a particular administrative tribunal and more on the specific procedural protections that were appropriate for a particular situation. In addition, the subsequent cases have moved away from a distinction between the principles of natural justice and the principles of fairness in determining the procedural requirements for all administrative tribunals. For example, in *Martineau v. Matsqui Institution (Disciplinary Board)*,[15] the Supreme Court of Canada stated the following:

> In general, Courts ought not to seek to distinguish between the two concepts, for the drawing of a distinction between a duty to act fairly, and a duty to act in accordance with the rules of natural justice, yields an unwieldy conceptual framework.
>
> . . . . .
>
> It is wrong, in my view, to regard natural justice and fairness as distinct and separate standards and to seek to define the procedural content of each.

Similarly, in *Syndicat des employés de production du Québec et de l'Acadie v. Canada (Canadian Human Rights Commission)*,[16] the Supreme Court of Canada stated the following:

> Both the rules of natural justice and the duty of fairness are variable standards. Their content will depend on the circumstances of the case, the statutory provisions and the nature of the matter to be decided. The distinction between them therefore becomes blurred as one approaches the lower end of the scale of judicial or *quasi*-judicial tribunals and the high end of the scale with respect to administrative or executive tribunals.

The basic purpose of the principles of fairness is to ensure that individuals are given an opportunity to participate in the decision-making process. This is required so that they could inform the decision-maker about any fact or argument that an administrative tribunal would need in order to make a fair decision. The procedural protections that are needed to achieve this purpose must allow the administrative tribunal to fulfill its duties under the governing statute effectively and efficiently.

To some extent, the courts still classify the function of the administrative tribunal. Classification of function is important for determining the content of the duty of fairness in particular situations. The courts have recognized that the decisions of administrative tribunals fall along a spectrum between administrative

---

[15] (1979), 106 D.L.R. (3d) 385 at pp. 410-11, [1980] 1 S.C.R. 602, 50 C.C.C. (2d) 353, 13 C.R. (3d) 1, 30 N.R. 119.

[16] (1989), 62 D.L.R. (4th) 385 at p. 425, [1989] 2 S.C.R. 879, 11 C.H.R.R. D/1, 89 C.L.L.C. ¶17,023, 100 N.R. 241.

and judicial functions which require different types of procedural protections. For example, an administrative tribunal which primarily sets policy will not be required to provide the same type of procedural protections as an administrative tribunal which primarily makes decisions affecting persons' rights, privileges or interests.

What this means in practice is that at one end of the spectrum, an administrative tribunal may not be required to hold an oral hearing and parties may only be able to make submissions in writing. At the other end of the spectrum, an administrative tribunal may be required to hold an oral hearing. At the hearing, the parties will be entitled to present evidence and cross-examine witnesses, to be represented by counsel, and the same rules of evidence that would apply in a court would have to be enforced. This same kind of administrative tribunal may also have the right to issue summonses to compel witnesses to attend at the hearing to give evidence and may be entitled to have its orders enforced in court.

When an administrative tribunal has the right to revoke or cancel a licence such as a taxi licence or even a licence to practise a particular profession, it will be required to follow more comprehensive procedural requirements than other administrative tribunals which do not have that power. As a result, the licensee will be given procedural protections that are close to those which are given at a trial.

More recently, the courts seem to have abandoned any classification of the function of the administrative tribunal in determining the content of the duty of fairness in particular situations. Instead, the courts have started to use a contextual approach to determine the content of the duty of fairness. For example, in *Baker v. Canada (Minister of Citizenship and Immigration)*,[17] the Supreme Court of Canada identified several factors to be considered in determining the specific procedural protections that will be applied in a particular situation. These factors include:[18]

(a) the nature of the decision being made by the administrative tribunal and the process followed in making that decision;
(b) the nature and the terms of the governing statute of the administrative tribunal;
(c) the importance and impact of the decision by the administrative tribunal to the individual or individuals affected;
(d) the legitimate expectations of the person challenging the decision of the administrative tribunal; and
(e) the choices of procedure made by the administrative tribunal.

---

[17] (1999), 174 D.L.R. (4th) 193, [1999] 2 S.C.R. 817, 14 Admin. L.R. (3d) 173, 1 Imm. L.R. (3d) 1, 243 N.R. 22.
[18] *Supra*, at pp. 838-40 (S.C.R.).

(4) Statutory Powers Procedure Act and Administrative Procedures Act

In Ontario and Alberta, there are general statutes which provide the minimum procedural requirements for proceedings of administrative tribunals. For example, in Alberta, the general statute, the *Administrative Procedures Act* ("APA"), applies to an administrative tribunal that exercises a "statutory power".[19] The phrase "statutory power" is defined in the Act. In Ontario, the statute is the *Statutory Powers Procedure Act* ("SPPA") and applies to administrative tribunals which are required to hold a hearing and which exercise a "statutory power of decision". The phrase "statutory power of decision" is also defined in the Act. Once it is determined that there is a statutory power of decision and there is a requirement to hold a hearing, the decision-maker must follow the procedural requirements in the SPPA.[20]

These procedural requirements in the SPPA include things such as the right to be represented by counsel or an agent, the right to reasonable notice of the hearing, the right to call and examine witnesses, and the right to reasons for decision if requested by a party.

Not all decisions will meet the threshold requirement and attract the minimum procedural requirements in the SPPA. For example, a decision to close down a school has been determined not to be a statutory power of decision. Therefore, the Act does not apply. Similarly, a decision in internal discipline proceedings at a university dealing with academic dishonesty, such as cheating by students, has

---

[19] The APA applies to a much smaller number of administrative tribunals than the SPPA. It only applies to the administrative tribunals that are listed in a schedule to the Act (approximately 10) and some other administrative tribunals whose governing statutes incorporate this Act into their governing statute. In contrast, the SPPA applies to all administrative tribunals that meet the requirements in the Act, which means that a much larger number of administrative tribunals are required to follow this Act.

[20] The SPPA now has exceptions to this automatic duty to hold a hearing. The SPPA now allows an administrative tribunal to postpone holding a hearing until certain procedural requirements have been satisfied if the administrative tribunal has made rules regarding postponement (s. 4.5). If documents are incomplete, documents are received after the deadline for commencing a proceeding, the required fee for commencing a proceeding is not paid, or there is some other technical defect in commencing a proceeding, an administrative tribunal can postpone holding a hearing. Also, the Act gives administrative tribunals the authority to dismiss a proceeding without holding a hearing under certain circumstances if an administrative tribunal has made rules regarding dismissal (s. 4.6). If a proceeding is frivolous or vexatious or is commenced in bad faith, the proceeding relates to matters that are outside the authority of the administrative tribunal, or some aspect of the requirements in the governing statute for bringing the proceeding has not been met, an administrative tribunal can dismiss a proceeding without holding a hearing. In both situations, the administrative tribunal has to give notice of its decision of postponement or dismissal including the reasons for this decision and provide the party with a chance to fix the procedural deficiency or to convince the administrative tribunal that its decision to dismiss is wrong.

been determined not to be a statutory power of decision. Nevertheless, the common law duty of fairness may still apply.

On the other hand, a decision about whether to issue a liquor licence is considered a statutory power of decision and the SPPA would apply. As a result, the decision-maker would be required to comply with the various procedural requirements in the Act.

The SPPA also indicates what evidence is admissible or allowed to be considered at a hearing to which the Act applies. For example, hearsay evidence is admissible at a hearing to which the Act applies. It is important to note that hearsay is inadmissible in a court.

However, certain statutes which create administrative tribunals to which the SPPA applies, expressly indicate that the rules of evidence applicable in a court apply to the hearing rather than the rules under the Act. Those administrative tribunals are usually the ones that hear more serious matters such as allegations of professional misconduct or unprofessional conduct. The legislatures in creating these statutes which provided for discipline proceedings have recognized that the potential penalties for a finding of professional misconduct or unprofessional conduct are so great that the finding must be based only on the most reliable evidence. As a result, only first-hand or direct evidence is usually admissible as it is in a civil or criminal trial and a witness would not ordinarily be able to give evidence about what he or she was told by a third person. The relaxed rules of evidence applicable at a SPPA hearing are not appropriate in those cases because of the nature of the decision to be made.

The SPPA also requires an administrative tribunal to give reasons for its decision if requested by a party. Even in places without a general procedural statute, it is preferable that an administrative tribunal gives reasons for its decision. Courts have stated that they will show more deference or respect to decisions of administrative tribunals which are accompanied by reasons when they review these decisions. This is because the reasons allow the court to determine how the administrative tribunal came to its decision. Without reasons, a court will probably scrutinize the decision of the administrative tribunal very carefully. Courts are often critical of administrative tribunals that do not give reasons, especially when the decision is not an obvious one, when findings of credibility were made, or when the decision is different from past decisions made by the same administrative tribunal in similar cases.

In contrast to the SPPA, the APA is not as detailed and does not require administrative tribunals to follow the same degree of procedural requirements. For example, under the APA, the right of a party to make representations does not necessarily involve a right to make oral representations or to be represented by counsel. If an administrative tribunal determines that a party can adequately make representations in writing, then the administrative tribunal has the authority under the APA to limit the party to making only written submissions. As another example, under the APA, the right to cross-examine is qualified because the party must first convince the administrative tribunal that "a fair opportunity" to "contradict or explain" facts or allegations made against that person requires that the person(s) making the factual statements or allegations be cross-examined. Under the SPPA, the right to cross-examine is also qualified but not to the same extent. A party has the automatic right to conduct a cross-examination that is "reasonably required for a full and fair disclosure of all matters relevant to the issues in the proceeding".

As an exception, there is one section in the APA which is more detailed than the corresponding section in the SPPA. The section in the APA dealing with the requirement to provide reasons requires an administrative tribunal to provide not only reasons for its decision (as the SPPA does) but also the findings of fact on which the administrative tribunal based its decision. However, this section is only triggered when an administrative tribunal exercises a "statutory power" that adversely affects the rights of a party. The corresponding section in the SPPA is triggered whenever there is a request by a party.

(5) Substantive Principles: Jurisdiction and Discretion

In addition to following proper procedures when making decisions, administrative tribunals must act within the scope of the authority or jurisdiction given to them by their governing statute. In the governing statute, an administrative tribunal's authority to act is expressed in terms of duties and powers. An administrative tribunal under a duty to act has no discretion and must act whenever that duty arises, while an administrative tribunal with a power to act has discretion and can act if the administrative tribunal feels it is appropriate. In the governing statute, a duty to act is usually expressed by using words such as "shall" or "must" while a power to act is usually expressed by using words such as "may".

(6) Jurisdiction

Jurisdiction means authority of the administrative tribunal. The authority of an administrative tribunal is located in the statute which establishes that administrative tribunal. In addition, the limits placed on that authority are also described in the statute because all delegated authority is restricted in some way. Because this statute governs what an administrative tribunal can and cannot do, it is called the governing statute. Similarly, since this statute enables the administrative tribunal to act and make decisions, it is often described as the enabling statute. Without authority from the enabling statute, the administrative tribunal would not be able to do anything. This is why administrative tribunals are often called "creatures of statute".

The governing statute gives an administrative tribunal its authority to act by setting out the objective or purposes of the administrative tribunal, procedures to be followed in making decisions, subject matter for making decisions, and remedies that can be granted. Since all statutes are different, it is important and necessary to refer to the actual governing statute for a specific administrative tribunal. The discussion, which follows, will only focus on the general principles for all administrative tribunals.

The courts review what an administrative tribunal does to ensure that its actions and decisions are legal/lawful by being within the authority of that administrative tribunal. The courts determine whether an administrative tribunal's actions and decisions are legal/lawful by reviewing and then interpreting, among other things, the objective or purposes of the administrative tribunal. This allows the courts to be able to decide if the administrative tribunal has acted within its authority (*intra vires*) or acted outside of its authority (*ultra vires*). This can be a very difficult and time-consuming exercise for a court because the words in a statute can have different meanings and judges rely on a variety of different factors in reviewing the actions and decisions of administrative tribunals.

There are two types of jurisdiction: jurisdiction in the narrow sense and jurisdiction in the broad sense. Jurisdiction in the narrow sense is the authority to initiate an inquiry on a particular subject. This involves determining whether an administrative tribunal has the authority to act or make decisions on the particular subject matter that it is confronted with in a given case. As part of deciding this question, the court will examine and analyze the governing statute. This is done in order to determine certain things such as the nature of the issue or problem that is before the administrative tribunal, the purpose and wording of the governing statute, and the characteristics of the administrative tribunal. It is important to remember that an administrative tribunal cannot have authority over all subject matter but must have certain identifiable limits and the court's function is to determine what are these limits. It is not appropriate to permit the administrative tribunal to determine its own limits because this would allow the administrative tribunal to extend its jurisdiction which is unlawful or illegal.

Jurisdiction in the narrow sense includes things such as whether the members of the administrative tribunal have the required qualifications, whether the composition of the administrative tribunal is proper, and whether the administrative tribunal has the authority to decide the particular question. For example, in regard to whether the administrative tribunal has the authority to decide a particular question, this requires the court to determine whether the federal Parliament or the provincial legislature intended that the administrative tribunal decide the particular question. If the answer is yes, it is considered *intra vires* and the administrative tribunal acted within its jurisdiction. If the answer is no, it is considered *ultra vires* and the administrative tribunal acted outside of its jurisdiction.

Even if an administrative tribunal has jurisdiction in the narrow sense to initiate an inquiry dealing with a particular subject matter, it may lose its jurisdiction to continue. An administrative tribunal may lose its jurisdiction by making an error in how it uses the authority that has been granted by the governing statute. This can occur by not providing fair procedures or exercising its discretion improperly (see the next section). This is called jurisdiction in the broad sense. In order to determine whether an administrative tribunal will lose its jurisdiction, the court will need to look at how it uses its authority to determine whether the administrative tribunal has acted unreasonably or unfairly. This will require that the court look at the entire conduct of the administrative tribunal and determine whether the administrative tribunal lost its authority because the administrative tribunal either failed to do something or did something wrong during the inquiry. When an administrative tribunal loses its jurisdiction, it no longer has any authority and the decision that is ultimately made by the administrative tribunal will be considered to be void and have no legal force or effect.

(7) Discretion

Discretion means choice. In the governing statute, discretion is defined on a subjective and broad basis such as "the administrative tribunal may do what is appropriate in the circumstances" or discretion is defined on an objective and narrow basis such as "the administrative tribunal may do one or more of the following". An administrative tribunal has more choice in terms of its actions and decisions when discretion is defined on a subjective basis but even then there are limits placed on the administrative tribunal's powers. This means that, when evaluating the actions or decisions of the administrative tribunal, the court will infer that the lawmakers placed limits on the administrative tribunal's powers of discretion. The court will also infer that the lawmakers expressed these limits by the words used in the governing statute such as in the purpose or objects section of the governing statute. Failure to do so is sometimes called "palm tree justice" which conjures up an image of arbitrary decisions being made by a dictator sitting under a palm tree.

Discretion also exists when the governing statute does not discuss a particular aspect of its authority to act, such as the procedures to be followed in making decisions.

In examining and analyzing the actions and decisions of an administrative tribunal, the courts determine whether the particular administrative tribunal is properly exercising its discretion. This involves determining whether the administrative tribunal has acted reasonably. This means that an administrative tribunal should exercise its discretion unfettered or unaffected by general policies of that administrative tribunal or directions from another administrative tribunal. This does not mean that administrative tribunals should avoid developing policies or guidelines to promote consistency and fairness in decision-making. It only means that administrative tribunals must ensure that these policies are not binding and that they do not follow them so strictly that it prevents them from making a decision in each case on an individual basis. Courts have also required that when an administrative tribunal has a discretion, it must be exercised by that administrative tribunal and not by anyone else. This means that the administrative tribunal must conduct the hearing and then make its own decision.

In addition, the courts also review the objective of the administrative tribunal as expressed in the governing statute to ensure that the administrative tribunal has not used its powers for improper purposes or failed to consider relevant factors when making its decision. Therefore, it is recommended that an administrative tribunal prepare reasons for its decision and set out its reasoning in as much detail as is possible so that a court reviewing its decision can see the thought process for the decision made by the administrative tribunal.

4

Decisions of Administrative Tribunals

(1) What is a Decision?

It is very common to use the word "decision" in place of the term "reasons for decision" and to use the term "reasons for decision" instead of the word "decision" but there are differences between a "decision" and the "reasons for decision". The "decision" is what the administrative tribunal has either found as fact or has ruled should be done in response to an investigation or any other proceeding that has been brought before it. In making this determination, the administrative tribunal will consider the facts and the law that are relevant to the situation. The subject matter of what a decision deals with is quite broad. It ranges from responding to a request for or even a claim to something to establishing a duty or imposing a penalty on someone.

It is also common to use the words "decision" and "order" interchangeably but there are differences between a "decision" and an "order". These differences are usually reflected in the different governing statutes of administrative tribunals. For example, some governing statutes define the word "order" as meaning the format of the decision. This means that the "decision" is what the administrative tribunal has determined should be done and the "order" is the piece of paper that contains the decision.

(2) What is the Difference Between a Final and an Interim Decision?

In any proceeding that is brought before an administrative tribunal, the administrative tribunal will eventually make a decision which finishes or completes that proceeding. Decisions which finish or complete proceedings that are brought before an administrative tribunal are considered final decisions. Examples of final decisions include the following:

43

- to deny or grant a licence,[1]
- to impose terms, conditions or limitations on a licence,
- to remove or modify the terms, conditions or limitations on a licence,
- to suspend a licence,
- to revoke a licence,
- to remove a suspension or to reinstate a licence,
- to refuse to hear a case,
- to dismiss a complaint, and
- to not investigate a complaint when the complaint is determined to be frivolous, vexatious, made in bad faith, or an abuse of process.

Courts tend to give a very broad scope to final decisions. For example, courts consider a decision to be a final decision if it finishes or completes the proceeding for one person even though the proceeding continues for one or more other persons. This means that an administrative tribunal may decide to not allow a person to participate in a hearing even though the hearing will continue for the parties to the hearing. This decision to not permit that person to participate is considered a final decision for that person because the proceeding is finished for him or her before that administrative tribunal. Also, courts consider a final decision to be final even if reasons for that decision have not been given.

In contrast to a final decision, an administrative tribunal will often make many decisions during a proceeding. Decisions that are made during a proceeding and which deal with matters that are secondary to the issues that must be decided by the administrative tribunal are considered interim decisions. Examples of interim decisions include the following:

- to limit or expand the scope of an investigation,
- to allow a person to participate in a hearing or add a person as a party to the hearing,
- to deny or grant an adjournment,
- to order or deny disclosure of the evidence,
- to order or deny disclosure of the complainant's clinical or psychiatric records,
- to disqualify a member of the administrative tribunal from hearing the case on the grounds of bias,
- to close or open a hearing or a portion of a hearing,
- to order a physical or mental examination, and
- to admit or refuse to admit certain evidence.

The word "interim" is also used to describe decisions which are made by an administrative tribunal as a temporary measure until a final decision is made. An example of this kind of interim decision is a decision to grant a temporary rate

---

[1] The use of the word "licence" is meant to also include other documents such as a certificate of registration.

increase for telephone services to Bell Canada pending the final decision of the Canadian Radio-television and Telecommunications Commission (the "CRTC"). Another example is a decision to suspend a nurse's certificate of registration pending the final decision of the Discipline Committee of the College of Nurses of Ontario. These types of interim decisions are commonly made to provide temporary relief against the potentially harmful effects arising from the length of time it takes for an administrative tribunal to conduct a hearing and make a final decision, especially if the hearing before the administrative tribunal is expected to take a long time to complete.

Interim decisions of administrative tribunals are also occasionally referred to as interlocutory decisions. The use of the word "interlocutory" to refer to an "interim" decision of an administrative tribunal is problematic because there can be confusion since the Rules of Court in many provinces use the term "interlocutory". Under these Rules of Court, an interlocutory decision is considered more similar to a final decision than to an interim decision.

It is important to realize that there are differences between a final and an interim decision — and be able to determine when a decision is final or interim — because a person has different rights, and an administrative tribunal has different requirements, depending on whether a decision is considered to be interim or final.

For example, if there is a right to appeal in the governing statute of the administrative tribunal, a person can generally only appeal a final decision of the administrative tribunal not an interim decision. Similarly, the courts do not often agree to hear an application for judicial review[2] of interim decisions. The courts will consider applications for judicial review of interim decisions of an administrative tribunal as being premature and require the person to wait until the administrative tribunal has given a final decision before the court will be willing to intervene.

Also, the governing statute of an administrative tribunal usually places different requirements on an administrative tribunal when it makes a final decision as compared to an interim decision. For example, many governing statutes of administrative tribunals require an administrative tribunal to prepare reasons for decision only when making a final decision and not an interim decision. In addition, the *Statutory Powers Procedure Act*[3] (the "SPPA"), the general procedural statute in Ontario, indicates that interim decisions need not be accompanied by reasons for decision.[4]

---

[2] For the most part, judicial review is initiated by an application for judicial review. However, for some provinces and territories, a variety of different documents such as a petition or notice of motion initiates judicial review. Nevertheless, for the rest of the book, the term application for judicial review will be used in all cases.

[3] R.S.O. 1990, c. S.22.

[4] See s. 16.1 of the SPPA.

(3) Is There a Required Format for a Decision?

Unless the administrative tribunal's governing statute, or any other statute which is applicable to the administrative tribunal, requires a particular format for decisions,[5] the decision can be oral or written.

Generally, interim decisions of administrative tribunals are oral as administrative tribunals usually do not prepare written decisions regarding requests for things such as disclosure of the evidence against the professional or allowing a person to participate in the hearing. Yet, an administrative tribunal should try to prepare written interim decisions because this allows the participants in the proceeding before the administrative tribunal, and possibly the court if it agrees to hear a judicial review application, to be clear about the decision that has been made by the administrative tribunal. There are also other options for an administrative tribunal if it determines that it does not want to prepare an interim written decision, especially if there have been multiple interim decisions. For example, an administrative tribunal can set out any interim decisions in a small section, even a short paragraph, of its final written decision.

In contrast, it is very common for administrative tribunals to prepare written final decisions. For administrative tribunals that do not usually prepare written final decisions, it is strongly recommended that they prepare written final decisions in order to ensure that the participants and possibly the court are clear about the decision. It is especially important to prepare final decisions in writing when these decisions can be reviewed or appealed or even when these decisions will need to be enforced. For example, an oral final decision that is unclear or ambiguous will probably not be able to be enforced by a court.

It is also important to prepare final decisions in writing when a person or persons will be required to do or be prohibited from doing something. For example, if an administrative tribunal makes a final decision awarding a person disability benefits, it is helpful for the person to have a written decision stating that he or she has been awarded disability benefits and any other relevant aspects to the decision, such as the amount and the duration of the disability benefits. This is important because, when a final decision is given orally by an administrative tribunal, the participants to the hearing often cannot remember the entire decision or even the key aspects of the decision. Also, participants may attempt to write down the key aspects of the decision but they cannot write them down fast enough to keep up as the decision is being read orally.

In addition to determining whether a decision should be oral or written when there is no required format for a decision, an administrative tribunal has to decide whether its decision and reasons for that decision will be in the same document or in separate documents. There are several advantages of having separate documents for the decision and the reasons for that decision. The advantages of a sep-

---

[5] Section 17 of the SPPA requires an administrative tribunal to give its final decision in writing.

arate document for the decision are that it can be drafted more precisely, it can be drafted by the Discipline Committee's lawyer, and it can be delivered before the reasons for decision have been finished.

The format of a decision does not turn something into a decision. Something becomes a decision if it contains what the administrative tribunal has either found as fact or has ruled should be done in response to an investigation or any other proceeding that has been brought before it. Therefore, a one-paragraph letter from an administrative tribunal that imposes a duty, benefit or penalty on someone, can be considered a decision. Similarly, a form letter or a standard form with boxes checked off can be considered a decision. In contrast, a letter from a staff member of an administrative tribunal might not be considered a decision if it does not accurately communicate what the administrative tribunal has decided to do.[6] In addition, a letter from a staff member of an administrative tribunal that notifies a person about things such as the process for the hearing or the applicable law to the case will probably not be considered a decision because the letter only provides information and does not make any decision.

Regardless of the format of the decision, all decisions made by an administrative tribunal must be clear about what the administrative tribunal has decided to do. This is especially important when a person or persons is required to do or is prohibited from doing something. In that case, the decision must be clear enough so that the person or persons can be aware of what they are required or prohibited from doing.

(4) What are Reasons for Decision?

All decisions regardless of whether they are final or interim, oral or written, must have reasons. An administrative tribunal cannot make a decision without having a reason or reasons for making that decision.

Reasons for decision are not the same thing as the decision. The decision is *what* the administrative tribunal has either found as fact or has ruled should be done in response to an investigation or any other proceeding that has been brought before it. In contrast, the reasons for decision are *why* the administrative tribunal determined something should be done. Reasons for decision represent the method that the administrative tribunal uses to communicate why it made a

---

[6] For example, in the recent decision of the Federal Court of Appeal in *Centre for Research-Action on Race Relations v. Canadian Radio-television and Telecommunications Commission* (2000), 266 N.R. 344, the court reaffirmed the decision of the CRTC that a letter by a CRTC staff member indicating an opinion about a complaint was not considered a decision of the Commission. In this letter, the Executive Director had indicated that the complaint regarding the television program had been examined and that this program did not constitute a violation of the law or regulations. The CRTC had determined that this letter was not a decision because no member of the Commission had considered the matter and the letter only represented the views of certain officers. Similarly, the court determined that this letter was not a decision because the Executive Director was not a member of the CRTC.

specific decision. Reasons for decision provide an explanation for the decision so that the person or persons reading the decision can understand why the administrative tribunal made a certain decision.

(5) Why Give Reasons?

Whenever an administrative tribunal makes a decision, it should try to give a reason or reasons for its decision, unless this is impractical or even impossible, because reasons fulfill a lot of useful purposes.

In the article entitled "Good Agency Decisions: A Judge's Perspective",[7] the Honourable Mr. Justice Barry Strayer illustrates the importance of giving reasons. He stated:

> But if an agency is subject to review by a court, then it is important that it explain itself so that the court may understand what is decided and why. Most judges are not anxious to disturb agency decisions if they can perceive a rational basis for the result in question, even if it is not the result they might have chosen. The agency is in the best position to know why it reached the conclusion it did, what evidence, what criteria, and what arguments it took into account in the process. It is also best able to explain the procedure employed by it. In the absence of such explanations it is open to counsel, in attacking the agency decision before a reviewing court, to speculate as to those reasons, to colour events which transpired before the agency, and even to characterize agency decisions as based on ignorance, stupidity, or bad faith. One cannot always count on opposing counsel who are there to support the agency's decision to be able to explain it correctly or effectively, particularly when the agency has not explained itself. The agency itself will often not be represented before the courts and where it is, the role of the agency's counsel may be seriously limited.

Many of the purposes for providing reasons were described by the Supreme Court of Canada in its recent decision in *Baker v. Canada (Minister of Citizenship and Immigration)*:[8]

1. Reasons foster better decision-making by an administrative tribunal by ensuring that issues and reasoning are well articulated and, therefore, more carefully thought out.
2. The process of writing reasons for a decision by itself may be a guarantee of a better decision by an administrative tribunal.
3. Reasons allow parties to see that the applicable issues have been carefully considered.
4. Reasons are invaluable if a decision by an administrative tribunal is to be appealed, questioned or considered on judicial review.
5. Those affected by a decision of an administrative tribunal may be more likely to feel they were treated fairly and appropriately if reasons are given.

---

[7] B.L. Strayer, "Good Agency Decisions: A Judge's Perspective" (1995), 1 *Administrative Agency Practice* 55, at pp. 55-6, reproduced with permission.

[8] (1999), 174 D.L.R. (4th) 193, [1999] 2 S.C.R. 817 at pp. 845-6, 14 Admin. L.R. (3d) 173, 1 Imm. L.R. (3d) 1, 243 N.R. 22.

Similarly, the Federal Court of Appeal in *Williams v. Canada (Minister of Citizenship and Immigration)*[9] described some of the purposes for giving reasons:

> I would first confirm, as have many courts over the years, that it is usually, if not always, preferable that both courts and tribunals give reasons for their decisions. There are many advantages in issuing reasons: they enable the parties to know why they have won or lost, a very important consideration; the articulation of reasons imposes a discipline upon a court or tribunal when it is obliged to justify the result; and they undoubtedly assist a court later in disposing of an appeal or exercising powers of judicial review.

In addition to the courts, authors who have written about the practice and procedure before administrative tribunals have identified additional purposes for giving reasons:[10]

1. Reasons fulfill an educational purpose because they can be used in future cases as guides for the public or as precedents for other administrative tribunals or even other decision-makers within the administrative tribunal that prepared the reasons.
2. Reasons may clarify the decision of the administrative tribunal when there is ambiguity in that decision.
3. Reasons may indicate how the decision of the administrative tribunal was expected to be applied where the application of that decision to a particular circumstance is not clear.
4. Reasons allow the decisions of administrative tribunals to be understood and accepted. For example, reasons can offer a party some assurance that the decision of the administrative tribunal was not made arbitrarily and that the relevant evidence and arguments have been considered. As a result, deci-

---

[9] (1997), 147 D.L.R. (4th) 93 at pp. 110-11, [1997] 2 F.C. 646, 129 F.T.R. 240*n*, 4 Admin. L.R. (3d) 200, 212 N.R. 63 (C.A.), leave to appeal to S.C.C. refused 150 D.L.R. (4th) viii, 224 N.R. 320*n*.

[10] J.M. Evans, H.N. Janisch and D.J. Mullan, *Administrative Law: Cases, Text, and Materials*, 4th ed. (Toronto: Emond Montgomery Publications Ltd., 1995), at pp. 479-80; G. Steele, "Reflections on Writing a Reasoned Decision" (1996), 2 *Administrative Agency Practice* 108, at p. 109; C. Gauk, "The Annotated Alberta *Administrative Procedures Act* — Section 7: The Duty to Give Reasons" (1995), 1 *Administrative Agency Practice* 49, at pp. 49-50; J. Swaigen, *A Manual for Ontario Adjudicators* (Courtice: Society of Ontario Adjudicators and Regulators, 2000), at pp. 161-2; Alberta, *Powers and Procedures for Administrative Tribunals in Alberta — Report No. 79* (Edmonton: Alberta Law Reform Institute, 1999), at p. 135; R.W. Macaulay and J.L.H. Sprague, *Practice and Procedure Before Administrative Tribunals* (Scarborough: Carswell Thomson Professional Publishing, 1997), at p. 22-55 (2000, release 4); J.L.H. Sprague, "Remedies for the Failure to Provide Reasons" (2000), 13 C.J.A.L.P. 209, at pp. 211-13; M.H. Morris, "Administrative Decision-makers and the Duty to Give Reasons: An Emerging Debate" (1998), 11 C.J.A.L.P. 155, at p. 157; R.A. Macdonald and D. Lametti, "Reasons for Decision in Administrative Law" (1990), 3 C.J.A.L.P. 123, at pp. 145-59.

sions with reasons are less likely to be challenged and even if there is a challenge, they are not likely to be reversed.

5. Reasons help to ensure that the administrative tribunal does not overlook relevant matters to its decision such as the evidence of a particular witness or the arguments of a party.
6. Reasons promote a sense of accountability in an administrative tribunal to members of the public.

(6) Are Reasons Required?

Aside from the practical purposes for providing reasons when an administrative tribunal makes a decision, it is important to determine whether reasons are required in a particular case. In determining whether reasons are required, there are two important sources which need to be looked at: the common law and the administrative tribunal's governing legislation or any other legislation which is applicable to the administrative tribunal.

(a) Common law

Traditionally, the principles of natural justice and fairness did not impose a general duty on an administrative tribunal to provide reasons for its decision.

However, in the past 10 years, the courts have shown an increasing willingness to require administrative tribunals to provide reasons for its decisions on the basis of the principles of natural justice and fairness. Examples of cases where the courts have determined that administrative tribunals are required to provide reasons for its decisions include the following:

- where a decision by an administrative tribunal affected a person's rights that were protected by s. 7 of the *Canadian Charter of Rights and Freedoms*[11] (the "Charter"),
- where an administrative tribunal exercises discretion in the course of making a decision,
- where the administrative tribunal's governing statute or any other applicable statute requires certain criteria or conditions to be met in order to make a particular decision,
- when an administrative tribunal's failure to provide reasons for its decision interferes with or even prejudices future legal remedies,
- where an administrative tribunal's failure to give reasons for its decision prevents a person from exercising his or her right to appeal,
- when an administrative tribunal's failure to provide reasons for its decision compromises a person's ability to demonstrate specific grounds for judicial review,

---

[11] Part I of the *Constitution Act, 1982*, being Schedule B of the *Canada Act 1982* (U.K.), 1982, c. 11.

- where an administrative tribunal makes a decision which is different from previous similar fact decisions made by that administrative tribunal,
- where there are substantial issues to be decided by the administrative tribunal and an administrative tribunal's reasons for its decision on those substantial issues are not apparent from a review of the record, and
- where an administrative tribunal makes a negative decision which adversely affects an individual and there is a concern that the decision was made on the basis of or influenced by irrelevant considerations.

Subsequently, in contrast to the traditional position of the Canadian courts, the Supreme Court of Canada gave a landmark decision in 1999 in *Baker v. Canada (Minister of Citizenship and Immigration)* when it recognized that administrative tribunals have a duty to provide written reasons in certain circumstances. The court stated:[12]

> In my opinion, it is now appropriate to recognize that, in certain circumstances, the duty of procedural fairness will require the provision of a written explanation for a decision. The strong arguments demonstrating the advantages of written reasons suggest that, in cases such as this where the decision has important significance for the individual, when there is a statutory right of appeal, or in other circumstances, some form of reasons should be required.

Despite the fact that this decision is significant because it expands the principles of fairness to include a duty on administrative tribunals to provide reasons for their decisions, there is not much direction from the Supreme Court of Canada about when the principles of fairness will require reasons for decision. The only direction that is provided by the Supreme Court is that reasons for decision will be required by the principles of fairness when the decision by the administrative tribunal has "important significance for the individual",[13] when there is a "statutory right of appeal", or "in other circumstances". Given the fact that these are very broad criteria, subsequent courts will need to determine the meaning of these criteria in the course of making a decision about whether a particular case will require reasons for decision.

(b) Legislation

Despite the fact that there is uncertainty in the common law about when an administrative tribunal will be required to provide reasons for decision, it has become very common to specify when reasons for decision are required in relevant legislation. This includes: the general procedural statutes in Ontario and Alberta, the governing statutes of administrative tribunals, any other statutes

---

[12] *Supra*, footnote 8, at p. 848.

[13] As an example, a court will likely determine that a decision by a Discipline Committee of an administrative tribunal regarding allegations of professional misconduct or incompetence will have important significance for the individual professional. It will likely require that Discipline Committee to give reasons for its decision even if its governing statute or any other applicable statute does not have a requirement to provide reasons.

which are applicable to the administrative tribunals, and even regulations made under any of these statutes. There is a wide variation in these statutes and regulations in terms of the requirement of reasons for decision. The requirement for reasons can be automatic or only on request. The requirement for reasons can be with respect to all actions taken or decisions made by the administrative tribunal or only with respect to certain actions taken or decisions made by the administrative tribunal. The requirement for reasons can impose a time limit for giving reasons or leave it open-ended. The requirement for reasons may specify people who are required to receive a copy of the reasons or it can be made available to the general public.

The following are some examples of the legislative provisions regarding decisions:

1. *Administrative Procedures Act*:[14]

> 7. When an authority exercises a statutory power so as to adversely affect the rights of a party, the authority shall furnish to each party a written statement of its decision setting out
> (a) the findings of fact on which it based its decision; and
> (b) the reasons for the decision.

2. *Statutory Powers Procedure Act*:[15]

> 17(1) A tribunal shall give its final decision and order, if any, in any proceeding in writing and shall give reasons in writing therefor if requested by a party.

3. *Certified General Accountants Act*:[16]

> 75. A hearing committee shall, within a reasonable time after the conclusion of a hearing, make a written decision on the matter, in which it shall
> (a) describe each finding made by it of unprofessional conduct,
> (b) state the reasons for each finding made by it, and
> (c) state any order made by it.

4. *Engineers and Geoscientists Act*:[17]

> 33(3) The discipline committee must give written reasons for any action it takes under subsection (2).

5. *Horse Racing Act*:[18]

> 16(3) The commission must, on request, give written reasons for any action taken under subsection (2)(b) to (e).

6. *Legal Profession Act*:[19]

> 38(3) A panel must
> (a) make a determination and take action according to this section,

---

[14] R.S.A. 1980, c. A-2.
[15] R.S.O. 1990, c. S.22, amended 1993, c. 27.
[16] S.A. 1987, c. C-3.6.
[17] R.S.B.C. 1996, c. 116.
[18] R.S.B.C. 1996, c. 198.
[19] S.B.C. 1998, c. 9.

(b) give written reasons for its determination about the conduct or competence of the respondent and any action taken against the respondent, and

(c) record in writing any order for costs.

7. *Nurses (Registered) Act:*[20]

43(3) A decision of the professional conduct committee under sections 42 and 43 must be in writing and must contain or be accompanied by the reasons for the decision, in writing.

43(4) The professional conduct committee must, within 30 days of the date of a decision made under this section or section 42, serve the member and the complainant referred to in section 44(1)(d) with

(a) a copy of the decision and the reasons, and

(b) notice of the right to appeal under section 44.

8. *Charitable Institutions Act:*[21]

9.11(15) The Appeal Board shall render its decision within one day after the end of the hearing and shall provide written reasons to the parties within seven days after rendering the decision.

9. *Ontario College of Teachers Act, 1996:*[22]

32(13) Subject to subsection (14), the Discipline Committee or Fitness to Practise Committee shall serve its decision, with reasons,

(a) on the parties; and

(b) where the matter was referred to the Discipline Committee or Fitness to Practise Committee as a result of a complaint under subsection 26(1), on the complainant.

32(14) Where the hearing was closed, the Discipline Committee or Fitness to Practise Committee may, in its discretion, serve its decision on the complainant without reasons.

10. *Regulated Health Professions Act, 1991:*[23]

54. A panel shall give its decision and reasons in writing to the parties and, if the matter had been referred to the Discipline Committee by the Complaints Committee, to the complainant in the matter.

11. *Canada Pension Plan:*[24]

82(11) A Review Tribunal may confirm or vary a decision of the Minister made under section 81 or subsection 84(2) or under subsection 27.1(2) of the *Old Age Security Act* and may take any action in relation to any of those decisions that might have been taken by the Minister under that section or either of those subsections, and the Commissioner of Review Tribunals shall thereupon notify the Minister and the other parties to the appeal of the Review Tribunal's decision and of the reasons for its decision.

83(11) The Pension Appeals Board may confirm or vary a decision of a Review Tribunal under section 82 or subsection 84(2) and may take any action in relation

---

[20] R.S.B.C. 1996, c. 335.

[21] R.S.O. 1990, c. C.9.

[22] S.O. 1996, c. 12.

[23] S.O. 1991, c. 18, Schedule 2, the *Health Professions Procedural Code.*

[24] R.S.C. 1985, c. C-8.

thereto that might have been taken by the Review Tribunal under section 82 or subsection 84(2), and shall thereupon notify in writing the parties to the appeal of its decision and of its reasons therefor.

12. *Immigration Act*:[25]

69.1(11)   The Refugee Division may give written reasons for its decision on a claim, except that
- (a) if the decision is against the person making the claim, the Division shall, with the written notice of the decision referred to in subsection (9), give written reasons with the decision; and
- (b) if the Minister or the person making the claim requests written reasons within ten days after the day on which the Minister or the person is notified of the decision, the Division shall forthwith give written reasons.

13. *National Energy Board Act*:[26]

28.2(7) At or after the conclusion of the hearing, the Board shall make the decision, give notice of it to each person who requested the hearing and, if the person requests reasons, publish or make available the reasons for the decision.

14. *Royal Canadian Mounted Police Act*:[27]

45.12(2) A decision of an adjudication board shall be recorded in writing and shall include a statement of the findings of the board on questions of fact material to the decision, reasons for the decision and a statement of the sanction, if any, imposed under subsection (3) or the informal disciplinary action, if any, taken under subsection (4).

45.23(2) A decision of a discharge and demotion board shall be recorded in writing and shall include a statement of the findings of the board on questions of fact material to the decision, reasons for the decision and a statement of the action taken by the board under subsection (3) or (4).

15. *Canada Lands Surveyors Regulations*[28] under the *Canada Lands Surveyors Act*:[29]

54. For every hearing held by the Discipline Committee, a record shall compile consisting of the allegation and the notice referred to in subsection 44(1), any rulings or orders made in the course of the proceeding, a summary of the oral evidence presented at the hearing, any copies of documents and things that were placed in evidence and the decision and the reasons therefor.

16. *P.S.S.R.B. Regulations and Rules of Procedure, 1993*[30] under the *Public Service Staff Relations Act*:[31]

83. The decision of an adjudicator or a board of adjudication shall contain
- (a) a summary of the grievance;

---

[25] R.S.C. 1985, c. I-2.
[26] R.S.C. 1985, c. N-7.
[27] R.S.C. 1985, c. R-10.
[28] SOR/99-142.
[29] S.C. 1998, c. 14.
[30] SOR/93-348.
[31] R.S.C. 1985, c. P-35.

(b) a summary of the representations of the parties; and

(c) the reasons for the decision.

(7) What Happens if You Fail to Give Reasons?

(a) No requirement to give reasons

If an administrative tribunal fails to give reasons even though there is no requirement to give reasons either in the common law or the administrative tribunal's governing legislation or any other legislation which is applicable to the administrative tribunal, a court will probably scrutinize the decision of the administrative tribunal very carefully.

Courts are often critical of an administrative tribunal that does not give reasons, especially when the decision is not an obvious one, when findings of credibility were made, or when the decision is different from past decisions made by the same administrative tribunal in similar cases.

Courts have stated that, when no reasons have been given, they may draw adverse inferences against the administrative tribunal, refuse to show deference to the decision of the administrative tribunal, or even interfere with the decision of the administrative tribunal. For example, the Newfoundland Court of Appeal in *Hallingham v. Workers' Compensation Commission (Nfld.)*[32] stated:

> Even if the Tribunal were not statutorily required to give reasons, its failure to demonstrate that it considered all relevant factors in arriving at its decision could lead to an inference that it did not consider them . . .

Similarly, the Newfoundland Supreme Court in *Jaswal v. Newfoundland Medical Board*[33] stated:

> Whilst the Board is not required to give reasons, the fact that it chooses not to do so may have the practical result of the court having greater reason to intervene because of a lack of apparent rationale for the penalty imposed.

(b) Requirement to give reasons — legislation

In contrast, if an administrative tribunal fails to give reasons when there is a requirement to give reasons in the administrative tribunal's governing legislation or any other legislation which is applicable to the administrative tribunal, there can be significant consequences for the administrative tribunal and its decision.

In terms of determining the consequences, the first place to look is the administrative tribunal's governing statute or any other statute which is applicable to the administrative tribunal. If any of these statutes set out the consequences to an administrative tribunal for failing to give reasons, those consequences will occur. For example, s. 48 of the *Labour Relations Act, 1995*[34] states:

---

[32] (1997), 158 Nfld. & P.E.I.R. 21 at p. 27 (Nfld. C.A.).

[33] (1996), 138 Nfld. & P.E.I.R. 181 at p. 193, 42 Admin. L.R. (2d) 233 *sub nom. Jaswal v. Medical Board (Newfoundland)* (Nfld. S.C.).

[34] S.O. 1995, c. 1, Sch. A.

48(11) If the arbitrator or arbitration board does not give a decision within the time described in subsection (7) or (8) or does not provide written reasons within the time described in subsection (10), the Minister may,

   (a) make such orders as he or she considers necessary to ensure that the decision or reasons will be given without undue delay; and

   (b) make such orders as he or she considers appropriate respecting the remuneration and expenses of the arbitrator or arbitration board.

This subsection makes it clear to the arbitrator or arbitration board under the *Labour Relations Act, 1995* that if it fails to give reasons, the validity of its decision will not be affected but the arbitrator or arbitration board will be confronted with potential consequences regarding remuneration and expenses.

If none of the relevant legislation set out the consequences for failing to give reasons, a court will need to determine whether the requirement to give reasons is intended to be mandatory or directory. In the course of determining whether the requirement is mandatory or directory, the court will consider the importance of providing reasons given the wording of the relevant statute(s) and surrounding circumstances and whether the failure to give reasons will lead to prejudice.

When the requirement to give reasons is considered to be mandatory, the court will invalidate the decision of the administrative tribunal by setting it aside or quashing it and then generally send the matter back to the administrative tribunal for a rehearing. The court will not always send the matter back for a rehearing. If the matter is sent back for a rehearing, the nature of the rehearing will vary depending on the instructions by the court in its decision and the administrative tribunal's governing statute. When the requirement to give reasons is considered to be directory, the court will not invalidate the decision. Nevertheless, the court may send the matter back to the administrative tribunal to give reasons for its decision. In other cases, the court may decide to do nothing.

A related issue involves determining the effect on an administrative tribunal and its decision when the administrative tribunal does not give reasons for its decision where there is a requirement in the relevant statute to give reasons but only on request of a party. In those cases including when s. 17 of the SPPA is applicable, there would be no effect on the administrative tribunal or its decision for not giving reasons for its decision if a party does not make a request for reasons for decision. This means that the court will not interfere with the decision of the administrative tribunal if it does not give reasons for its decision when a party has not requested reasons for decision. The court will not intervene because previous courts have determined that an administrative tribunal's duty to give reasons for its decision only develops when a party makes a request for reasons for decision.

If a party makes a request for reasons for decision but the request is not made within a reasonable length of time, there would also be no effect on the administrative tribunal or its decision for not giving reasons for its decision. This means that the court will not interfere with the decision of the administrative tribunal when a party has not requested reasons for decision within a reasonable length of time. There is a wide variation in the cases in terms of what is considered a reasonable length of time. But, the courts have identified various factors to be considered in determining what is a reasonable length of time. These factors include:

- the workload of the administrative tribunal at the time the request is made,
- the length of time since the administrative tribunal gave its decision,
- whether the members of the administrative tribunal who made the decision are still members of the administrative tribunal at the time the request is made,
- whether there is a transcript of the evidence from the hearing before the administrative tribunal, and
- whether any of the documents and materials from the hearing have been destroyed.

If a party makes a request for reasons for decision and the request is made within a reasonable length of time, there would probably also be no effect on the administrative tribunal's decision for not giving reasons for its decision. This means that the court will not likely interfere with the decision of the administrative tribunal even when a party has requested reasons for decision within a reasonable length of time. The court will not likely intervene because previous courts have determined that reasons for decision are not a prerequisite to making a decision by an administrative tribunal. An administrative tribunal's duty to give reasons for its decision only develops after the administrative tribunal has given a decision and a party makes a request for reasons for decision. Since there is no duty to give reasons for decision when the administrative tribunal makes its decision, the administrative tribunal's original decision probably cannot be invalidated if the administrative tribunal fails to observe its subsequent duty to give reasons. Nevertheless, the court may send the matter back to the administrative tribunal to give reasons for its decision.

(c) Requirement to give reasons — common law

If an administrative tribunal fails to give reasons when there is a requirement to give reasons in the common law on the basis of the principles of natural justice and fairness, there can be significant consequences for the administrative tribunal and its decision.[35]

The cases indicate that when a court determines that an administrative tribunal has a common law duty to provide reasons for its decision and that administrative tribunal does not give reasons for its decision, the court will invalidate the decision of the administrative tribunal by setting it aside or quashing it and then generally send the matter back to the administrative tribunal for a rehearing. The

---

[35] As an exception, there will probably be no consequences for an administrative tribunal and its decision if the tribunal fails to give reasons when there is a common law requirement to give reasons if the party to the proceeding, explicitly or implicitly, waives his or her right to reasons.

court will not always send the matter back for a rehearing. If the matter is sent back for a rehearing, the nature of the rehearing will vary depending on the instructions by the court in its decision and the administrative tribunal's governing statute.

(8) What Happens if the Reasons are Inadequate?

If an administrative tribunal gives inadequate reasons, there are a variety of different consequences for the administrative tribunal and its decision which will vary depending on the nature or degree of the inadequacy.

If the reasons are inadequate, the court may send the matter back to the administrative tribunal to give appropriate reasons, whereas, in other cases, the court may decide to do nothing. In contrast, if the reasons disclose that the administrative tribunal made an error in how it exercised the authority that had been granted by the governing statute, the court may invalidate the decision of the administrative tribunal by setting it aside or quashing it and then will generally send the matter back to the administrative tribunal for a rehearing. The court will not always send the matter back for a rehearing. If the matter is sent back for a rehearing, the nature of the rehearing will vary depending on the instructions by the court in its decision and the administrative tribunal's governing statute.

(9) Who are Your Audiences?

The purpose of writing a decision is to inform others about *what* the administrative tribunal has either found as a true fact or has ruled should be done in response to an investigation or any other proceeding that has been brought before it. In contrast, the purpose of writing reasons for decision is to explain *why* the administrative tribunal decided something should be done. In order to accomplish these purposes, it is important for the administrative tribunal to become aware of and actually identify the potential readers of its decision and reasons for decision[36] or its possible audiences. It is also important for the administrative tribunal to think about and attempt to understand the questions that each audience brings to the decision and reasons for decision. It is very important that the administrative tribunal does these things before the hearing takes place so that the administrative tribunal keeps these audiences and their questions in mind during the course of the hearing. In addition, after the hearing takes place, it is important that the member of the administrative tribunal who is responsible for preparing the decision and reasons for decision keeps these audiences and their questions in mind when preparing the decision and reasons for decision.

---

[36] The term "decision and reasons for decision" refers to the document that is given to the parties to the proceeding before the administrative tribunal and it contains all the elements of a decision including the final decision and the reasons for that decision.

(a) The parties

The primary audience for the administrative tribunal's decision and reasons for decision are the parties to the proceeding before that administrative tribunal. Parties want to know why they won or lost, succeeded or failed. Parties want to know what the administrative tribunal thought of their submissions, arguments and evidence. Parties also usually care about the administrative tribunal's opinion of them such as whether the party was truthful, sincere, capable and thoughtful.

It is important to remember that the administrative tribunal cannot make all the parties to the proceeding happy with its decision and reasons for decision but the administrative tribunal can often leave all the parties with the feeling that the administrative tribunal listened to their submissions, arguments and evidence. This can be done by the way that the administrative tribunal approaches its decision and reasons for decision and the actual wording it uses in its decision and reasons for decision. It is especially important that the losing party feels that the administrative tribunal listened to his or her submissions, arguments and evidence so that he or she is not left with the impression that the administrative tribunal made an unfair and arbitrary decision.

It is also important for the administrative tribunal to ensure that its decision and reasons for decision are clear and understandable to the parties to the proceeding especially the losing party. This allows the parties to have a complete understanding of its effect on them and to evaluate on a realistic basis the merits of bringing an appeal or an application for judicial review.

(b) The courts

Another primary audience for the administrative tribunal's decision and reasons for decision are the courts. Every administrative tribunal must keep the courts in mind because the courts may review its decisions. When thinking about the courts, it is important to realize that administrative law is a fairly new area of law in Canada and is not yet well known. It is also important to realize that not many of the judges have been members of administrative tribunals, and proceedings before administrative tribunals should not be treated as if they were proceedings before courts given the differences between courts and administrative tribunals.

The courts need to be able to understand the thought process of the administrative tribunal in order to determine whether the decision was properly made. Of course, this makes administrative tribunals very nervous because they are afraid that if their thought process is revealed in too much detail in its decision and reasons for decision, there will be more for the court to criticize.

However, the general approach that the courts take is that they are less likely to criticize when an administrative tribunal provides a clear and understandable decision and reasons for decision. The courts are also less likely to set aside or quash the decision and send the matter back to the administrative tribunal for a rehearing when the decision and reasons for decision are clear and understandable. An administrative tribunal that regularly prepares a clear and understandable decision and reasons for decision is often given greater deference or respect than one which prepares a decision and reasons for decision that does not reveal or gives very little details about its thought process.

The courts have consistently indicated that they will not subject the decision and reasons for decision of an administrative tribunal to "painstaking scrutiny" and focus on every slip and omission.

(c) The provincial legislatures or federal Parliament

Many administrative tribunals in their decisions and reasons for decision consider and discuss relevant legislation, whether it is the governing statute of the administrative tribunal or any other statute that is applicable to the tribunal, including a general procedural statute. Therefore, an administrative tribunal must always consider the relevant members of the provincial legislature(s) or the federal Parliament to be part of its audiences.

In addition, the relevant provincial legislature(s) or the federal Parliament may be influenced in various ways by the decision of the administrative tribunal. Therefore, it is important when you comment on relevant legislation, especially when you make a recommendation to change the legislation, you ensure that your comments are always clear and understandable.

Making comments on relevant legislation can lead to a positive influence on the relevant provincial legislature(s) or the federal Parliament if there is recognition that the administrative tribunal's comments including any recommendations for change are necessary. However, making comments on relevant legislation can also have a negative influence if these comments lead to a determination by the relevant provincial legislature(s) or the federal Parliament that the administrative tribunal is not capable of effectively regulating the particular industry or profession.

(d) The involved ministry

Almost every administrative tribunal is required to report to a government ministry. Therefore, an administrative tribunal must always consider the relevant government ministry to be part of its audiences. As a result, it is important to ensure that the relevant government ministry understands the decision of the administrative tribunal, what the decision is intended to accomplish, and why that particular decision was made. This will help ensure that the relevant government ministry has confidence in the work of the administrative tribunal, including its decisions.

(e) The industry or profession being regulated

Administrative tribunals play a significant if not comprehensive role in the regulation of industries and professions in Canada. Therefore, it is very important that the relevant industry or profession should be considered by the administrative tribunal. It is also important that the administrative tribunal uses clear words in its decision and reasons for decision so that the relevant industry or profession understands the impact of the decision. Industries or professions follow, at least in a general way, the decisions of the relevant administrative tribunal(s). This type of monitoring is usually by word of mouth and by reviewing summaries or commentaries on the decisions of the relevant administrative tribunal(s) in various publications including the administrative tribunal's newsletter or annual report.

Decisions and reasons for decision of administrative tribunals are a very effective method of communicating to or "educating" the relevant industry or profession, the expected values of that industry or profession. For example, unacceptable conduct by a particular industry or profession or by a member of the particular industry or profession can be communicated through an administrative tribunal's decision and reasons for decision. This will hopefully prevent similar cases in the future or at least lead to agreements and settlements in similar proceedings in the future.

(f) Other industries or professions

Industries or professions will be interested in the decisions and reasons for decisions of an administrative tribunal even when they are not being regulated by that administrative tribunal. For example, a decision of an administrative tribunal dealing with general procedures will be important to any industry or profession. In addition, decisions of an administrative tribunal on general topics will have an impact on many industries and professions other than the parties involved.

(g) The media

The media is very interested in the decisions and the reasons for decision of administrative tribunals. However, because the media must review an enormous amount of paper on a daily basis, it is crucial that an administrative tribunal makes its decision and reasons for decision clear and understandable and of course as short as possible. Where it is not possible to prepare a short decision and reasons for decision, it is a good idea to prepare a summary at the beginning or at the end of the document.

It is important to recognize that the length of time it takes until the decision and reasons for decision is released will impact how the media responds to the decision. For example, if an administrative tribunal takes two years to release a decision and reasons for decision, the administrative tribunal will likely receive negative publicity from the media. In contrast, if an administrative tribunal releases its decision and reasons for decision within a reasonable period of time after the hearing has been completed, the administrative tribunal will likely either receive positive publicity from the media or no publicity at all.

In addition to the length of time, the quality of the decision and the reasons for decision will often have an impact on how the media responds to the decision.

For example, if the quality is poor because the decision or reasons for decision is not clear or understandable, the media will likely focus on the incompetence or insensitivity of the administrative tribunal. In contrast, if the quality is good, the media will likely focus on the conduct of the person which resulted in the hearing as disclosed in the decision and reasons for decision of the administrative tribunal.

(h) Law journals

There are many law journals which publish the important decisions made by administrative tribunals in Canada. Therefore, the relevant law journal should be kept in mind by the administrative tribunal. It is important to remember that the editor of a law journal has more time to read and consider the decision and reasons for decision of an administrative tribunal than the media. This means that if a particular law journal is one of the targeted audiences, this may require the administrative tribunal to prepare a more detailed decision and reasons for decision.

(i) Special interest groups

Most regulated industries or professions have special interest groups that will carefully review and scrutinize the decisions and reasons for decision of the administrative tribunals from the perspective of their group's interests. Special interest groups often have the resources and the ability to make things difficult for administrative tribunals by involving the media and by intervening in or even funding individual cases, applications for judicial review, or appeals from decisions of administrative tribunals. Therefore, if possible, it is important for an administrative tribunal to address the concerns of special interest groups in its decision and reasons for decision in order to avoid any undesirable action by the special interest groups.

(j) Universities and libraries

Universities and libraries collect and distribute decisions and reasons for decision of administrative tribunals. For example, university professors for courses in administrative law will collect and then distribute to its students the relevant decisions and reasons for decision. As part of teaching specific administrative law concepts, the professors will often critique the decisions and reasons for decision of administrative tribunals as part of class discussions. In addition, the decisions and reasons for decision of many of the administrative tribunals are stored in an electronic data bank (*i.e.*, Quicklaw). Therefore, this is another reason for administrative tribunals to prepare clear and understandable decisions and reasons for decision.

(k) Other administrative tribunals

It is important for an administrative tribunal to recognize that other administrative tribunals across Canada, especially ones that are in the same industry or profession, will be reviewing its decisions and reasons for decision. This allows that industry or profession to be kept current on all the decisions which have a direct or even an indirect impact on that industry or profession.

(l) Lawyers and agents appearing before the administrative tribunal

Most administrative tribunals have the same group of lawyers and agents who appear before them on a regular basis. Therefore, this is another reason for administrative tribunals to prepare clear and understandable decisions and reasons for decision. Clear and understandable decisions and reasons for decision can educate these lawyers and agents regarding the likely result of similar cases in the future, leading to agreements and settlements and avoiding the necessity of conducting long hearings. Even lawyers and agents who have never appeared before a particular administrative tribunal can educate themselves and their clients about the administrative tribunal's approach to cases by reading prior decisions and reasons for decision especially ones with similar facts and issues. This can help these lawyers and agents to avoid time-consuming and detrimental mistakes by allowing them to be clear about the issues they will face, be aware of the type of evidence the administrative tribunal will want to hear, and be able to develop grounds for distinguishing similar cases. Therefore, clear and understandable decisions and reasons for decision can be an important way for an administrative tribunal to reduce its workload, particularly dealing with routine matters.

(m) The general public

In general, the public is affected by many of the decisions made by administrative tribunals because they are considered in the public interest. The basic duty for most administrative tribunals is to serve and protect the public interest. Therefore, the general public must be kept in mind and should really be carefully considered when preparing the decision and reasons for decision for every administrative tribunal.

(n) The administrative tribunal

The administrative tribunal itself will often review and rely on its past decisions and reasons for decision when deciding future cases with similar facts and issues. Therefore, it is important for an administrative tribunal to always prepare clear and understandable decisions and reasons for decision in order to ensure consistent decisions and reasons for decision in the future. In contrast, unclear decisions and reasons for decision may place an administrative tribunal in a difficult situation of having to decide whether to disregard a past decision even if it is based on similar facts and issues.

For example, there have been cases where an administrative tribunal has imposed a lighter penalty for serious professional misconduct in order to avoid an appeal of its decision because of difficult or questionable rulings made by the administrative tribunal during the course of the hearing. However, when that particular administrative tribunal has to decide a case in the future involving a similar type of professional misconduct, the administrative tribunal will be faced with the precedent it set in the earlier case. The administrative tribunal will have to decide whether it will impose the penalty that the conduct deserves and run the risk of an appeal on penalty or impose the lighter and inadequate penalty.

(10) How do You Ensure an Accurate and Complete Decision and Reasons for Decision?

After an administrative tribunal identifies its possible audiences and thinks about and attempts to understand the questions that each audience brings to the decision and reasons for decision, an administrative tribunal must consider how it can ensure that its decision and reasons for decision are accurate and complete. It is very important that the administrative tribunal thinks about ways for ensuring that its decision and reasons for decision are accurate and complete before the hearing takes place because there are many things that the administrative tribunal can and should do during and after the hearing.

One of the most important things that an administrative tribunal should do during the hearing to ensure an accurate and complete decision and reasons for decision is to take notes. The notes made by an administrative tribunal during the hearing are the basis on which an accurate and complete decision and reasons for decision are created because they contain the information regarding what took place at the hearing including the evidence of the witnesses.

Taking notes of the evidence of the witnesses at the hearing is crucial. If an administrative tribunal fails to take notes or takes poor notes and then makes a mistake when it refers to or describes the evidence of any of the witnesses, it can have a detrimental effect. For example, on an appeal, a court may decide to set aside or quash a decision if an administrative tribunal makes a mistake regarding the evidence of any of the witnesses. Mistakes dealing with the evidence of any of the witnesses are easy to establish on an appeal when transcripts have been prepared for the hearing. An administrative tribunal rarely has transcripts available to it when it is preparing its decision and reasons for decision because of the high cost of transcripts and the time constraints on an administrative tribunal for preparing its decision and reasons for decision.

There are many different ways that an administrative tribunal can take notes during the hearing but there are some basic features which are common to all methods of effective note taking. These features include the following:

1. *A daily list of all the participants who attended at the hearing.* This list will help members of the administrative tribunal remember the role of each of the participants. It also allows members of the administrative tribunal to know and keep track of any of the participants who do not attend at the hearing on certain days. This is very important because a court will not look favourably on an administrative tribunal if it states or implies that a participant was

present during the entire hearing when he or she was not present during the entire hearing.

2. *The notes should record the times of the key events during the hearing.* For example, the times when the hearing begins and ends each day and the times of each break should be recorded. Also, the times that a witness begins and stops his or her examination in chief, cross-examination or re-examination should be recorded. These time records will help members of an administrative tribunal refresh their memories when preparing the decision and reasons for decision. These time records also allow an administrative tribunal to order a transcript of a particular witness's evidence or even an important portion of the evidence of a particular witness. This can potentially be a tremendous cost saving for an administrative tribunal.

3. *An asterisk sign, highlighting or underlining should be used to identify important pieces of evidence.* This is very important because it helps an administrative tribunal ensure that important pieces of evidence are reviewed before and during the preparation of its decision and reasons for decision. It also helps ensure that an administrative tribunal discusses important pieces of evidence in its reasons for decision.

4. *Impressions of a witness should be recorded in square or round brackets.* It is a good idea to record them in brackets because it prevents members of the administrative tribunal from having any confusion later on between a person's subjective observations of a witness and the actual evidence given by a witness. These notations are very important and very useful for an administrative tribunal when it prepares its reasons for decision because they assist in determining the credibility of witnesses.

5. *The notes of the evidence of the witnesses should be as detailed and complete as is possible.* Members of an administrative tribunal often do not know at the time that a particular witness gives evidence whether that evidence will ultimately be important or significant.

6. *Exhibits with their identifying letter or number and a short description should be listed chronologically in the notes to show when they were identified or introduced into evidence.* It is also helpful to have a separate list of exhibits, especially when the hearing takes place over a long period of time and there are a large number of witnesses. In this separate list of exhibits, it is useful to identify which party introduced the exhibit in case some or even all of the exhibits must be returned to the respective parties.

In addition to taking notes during the hearing, there are many other things that an administrative tribunal can do after the hearing to ensure that its decision and reasons for decision are accurate and complete. These include the following:

1. The member of the administrative tribunal who is responsible for writing the decision and reasons for decision should prepare a comprehensive outline in point form of the decision and reasons for decision. This should be done as soon as possible after the hearing is completed and should set out an

overview of the case, the facts, issues, a tentative decision, and the reasons for decision.

2. The first draft of the decision and reasons for decision should be written by hand, typewritten, or entered into the computer. An administrative tribunal should avoid dictating the decision and reasons for decision because a dictated decision and reasons for decision tends to be less precise, longer and more inaccurate.

3. The member of the administrative tribunal who is responsible for writing the decision and reasons for decision should have the notes which were taken during the hearing by the other members of the administrative tribunal when writing the decision and reasons for decision. This allows the member of the administrative tribunal who is writing the decision and reasons for decision to double-check the accuracy of any references in the reasons for decision that he or she makes to the evidence of the witnesses. Also, he or she can review the portions of the notes of the other members of the administrative tribunal which identify the important pieces of evidence and record the impressions of the witnesses. This will assist him or her in writing a complete decision and reasons for decision and making any credibility findings regarding the witnesses.

4. When writing the reasons for decision, the member of the administrative tribunal should avoid quoting specific evidence given by a witness unless he or she is certain that the quote is completely accurate. A summary of the evidence given by a witness is just as persuasive and is not easily proven to be inaccurate.

5. The original draft of the decision and reasons for decision should be circulated among all the members of the administrative tribunal for their comments.

6. All members of the administrative tribunal should proofread the decision and reasons for decision to ensure that they are complete and accurate. The member of the administrative tribunal who wrote the decision and reasons for decision should carefully proofread the final version of the decision and reasons for decision against the original draft to ensure that it is complete and accurate. It also might be a good idea to have another member of the administrative tribunal compare the final version with the original draft as an additional measure to ensure completeness and accuracy.

(11) When Should the Decision and Reasons for Decision be Prepared?

The first draft of the decision and reasons for decision of the administrative tribunal should be prepared as soon as possible after the hearing is finished.

First, the parties to the hearing and the general public should be told about the decision of the administrative tribunal as soon as possible after the hearing is finished. This is because the decision may have an impact on a person's rights or duties. Also, for most decisions, the public interest is also affected. It is also important to remember that the parties may see the result as more acceptable if the decision and reasons for decision is prepared on a timely basis.

Any delay in coming to a decision, especially if it is a long and unexplained delay, will lead to an increase in the expectations of the parties to the hearing and the general public about the decision. It can also lead to a suspicion that the entire evidence of certain witnesses or a portion of the evidence of a particular witness was ignored or even forgotten. Any delay in coming to a decision will also intensify disappointment in the decision, especially if the decision is unfavourable, and will probably lead to a higher rate of appeal.

Second, it will be easier to write the decision and reasons for decision when the memories of what took place at the hearing and the evidence of the witnesses are still fresh because memories decrease over time. Even a week after the hearing is completed, members of the administrative tribunal confuse or even forget the details of the hearing.

These fresh memories will also allow the member of the administrative tribunal who is writing the decision and reasons for decision to finish writing the decision and reasons for decision earlier than if he or she waited for a period of time, such as a month or even six months, to begin preparing the decision and reasons for decision.

As the memories decrease over time, it will take the member of the administrative tribunal who is writing the decision and reasons for decision a longer period of time to review his or her notes and the notes of the other members of the administrative tribunal, especially the evidence of the witnesses, which were taken during the hearing.

Even though it is desirable to prepare a first draft of the decision and reasons for decision as soon as possible after the hearing has been completed; it is not always possible, especially, if the administrative tribunal has a very heavy workload. If this occurs, it is even more important that every member of the administrative tribunal take very detailed notes during the hearing and that a comprehensive outline is prepared after the hearing is completed by the member of the administrative tribunal who is responsible for writing the decision and reasons for decision.

(12) What is the Role of Staff in Preparing the Decision and Reasons for Decision?

Traditionally, there was a public perception that legal counsel or staff of the administrative tribunal had a very limited involvement in the deliberations by the administrative tribunal after the completion of the hearing or in the preparation by the administrative tribunal of the decision and reasons for decision. This perception was reinforced by the courts who felt that staff of the administrative tribunal had to be excluded from participation in the administrative tribunal's deliberations and that staff, including legal counsel, were prohibited from being able to assist the administrative tribunal in writing its decision and reasons for decision.

However, over the last decade, the courts including the Supreme Court of Canada[37] have taken a more liberal and flexible approach by allowing the staff of the administrative tribunal to participate in the deliberations and the writing of the decision and reasons for decision by the administrative tribunal. This more liberal and flexible approach has occurred, in part, to ensure consistency in the decisions and reasons for decision of an administrative tribunal. As a result, a number of principles can be drawn from the case law regarding the role of staff in the deliberations and the writing of the decision and reasons for decision by the administrative tribunal. These include the following:

1. The members of the administrative tribunal who heard the case must make the actual decision.
2. The staff of the administrative tribunal, including legal counsel, can assist the members of the administrative tribunal in writing the decision and reasons for decision.[38] This assistance can include:
   (a) editing by staff for spelling or grammatical errors or matters of style;
   (b) checking by staff, including legal counsel, to ensure that references to exhibits are correct and that any references to cases or legislation are appropriately cited;
   (c) commenting on the draft by legal counsel about possible incorrect references to the evidence of a particular witness or the need to make additional references to the evidence of other witnesses;
   (d) advising about previous cases decided by the administrative tribunal that may be relevant to the proposed decision;
   (e) reviewing the wording of the final decision to ensure that it is clear and complete; and
   (f) discussing the policy implications of the decision and reasons for decision, not the findings of fact made by the administrative tribunal, with members of the administrative tribunal who were not part of the hearing and staff.

---

[37] In the recent decision of *Ellis-Don Ltd. v. Ontario (Labour Relations Board)* (2001), 194 D.L.R. (4th) 385, [2001] 1 S.C.R. 221, 52 O.R. (3d) 160n, 140 O.A.C. 201, 26 Admin. L.R. (3d) 171, 2001 C.L.L.C. ¶220-028, 66 C.L.R.B.R. (2d) 216, [2001] O.L.R.B. Rep. 236, 265 N.R. 2, 2001 SCC 4, the Supreme Court of Canada determined that there was nothing improper with a panel of the Ontario Labour Relations Board hearing a grievance and drafting a decision dismissing the grievance but then engaging in discussions with the full Board about the draft decision that ultimately lead to significant changes to the decision, including a final decision upholding the grievance.

[38] The Workers' Compensation Appeals Tribunal, now called the Workplace Safety and Insurance Appeals Tribunal, has developed guidelines for the review of draft decisions and reasons for decision. A copy of those guidelines is in Appendix J: Guidelines for Review of Draft Decisions.

3. The assistance of staff of the administrative tribunal including legal counsel should be requested on a voluntary basis by the members of the administrative tribunal who heard the case. Assistance should not be expected or even required by an internal rule or policy of the administrative tribunal. Also, the assistance cannot be demanded or imposed by any of the staff or officers of the administrative tribunal.

4. The member of the administrative tribunal who is responsible for writing the decision and reasons for decision should have a discussion with the other members of the administrative tribunal who heard the case before requesting the assistance of staff.

5. No assistance should be requested from staff of the administrative tribunal, including legal counsel, who were involved in the hearing process unless the involvement was limited to providing legal advice or handling the procedural aspects of the hearing. The staff who are responsible for investigating or prosecuting the case should not provide any assistance with the decision and reasons for decision. This is important to avoid the appearance or apprehension of bias.

6. The assistance should be given in a manner that does not pressure the members of the administrative tribunal to make a certain decision or change their decision. The members of the administrative tribunal must always feel they can make their own decision. This means that members of the administrative tribunal who did not hear all the submissions and evidence of the parties at the hearing and staff of the administrative tribunal should not take part in any vote by the administrative tribunal in the course of making its decision. In addition, minutes of the discussion with the members of the administrative tribunal who did not hear the case and the staff of the administrative tribunal should not be kept and attendance should not be recorded.

7. Administrative tribunals that hold hearings involving factual allegations of professional misconduct or incompetence should have the least assistance from staff of the administrative tribunal whereas administrative tribunals that hold hearings on policy issues can obtain more assistance.

8. Parties to the hearing before the administrative tribunal must be notified of any new facts or grounds of argument that are raised as a result of any assistance that is provided, and given an opportunity to make submissions.

9. At a minimum, the administrative tribunal should write the decision and the first draft of the decision and reasons for decision document with no assistance at all.

10. Staff of the administrative tribunal including legal counsel should only make comments about the draft(s). These comments should be in the form of questions rather than suggested changes to reduce the chance of improper influence over the administrative tribunal such as: Can you give an example why you found witness x not to be credible?

11. All comments about the draft(s) should go back to the administrative tribunal for consideration.

12. The administrative tribunal should make all the changes to the draft(s). This should be done by the member of the administrative tribunal who is responsible for writing the decision and the reasons for decision.
13. Each of the members of the administrative tribunal should sign the final decision and reasons for decision. These signatures act as a record of the approval of the decision and reasons for decision by each member of the administrative tribunal.

(13) Do You Have to Give Notice of the Decision and Reasons for Decision?

An administrative tribunal must give notice of its decision and reasons for decision to the parties to the proceeding before the administrative tribunal. The method of giving notice of its decision and reasons for decision will depend on whether the administrative tribunal's governing statute or any other statute which is applicable to the administrative tribunal specifies the method or methods of giving notice. If the administrative tribunal's governing statute or any other statute which is applicable to the administrative tribunal does not specify the method of giving notice, any method that is effective can be used even though the most common method of giving notice is by mail.

The SPPA, the general procedural statute in Ontario, has a specific section dealing with notice. Section 18 of the SPPA requires an administrative tribunal to send a copy of its final decision, including its reasons for decision, to each party who participated in the proceeding. This means that an administrative tribunal has no obligation to send a copy of any interim decisions that are made during the proceeding. This section gives the administrative tribunal the option of sending a copy of its final decision to either the party or the party's counsel or agent.

The requirement in s. 18 to send a copy of its final decision only applies to parties not witnesses, and it only applies to parties who participated in the proceeding before the administrative tribunal. This means that a party is not entitled to receive a copy of the final decision if he or she did not participate in the proceeding before the administrative tribunal.

Section 18 provides many different methods of sending a copy of the final decision of the administrative tribunal to the parties who participated in the proceeding. These methods include the following: mail, e-mail, fax and some other method that allows proof of receipt if the administrative tribunal has made rules of practice and procedure under s. 25.1 of the SPPA that deal with the method of giving notice of a decision.

The last method of giving notice of a final decision gives an administrative tribunal considerable flexibility to develop rules of practice and procedure dealing with methods of giving notice which can address new forms of technology.

Section 24 provides an alternate method for giving notice of a final decision. When the administrative tribunal believes that the parties to the proceeding before the administrative tribunal are numerous or for any other reason it is impractical to send a copy of its final decision by one of the methods provided for in s. 18, notice of the final decision can be given by public advertisement. Notice of a final decision by public advertisement must inform the parties where copies of the final decision and reasons for decision may be obtained. This section is very useful when the proceeding involves environmental matters or zoning where many people are parties to the proceeding before the administrative tribunal. Notice in these cases would usually be given by newspaper.

Section 18 goes on to indicate when a final decision is deemed to have been received for the various methods of giving notice of a final decision. If a copy of the final decision is sent by mail, it must be sent to the most recent address that is known to the administrative tribunal and it is deemed to be received by the party on the fifth day after it is mailed. If a copy of the final decision is sent by e-mail or fax, it is deemed to be received on the day after it is sent unless that day is a holiday and then it is deemed to be received the next day that is not a holiday. If a copy of the final decision is sent by a method provided for by the rules of practice and procedure of the administrative tribunal, these rules will determine when it is deemed to be received.

The date of receipt can become very important if a party wants to appeal the decision of the administrative tribunal. Some governing statutes of administrative tribunals have a specific time period for bringing an appeal after the decision has been received. If an appeal is not brought within this time period, a court will likely quash or set aside the appeal. The rules in s. 18 regarding when a final decision is deemed to have been received do not apply if a party can show that he or she has acted in good faith. A party has acted in good faith if he or she has not done anything such as turning off the fax machine to deliberately avoid receiving a copy of the final decision. The party must also show that because of something beyond his or her control, such as an accident or illness, he or she did not receive the copy of the final decision until later than the deemed day of receipt. If both of these requirements are met, then the date of receipt will be the actual date that the party received the final decision.

Adequate notice of the decision and reasons for decision of an administrative tribunal is very important. As a result, the administrative tribunal must ensure that it complies with any requirements for giving notice of its decision and reasons for decision in the administrative tribunal's governing statute or any other statute which is applicable to the administrative tribunal. An administrative tribunal must still comply with these requirements even if the parties to the proceeding become aware of the decision which has been made by the tribunal by some other method.

An officer or staff member of the administrative tribunal may give notice of a decision made by an administrative tribunal. Notice does not have to be given by a member of the administrative tribunal who took part in the proceeding.

For practical reasons, notice of a decision made by an administrative tribunal should be sent at the same time to all parties and as soon as possible after a decision has been made. This will help to ensure that all parties receive the same document so that if a mistake has been made, such as a missing page, all parties will have received the incomplete document. This will also eliminate the risk of forgetting to give notice to a particular party. This becomes especially important when there are time limits for bringing an appeal because, if there is a delay in giving notice which goes past the time limit, a court may invalidate the decision of the administrative tribunal by setting it aside or quashing it. The court may also send the matter back to the administrative tribunal for a rehearing.

(14) What are the Key Elements of the Decision and Reasons for Decision?

(a) Outline

After the hearing is completed, the member of the administrative tribunal who is responsible for writing the decision and reasons for decision should prepare a comprehensive outline. An outline with the use of subheadings can assist the member of the administrative tribunal who is responsible for writing the decision and reasons for decision to prepare a clear, organized and complete decision. In contrast, if an outline is not prepared or if an outline is prepared but it is complicated or even inadequate, this can lead to confusion for the readers of the decision and reasons for decision. It can also result in the same information being repeated in different parts of the decision and reasons for decision or it can even result in certain information or important elements being omitted from the decision and reasons for decision.

The traditional outline for a court decision contains five parts:

1. Nature of the case — identification of the parties, the history or background of the case, how the case came before the court, and what the court needs to decide.
2. Facts — a summary of the facts which are material or important to understanding the decision.
3. Issues — the factual or legal issues which are necessary to deciding the case.
4. Law and reasoning — the law which applies to the factual and legal issues.
5. Holding — the court's intent about how it decides the case.

This type of outline is appropriate when it is important to identify and establish legal principles to be used in making decisions in the future. For most administrative tribunals, their decisions and reasons for decision do not establish legal principles but, instead, focus on making findings of fact or applying policy. Also, administrative tribunals do not make decisions as often as courts do and may not adequately explain their thinking process, including why a certain decision was made by using this type of outline.

As a result, a more appropriate outline for administrative tribunals who are making findings of fact should contain the following five key elements:

- overview of the case,
- facts,
- issues,
- decision, and
- reasons for decision.

(b) Overview of the case

The first section identifies the parties and explains the nature of the proceeding before the administrative tribunal. This is usually set out in one short paragraph using very simple and straightforward language so that the reader can get a quick and easily understandable introduction to the case. This introductory paragraph may also refer to the relevant section or sections of the governing statute of the administrative tribunal and any other applicable statute.

In order to spark the reader's attention in the rest of the decision and reasons for decision, a story-telling approach can be used to provide the overview of the case. However, it usually takes a lot of practice to use this approach effectively. As a result, it probably should be reserved for more experienced administrative tribunals who make decisions on a frequent basis.

(c) Facts

This section sets out a summary of the relevant or important facts so that the reader can understand the rest of the decision and reasons for decision of the administrative tribunal. This often includes identifying the witnesses who gave evidence at the hearing and referring to the exhibits that were introduced at the hearing unless there is a long list of exhibits. This is an easy way for an administrative tribunal to communicate to the reader that all the evidence that was heard was considered in the course of preparing its decision and reasons for decision. However, if the administrative tribunal is going to list the witnesses who gave evidence, the administrative tribunal must be very careful to ensure that all the witnesses are included in this list. If one or more witnesses are not included, this can give the reader the wrong impression that a particular witness's evidence was not considered or was ignored.

In addition to ensuring that a complete list of witnesses is prepared, it is very important that the summary of the relevant facts be as accurate as possible. If an administrative tribunal makes a mistake when it refers to or describes the evidence of any of the witnesses, it can have a detrimental effect. For example, on an appeal, a court may decide to set aside or quash a decision if an administrative tribunal makes a mistake regarding the evidence of any of the witnesses.

The summary of the relevant facts can be prepared in a variety of different ways:

1. The facts can be set out in chronological order either as a story or in a list. Setting out the facts in chronological order may not be easy if many different witnesses have given evidence about the same event throughout the hear-

ing. Where there are no disputes or contradictions about the evidence, all of the evidence should be set out as one set of events instead of writing: "He testified that . . ." or "she testified that . . .".

2. The facts can be combined with the overview of the case.
3. The facts can be combined with the issues.
4. The facts can set out a summary of the relevant evidence of the witnesses. This method is particularly helpful where one or more of the witnesses have given conflicting evidence.

(d) Issues

This section sets out the issues in the case. In other words, it sets out what must be decided by the administrative tribunal using language that is concise and specific to the case. By setting out the issues in the course of the decision, it helps the administrative tribunal to identify and understand the issues which must be decided, it makes it easier to prepare the rest of the decision and reasons for decision, and it provides a road map for the reader.

The issues in a particular case usually have both a factual component (what happened) and a legal component (what consequences flow from these facts). Administrative tribunals sometimes forget one or the other of these components.

This section may also include a statement of what are not the issues of the case, unless there is a long list of things which should not be decided by the administrative tribunal. This helps the administrative tribunal to stay focused on the issues in the case.

(e) Decision

This section sets out the decision or the ultimate finding of the administrative tribunal. It is important for the member of the administrative tribunal who is responsible for preparing the decision and reasons for decision to set out its decision before its reasons for making that decision. This will help the administrative tribunal to ensure that it properly explains its thought process in coming to a decision. Otherwise, the administrative tribunal may summarize the evidence and then immediately set out its decision without providing the reasons for making that decision.

The decision made by the administrative tribunal is considered a legally binding order that can be enforced by a court. Section 19 of the SPPA allows the administrative tribunal or a party to the proceeding before the administrative tribunal to file a certified copy of the administrative tribunal's decision in the court office. Once it has been filed, it is automatically deemed to be an order of the court and can be enforced as a court order.

As a result, the wording of the decision should be simple, clear and very precise. This will help avoid any confusion among the parties to the proceeding in attempting to follow any requirements in the decision and it will make it easier for a court if it needs to interpret all or any part of the decision in the future.

The wording of the decision should follow the wording that is used in the administrative tribunal's governing statute. For example, if the governing statute refers to findings of guilt, the wording of the decision should be: "The administrative tribunal finds the member guilty of . . ." or "The administrative tribunal finds the member not guilty of . . .". As another example, if the governing statute refers to findings of professional misconduct, the wording of the decision should be: "The administrative tribunal finds the member has committed the following acts of professional misconduct . . ." or "The administrative tribunal finds the member has not committed the following acts of professional misconduct . . .".

Following the wording of the administrative tribunal's governing statute is crucial when dealing with the penalty portion of the decision. For example, some governing statutes use the term "disbarment" while others use the term "revocation" or "cancellation". As another example, some governing statutes give an administrative tribunal authority to impose "terms, conditions and limitations" while others give an administrative tribunal the authority to impose only one of these, such as "terms". This example illustrates the importance of being precise with the wording because it will help an administrative tribunal to avoid making any errors in the penalty portion of the decision by not including a form of penalty that it has no authority to impose.

When preparing the penalty portion of the decision, it is important to review the penalty that is being imposed by the administrative tribunal to ensure that it is not completely different from the penalty proposed by the parties to the proceeding in closing arguments. For example, this can occur when the prosecutor asks for re-education and supervision and the defence counsel asks only for re-education but the administrative tribunal wants to impose a suspension. If the penalty is completely different from the penalty proposed by the parties to the proceeding in closing arguments, the next thing which must be considered is whether the parties have been informed about the proposed penalty to be imposed by the administrative tribunal and asked to comment on it. If this has already occurred, the rest of the decision and reasons for decision can be prepared. In the decision and reasons for decision, the administrative tribunal should identify the penalty proposed by the parties and explain why it imposed a different penalty. If this has not occurred, the administrative tribunal must tell the parties what it is proposing and the reasons why and then ask the parties if they have any comments. After considering these comments, the administrative tribunal can impose the proposed penalty and prepare the rest of the decision and reasons for decision. Otherwise, on an appeal, a court may set aside or quash the penalty portion of the decision on the basis that the administrative tribunal did not follow the principles of natural justice or fairness.

Once the member of the administrative tribunal who is responsible for preparing the decision and reasons for decision begins to write the final decision, he or she should ensure that the decision is detailed enough and adequately deals with all relevant issues or problems that may arise. For example, if the administrative tribunal "directs the member to successfully complete a course in ethics", the decision should also indicate:

    (a) who decides what is an acceptable course in ethics;

    (b) when must the course be completed;

    (c) what does the word "successfully" mean;

    (d) what happens if the member does not successfully complete the course; and

    (e) what happens if the member does not take the course at all.

(f) Reasons for decision

This section sets out the thought process of the administrative tribunal by explaining why it made a particular decision. It is not appropriate for the administrative tribunal to summarize the evidence given by the witnesses and then immediately set out its decision without explaining why it made that decision. Courts tend to be very critical of administrative tribunals who only state the decision that they have made in a particular case without explaining how that decision was made.

This section is the hardest section to write because it is difficult to express an administrative tribunal's thought process in writing. It is also difficult to break an administrative tribunal's thought process into component parts to make it easier for the reader to understand the reasons why an administrative tribunal made a particular decision.

In order to ensure that the reasons for decision adequately explains why it made a particular decision, the administrative tribunal should first set out the issue to be decided and the conclusion on that issue. Then, the administrative tribunal should explain why it reached that conclusion by referring to the evidence of one or more of the witnesses and if possible giving an example. The administrative tribunal then goes on to explain why the opposing arguments and evidence were rejected. This procedure should be followed for each of the issues that must be decided by the administrative tribunal.

Responding to the opposing arguments and evidence is an important part of an administrative tribunal's reasons for decision because it helps the administrative tribunal to explain in a more clear and complete manner why it made a particular decision. If an administrative tribunal does not do so, on an appeal, a court may rely on that omission as a factor to be considered in deciding whether to set aside or quash its decision.

(i) *How do you make findings of credibility for witnesses?*

Making findings of credibility is very important because many decisions made by administrative tribunals turn on the credibility of one or more of the witnesses who gave evidence at the hearing.

Credibility involves the honesty of the witness. This means that a witness who does not tell the truth will be considered an unreliable witness. Credibility also involves the ability of that witness to give accurate evidence. This means that an honest witness who is confused or unsure about the event(s) that occurred which are relevant to the case will also be considered to be an unreliable witness. Therefore, findings of credibility can be made relating to the credibility of the witness or the credibility of the witness's testimony.

Courts have consistently recognized that an administrative tribunal who observed and heard the evidence of the witnesses at the hearing is in the best position to make findings of credibility. However, the administrative tribunal must ensure that in making findings of credibility, it explains in a clear and full manner why it found a particular witness or all or part of a witness's testimony to be credible or not credible by referring to the evidence which supports that finding. Otherwise, if an administrative tribunal does not do so, on an appeal, a court may set aside or quash its decision and then generally send the matter back to the administrative tribunal for a rehearing. The court will not always send the matter back for a rehearing.

In *Pitts v. Ontario (Director of Family Benefits Branch)*,[39] the Ontario Divisional Court described the factors for determining the credibility of witnesses and their testimony and suggested that administrative tribunals consider these factors when making findings of credibility. The court stated the following:

> In weighing the testimony of witnesses you are not obliged to decide an issue simply in conformity with the majority of the witnesses. You can, if you see fit, believe one witness against many. The test is not the relative number of witnesses, but in the relative force of their testimony. With respect to the testimony of any witness, you can believe all that that witness has said, part of it, or you may reject it entirely.
>
> Discrepancies in a witness' testimony, or between his testimony and that of others, do not necessarily mean that the witness should be discredited. Failure of recollection is a common experience and innocent misrecollection is not uncommon. It is a fact also that two persons witnessing an incident or transaction often will see or hear it differently. Discrepancies on trivial detail may be unimportant, but a falsehood is always serious.
>
> In determining the credit to be given to the evidence of a witness, you should use your good commonsense and your knowledge of human nature. You might, in assessing credibility, consider the following:
>
>> The appearance and demeanour of the witness, and the manner in which he testified. Did the witness appear and conduct himself as an honest and trustworthy person? It may be that he is nervous or confused in circumstances in which he finds himself in the witness box. Is he a man who has a poor or faulty memory, and may that have some effect on his demeanour on the witness stand, or on the other hand, does he impress you as a witness who is shifty, evasive and unreliable?
>>
>> The extent of his opportunity to observe the matter about which he testified. What opportunities of observation did he in fact have? What are his powers of perception? You know that some people are very observant while others are not very observant.
>>
>> Has the witness any interest in the outcome of the litigation? We all know that humanity is prone to help itself, and the fact that a witness is interested in the

---

[39] (1985), 51 O.R. (2d) 302, at pp. 311-12 (Div. Ct.).

results of the litigation, either as a plaintiff or defendant, may, and often does, quite unconsciously tend to colour or tinge or shade his evidence in order to lend support to his cause.

Does the witness exhibit any partisanship, any undue leanings towards the side which called him as a witness? Is he a relative, friend, an associate of any of the parties in this case, and if so, has this created a bias or prejudice in his mind and consequently affected the value of his testimony?

It is always well to bear in mind the probability or improbability of a witness' story and to weigh it accordingly. That is a sound commonsense test. Did his evidence make sense? Was it reasonable? Was it probable? Does the witness show a tendency to exaggerate in his testimony?

Was the testimony of the witness contradicted by the evidence of another witness, or witnesses whom you considered more worthy?

Does the fact that the witness has previously given a statement that is inconsistent with part of his testimony at trial affect the reliability of his evidence?

After weighing these matters and any other matters that you believe are relevant, you will decide the credibility or truthfulness of the witness and the weight to be given to the evidence of that witness.

From a review of this excerpt from the court decision, an administrative tribunal can consider the following factors in making findings of credibility:

1. *Ability to recall* — Does the witness have a poor or good memory of the event(s) that occurred? How much time has passed since the event(s)? Did the witness make notes at the time or shortly after the event(s)? Has the witness reviewed or refreshed his or her memory from notes or some other method since the event(s)? How recently did the witness review or refresh his or her memory before giving evidence? If the witness had difficulty recalling, was this in relation to trivial as compared to important details about the event(s)?

2. *Appearance and demeanour* — Did the witness appear to be an honest person? Did the witness appear to be unusually nervous or even confused when he or she gave evidence? Did the witness give responsive answers to the questions asked or was the witness evasive? What kind of tone did the witness use when answering the questions? Did the witness maintain eye contact with the questioner when answering the questions or did he or she look towards one of the parties? Did the witness exhibit any form of body of language when answering all or some of the questions?

3. *Ability to observe* — Was the witness able to accurately observe the event(s)? Was the witness concentrating on the event(s) or was he or she distracted? Is the witness an observant person?

4. *Motivation* — Does the witness (complainant vs. member) have anything to gain or lose from the outcome of the hearing? Is the witness a relative, friend, or employee of any of the parties and has this led this witness to tailor his or her evidence in favour of that party?

5. *Probability* — Did the witness give evidence that made sense or did it seem unreasonable? Was the evidence given by the witness probable or was it unbelievable? Did the witness appear to be exaggerating when he or she gave evidence?

6. *External consistency* — Was the evidence given by the witness contradicted by the evidence of one or more of the witnesses at the hearing? Does the evidence given by that witness contradict the contents of one or more documents introduced as an exhibit at the hearing? Was the evidence given by that witness contradicted in relation to trivial as compared to important details about the event(s)? Was the evidence given by that witness contradicted by the evidence given by another witness who you have determined in whole or in part not to be credible?

7. *Internal consistency* — Did the witness previously give a statement that was inconsistent with all or part of the evidence given at the hearing? Did the witness make a statement on cross-examination that is inconsistent with a statement made in his or her examination in chief? Was the inconsistency in relation to trivial as compared to important details about the event(s)?

When referring to any one of these factors in making a finding of credibility, an administrative tribunal must ensure that it explains in a clear and full manner why a particular factor was relevant.[40] For example, it is not appropriate for an administrative tribunal to indicate in its reasons that the witness had an improper motivation in giving evidence at the hearing and thus was not a credible witness. The administrative tribunal must go further and explain why it believed that the witness had an improper motivation.

One of the most difficult things that an administrative tribunal must do is to indicate that it found a particular witness not to be credible because he or she was not telling the truth. The following are some examples of how an administrative tribunal can be tactful when it wants to indicate that a particular witness was lying:

1. Witness X admitted on cross-examination that he is a business partner with the member. Witness X has a direct financial interest in the outcome of the hearing. This interest tended to influence his opinion of what occurred.

2. Witness Y's testimony was unreliable because she tended to give answers she thought the member would like and always changed her answers when she thought the member did not like them.

3. Witness Z was not considered to be credible because he repeated every question before giving an answer and consistently gave evasive answers to all the questions.

---

[40] The courts have indicated that the demeanour of a witness is not enough to make a finding of credibility; demeanour is only one of the factors to consider in assessing credibility.

4. The member appeared to be extremely nervous, squirming in his seat during the entire time that he was questioned. He never looked at the College's counsel, looking only at the floor, the walls, or the ceiling when he was questioned. He often had a defensive tone when he answered the questions and repeatedly gave extraneous or irrelevant information. As a result, the member's evidence was unbelievable.

(ii) *How do you deal with expert evidence?*

Dealing with expert evidence in its reasons is very important but it can be a difficult task for the administrative tribunal. The non-professional members may have some difficulty in understanding the expert evidence. Also, the professional members may have some problems if the expert testifies about something which is beyond their area of practice, making it hard to evaluate the validity of the opinion. Nevertheless, an administrative tribunal will have to address the expert evidence in its reasons because in most cases conflicting expert evidence is being provided by the different parties. The administrative tribunal will have to make a decision in its reasons for decision about whether all or part of an expert's evidence will be accepted or rejected.

The following are some of the factors to be considered by an administrative tribunal in evaluating and assessing the expert evidence to determine whether all or a part of it should be accepted or rejected:

1. *Qualifications of the expert* — An administrative tribunal can reject or place little weight on the opinion of one expert and accept the opinion of another expert who has more extensive qualifications. Qualifications include formal education and training, work experience, teaching, research, and publications.

2. *Relevance of the expert's qualifications* — An administrative tribunal can reject or place little weight on the opinion of an expert who has extensive qualifications but none or very little of these qualifications are relevant to the issue(s) to be decided by the administrative tribunal.

3. *Factual basis for the expert's opinion* — An administrative tribunal can reject or place very little weight on the opinion of an expert if the expert's opinion is based on incorrect assumptions regarding the facts. This can occur when an expert assumes certain facts that are different than the findings of fact made by the administrative tribunal. For example, an administrative tribunal may reject the opinion of an expert that is based on facts which are ultimately rejected by the administrative tribunal.

4. *Relevance of the expert's opinion* — An administrative tribunal can reject the opinion of an expert who gives evidence on a matter where that matter does not relate to any of the issues to be decided by the administrative tribunal.

5. *Necessity of the expert's opinion* — An administrative tribunal can reject the opinion of an expert when it is able to make a decision from the evidence of the other witnesses without relying on the expert's evidence.

6. *Familiarity or experience with the case* — An administrative tribunal can place more weight on the evidence of an expert who has had some prior involvement with the case. This can occur when an expert has conducted a recent examination of the member's mental status.

7. *Credibility of the expert* — An administrative tribunal can reject the opinion of an expert if it determines that he or she was not credible. This can occur when an expert appears to be partisan to one of the parties.

In dealing with the expert evidence, an administrative tribunal that adjudicates (as opposed to setting policy) must be careful to make a decision based on the evidence given at the hearing and not based on the knowledge or experience of one or more of the members of the administrative tribunal. An administrative tribunal can use its knowledge or experience to evaluate the credibility of the expert and his or her evidence but should not substitute its opinion for the opinion of the expert. Otherwise, on an appeal, a court may set aside or quash the decision of the administrative tribunal on the basis that the parties were not able to make submissions or give evidence because the opinion of the member of the administrative tribunal was unknown to the parties.

(iii) *How do you respond to specific issues?*

Responding to specific issues that arise before and during the hearing before the administrative tribunal can also be very difficult because most administrative tribunals do not have members with any legal background. Even if one or more of the members of the administrative tribunal have some legal background, it is rarely in the area of administrative law as it relates to the practice of law before administrative tribunals.

Issues that may arise before and during the hearing before the administrative tribunal include the following:

1. *Procedural issues* — Should the complainant's psychiatric records be disclosed to the member or his or her lawyer? Should an adjournment of the hearing be granted? Should a member of the administrative tribunal be disqualified from hearing the case on the grounds of bias? Should a non-party be allowed to participate in the hearing and, if so, to what extent should the person participate? Should public access to all or part of the hearing be restricted?

2. *Legal issues* — What is the meaning of a section or part of a section including a particular word in the administrative tribunal's governing statute? Does a particular section in the SPPA apply to the hearing before the administrative tribunal and, if so, how should it be interpreted? Does the administrative tribunal have the authority to proceed with a hearing? Is the composition of the administrative tribunal hearing the case proper?

3. *Constitutional issues* — Does the administrative tribunal have the jurisdiction or authority to determine whether the Charter has been violated? Have the member's rights under the Charter been violated? Does a particular sec-

tion in the administrative tribunal's governing statute or any other applicable statute such as the SPPA violate the member's rights under the Charter? If the member's rights under the Charter have been violated, can the administrative tribunal grant a remedy and, if so, what remedy should be granted?[41]

In responding to the issues that arise before or during the hearing, the administrative tribunal must ensure that it explains in its reasons in a clear and full manner why it made a certain decision on a particular issue. Otherwise, if an administrative tribunal does not do so or makes an error, on an appeal, a court may set aside or quash its decision and then generally send the matter back to the administrative tribunal for a rehearing. As a result, the administrative tribunal should consider adopting the following approach when responding to these issues in its reasons:

1. *Identify the general legal principles* — An administrative tribunal should identify the general legal principles that apply to the particular issue to be decided. For example, if the member asks for an adjournment of the hearing, the rights of the member to a fair hearing compared to the rights of the administrative tribunal and the public to a quick hearing are the general legal principles that should be considered.

2. *Apply the general legal principles* — After it identifies the general legal principles, the administrative tribunal should apply these principles to the facts of the case that relate to the particular issue to be decided.

3. *Do not do legal research* — The administrative tribunal should not do its own research to determine what cases may be helpful in responding to a particular issue. In addition, if an administrative tribunal becomes aware of other cases such as from a previous hearing, these cases should not be referred to in its reasons. In either case, it is unfair to the parties because they have not had an opportunity to make submissions about these cases. However, if the administrative tribunal asks the parties whether they are aware of a particular case(s) and then gives the parties the opportunity to make submissions about whether the case(s) apply, a court would probably consider this approach to be acceptable.

4. *Follow the format* — The reasons should be set out as in the "Reasons for decision" section.

5. *Avoid explaining the law* — The administrative tribunal can identify the names (using short forms or abbreviations) of the most important cases that the parties referred to in their submissions, but, it should avoid discussing or even quoting from these cases. Otherwise, the administrative tribunal may make an error and, on an appeal, the court may set aside or quash the decision.

---

[41] The Charter will be discussed in more detail in Chapter 6.

(15) How do You Determine that the Decision and Reasons for Decision are Adequate?

When the outline is being prepared, and during the course of writing the decision and reasons for decision, the member of the administrative tribunal who is responsible for writing the decision and reasons for decision should be thinking about how to ensure the decision and reasons for decision are adequate.[42] Also, once the decision and reasons for decision have been completed, all of the members of the administrative tribunal should proofread the decision and reasons for decision to ensure adequacy and completeness.

In order to determine whether a particular decision and reasons for decision are adequate, the courts have indicated that the following factors should be considered in making this determination:

(a) the governing statute of the administrative tribunal including any requirements set out in the governing statute pertaining to the content and form of the decision and reasons for decision;

(b) the nature of the case;

(c) the issue(s) which must be decided by the administrative tribunal;

(d) the evidence presented; and

(e) the administrative tribunal including any circumstances affecting the particular administrative tribunal.[43]

The importance of considering the nature of the administrative tribunal and any circumstances affecting it in determining the adequacy of the decision and reasons for decision was recently acknowledged by the Supreme Court of Canada in *Baker v. Canada (Minister of Citizenship and Immigration)*:[44]

> In my view, however, the reasons requirement was fulfilled in this case since the appellant was provided with the notes of Officer Lorenz. The notes were given to Ms. Baker when her counsel asked for reasons. Because of this, and because there is no other record of the reasons for making the decision, the notes of the subordinate reviewing officer should be taken, by inference, to be the reasons for decision.

---

[42] To make this task easier, an administrative tribunal may consider establishing a standard format for the contents of the decision and reasons for decision. Appendix I contains a Checklist for Decisions and Reasons for Decision of Administrative Tribunals. In addition, an administrative tribunal may consider establishing a common set of guidelines or standards for the quality of the decision and reasons for decision. Appendix K contains the Hallmarks of Decision Quality, established by the Workers' Compensation Appeal Tribunal, now called the Workplace Safety and Insurance Appeals Tribunal.

[43] This may also include, in certain cases, the arguments made by the parties during the course of the hearing.

[44] (1999), 174 D.L.R. (4th) 193, [1999] 2 S.C.R. 817 at pp. 848-9, 14 Admin. L.R. (3d) 173, 1 Imm. L.R. (3d) 1, 243 N.R. 22.

Accepting documents such as these notes as sufficient reasons is part of the flexibility that is necessary, as emphasized by Macdonald and Lametti, *supra*, when courts evaluate the requirements of the duty of fairness with recognition of the day-to-day realities of administrative agencies and the many ways in which the values underlying the principles of procedural fairness can be assured. It upholds the principle that individuals are entitled to fair procedures and open decision-making, but recognizes that in the administrative context, this transparency may take place in various ways. I conclude that the notes of Officer Lorenz satisfy the requirement for reasons under the duty of procedural fairness in this case, and they will be taken to be the reasons for decision.

In addition to identifying the factors which must be considered in determining whether the decision and reasons for decision of an administrative tribunal are adequate, the courts have indicated what types of matters should be included in an administrative tribunal's decision and reasons for decision:

1. *Summary of the evidence of the witnesses* — It is not necessary that the administrative tribunal summarize all of the evidence of the witnesses, only the relevant evidence. This includes indicating the significance or weight that the administrative tribunal gives to the evidence which has been considered by them.

2. *Findings of fact* — When there are disputes or contradictions between the witnesses over the relevant facts, the administrative tribunal should make specific findings of fact. This includes indicating what evidence has been accepted and what evidence has been rejected and explaining why. It is not enough for an administrative tribunal to indicate that the evidence of the witnesses and the submissions made by the parties have been considered without indicating the specific evidence which has been accepted and rejected by the administrative tribunal.

3. *Findings of credibility* — In making a finding of credibility, an administrative tribunal must explain in a clear and full manner the reasons why it found a particular witness or all or part of the witness's testimony to be credible or not credible including referring to the evidence which supports that finding.

4. *Arguments made by the parties* — An administrative tribunal should ensure that it responds to the arguments made by the parties which are relevant to the issue(s) to be decided. This is especially important when it intends to reject an argument that has been made.

5. *Reasons for decision* — An administrative tribunal must explain its thought process so that the reader can understand the reasons why it made a particular decision. This becomes especially important when one of the parties needs to be able to determine whether there are grounds for an appeal or an application for judicial review.

6. *Proof of the charges/allegations* — An administrative tribunal must make a determination about whether the specific charges/allegations have been proven.

7. *Finding of professional misconduct or incompetence* — If an administrative tribunal determines that the charges/allegations have been proven, it must

make a determination about whether that conduct constitutes professional misconduct or incompetence. This includes indicating what conduct constitutes professional misconduct or incompetence.

8. *Penalty* — If an administrative tribunal makes a finding of professional misconduct or incompetence, it must make a determination about the appropriate penalty. This includes addressing the various mitigating and aggravating factors affecting the penalty.

(16) What are the Basic Rules for Writing an Effective Decision and Reasons for Decision?

During the course of writing the decision and reasons for decision, the member of the administrative tribunal who is writing the decision and reasons for decision should always think about the basic rules of writing to ensure that the decision and reasons for decision are understood by all of its potential readers. In order to make this task easier; it is helpful to rely on a dictionary and a thesaurus. Also, once the decision and reasons for decision have been completed, all of the members of the administrative tribunal should proofread the decision and reasons for decision to ensure that these basic rules have been followed.

What are the basic rules of writing? Many authors have written articles, chapters in books, and even entire books on this topic. The following is a summary of some of the basic rules for ensuring that an administrative tribunal has written an effective decision and reasons for decision:

1. Use short, common and definite words.[45]
2. Eliminate unnecessary words that do not add anything to a sentence. For example, instead of using the phrase "the question as to whether or not", it is sufficient to use the phrase "the question whether" or even just the word "whether".
3. Use positive words and avoid negative phrases. For example, it is better to say "forgot" rather than "did not remember", "ignored" rather than "paid no attention", "inadmissible" rather than "not admissible", "inapplicable" rather than "not applicable", "uncertain" rather than "not certain", "unfamiliar" rather than "not familiar".
4. Use the same word throughout the decision and reasons for decision to communicate the same meaning even if this requires repeating that word frequently.
5. Make sure a singular verb is used with a singular noun and a plural verb is used with a plural noun. It is very easy to make the mistake of using a plural verb with a singular noun. For example, it is incorrect to say: "A stack of medical charts were left open on Dr. Y's desk." Instead, it is correct to say: "A stack of medical charts was left open on Dr. Y's desk."

---

[45] See Appendix L for a Table of Simple Word Substitutes.

6. Use strong active verbs and avoid weak passive verbs. For example, it is better to say: "to infer" rather than "to make an inference", "to consider" rather than "to take into consideration", "to conclude" rather than "to provide conclusions".

7. Avoid the passive tense, use the active tense instead. The passive tense uses more words than the active tense, making the sentence not as clear and concise. For example, instead of "The complaint was made by Ms. X to the College", it is better to say "Ms. X made a complaint to the College".

8. Avoid using too many references to cases and footnotes. If possible, try not to use any footnotes.

9. Use headings to identify the elements of the decision and reasons for decision. In order to make these headings stand out, use a larger type size and underline or make them bold.

10. Use maps and diagrams. This can be done by either attaching a photocopy of an exhibit such as a map or drawing your own map. This can be particularly effective in making the "Facts" section of the decision and reasons for decision shorter.

11. Avoid using legal terms unless it is necessary. If legal terms are used, make sure that they are used properly. For example, instead of "Witness A was summonsed to appear before the administrative tribunal but did not appear", it is correct to say "Witness A was summoned to appear before the administrative tribunal but did not appear".

12. Avoid using Latin words and phrases. If they are necessary, underline or italicize them.

13. Use short sentences. Sentences that have more than 25 words must be written very carefully to avoid losing the reader's attention. If a long sentence is necessary, split the sentence by listing the items that are identified in the sentence.

14. Make sure you restrict each paragraph to one main thought or idea and each sentence in that paragraph should relate directly to that main thought or idea. If a sentence does not relate directly to the main thought or idea, eliminate it.

15. Ensure that each paragraph logically flows from the previous paragraph. To ensure that the paragraphs flow, use transition words to connect the paragraphs.[46]

16. Avoid repeating the same information in different parts of the decision.

17. Refer to the parties and witnesses by their names not by their titles. When the subject matter of the decision is sensitive and personal, abbreviations (such as initials) or first names should be used. When referring to a party or witness by a name or an abbreviation, be consistent by using the same name or abbreviation throughout the decision and reasons for decision.

18. Make sure the tone of the decision and reasons for decision is objective and impartial.

---

[46] See Appendix M for a Table of Transitional Words.

19. Try to keep the decision and reasons for decision as short as possible without eliminating essential information. However, it is not a good idea to single space the decision and reasons for decision in order to make it shorter.
20. Prepare as many drafts as are necessary to have a clear and organized decision and reasons for decision. It is almost impossible to achieve a clear and organized decision and reasons for decision on the first draft.
21. Check the governing statute and any other applicable statute such as the SPPA to make sure you have spelled the words in the decision and reasons for decision correctly. There are often different ways to spell a word and it is important to follow the approach that is used in the relevant statute.

5

How are Decisions of Administrative Tribunals Reviewed?

(1) Judicial Review

(a) What is judicial review?

Judicial review means review by a court of the actions and decisions of administrative tribunals. Because of this definition, most people think that judicial review is very similar to an appeal. In fact, judicial review is very different from an appeal. For example, a party only has a right to an appeal if the governing statute or another statute specifically indicates that there is a right to appeal. Also, since the governing statute gives a right to appeal, the scope of review on an appeal is usually broader. In contrast, the governing statute does not give a right to judicial review because it originates automatically from the authority of the courts to review state action including the actions of administrative tribunals.

Judicial review deals with the right of an individual to apply to a court to review the actions and decisions of administrative tribunals. This right originates from the basic legal principle known as the "Rule of Law". It recognizes the right of every individual to apply to the courts to ensure that an administrative tribunal's authority to act is set out in legislation and that the administrative tribunal stays within the limits of authority that are granted to it by the legislation.

Over the years, the extent to which the courts apply this legal principle has changed considerably. Traditionally, the courts decided that the right of an individual to judicial review could not be limited in any way. However, the more recent view of the courts is that the right of an individual to judicial review can be limited or even denied except when an administrative tribunal has acted outside of its jurisdiction. The courts have developed this new approach to judicial review because the courts recognize that most decisions by administrative tribunals require expertise in a particular area but the courts do not have this expertise. This means that the courts have recognized that they are not in the best position to evaluate certain decisions.

Some provinces such as Ontario,[1] British Columbia[2] and Prince Edward Island[3] have statutes which set out the procedure for judicial review. Other provinces such as Alberta, Saskatchewan and New Brunswick have rules that set out the procedure to be followed, and in Quebec, articles in its *Code of Civil Procedure*[4] set out the procedure.

The provincial statutes and rules only apply to the actions and decisions of provincial administrative tribunals. For judicial review of the actions and decisions of federal administrative tribunals, the procedure to be followed is set out in the *Federal Court Act*.[5] The *Federal Court Act* only permits the Trial Division, or the Court of Appeal,[6] to review decisions of federal administrative tribunals. This is true even where the federal Parliament has delegated or passed on authority to provincial administrative tribunals such as provincial transport or marketing boards. These provincial administrative tribunals would not be considered federal administrative tribunals because they were created by provincial legislation. In that situation, the applicable provincial statute or rule would apply and a provincial Superior or Supreme Court would hear the application for judicial review.

(b) Who can seek judicial review?

The right to seek judicial review of the actions and decisions of administrative tribunals is not available to every individual. The courts often use the term "standing" to describe the individuals who are able to seek judicial review. In order to have standing to seek judicial review, an individual must be either a party or directly affected by the actions or the decision of the administrative tribunal. It is not enough to be indirectly affected by the actions or the decision of the administrative tribunal.

There are two reasons for limiting who can seek judicial review. First, it helps to prevent the courts from being overloaded with cases where individuals only

---

[1] A copy of Ontario's *Judicial Review Procedure Act*, R.S.O. 1990, c. J.1, can be found in Appendix D.

[2] A copy of British Columbia's *Judicial Review Procedure Act*, R.S.B.C. 1996, c. 241, can be found in Appendix E.

[3] A copy of Prince Edward Island's *Judicial Review Act*, R.S.P.E.I. 1988, c. J-3, can be found in Appendix F.

[4] R.S.Q., c. C-25.

[5] R.S.C. 1985, c. C-7. Administrative tribunals in the territories are not considered to be federal administrative tribunals. Therefore, judicial review proceedings are supervised by the Supreme Courts of the territories through legislation established by the territories, not the *Federal Court Act*.

[6] Section 28 of the *Federal Court Act* lists 15 federal administrative tribunals whose decisions are reviewed by the Federal Court of Appeal. The Trial Division of the Federal Court reviews the decisions of all other federal administrative tribunals unless a federal statute including the governing statute requires the Federal Court of Appeal to hear the judicial review application. A copy of the *Federal Court Act* can be found in Appendix G.

have an indirect interest in the case. Second, it is assumed and expected that individuals who are directly affected by the actions or the decision of the administrative tribunal will be best able to present and argue the case.

The limits on who can seek judicial review will not usually apply in cases where an individual or a group meets the test for "public interest standing". There are three components to this test: there is a serious question or issue that needs be determined by the courts, the individual has a genuine interest, and there is no other reasonable and effective way of bringing the question or issue before the courts.

(c) Does a person have a "right" to judicial review?

A person does not have the right to judicial review. Whether to grant judicial review is in the discretion of the courts. A court may decide to not grant judicial review even though a person may feel that a remedy should be given. For example, judicial review will usually not be granted when there is an adequate alternative remedy such as an appeal.[7] A court may not grant judicial review when there has been a delay or the time requirements in a statute have not been met. Also, a court will usually not grant judicial review to correct a minor technical error made by the administrative tribunal when it caused no harm or prejudice.[8] In addition, a court will not grant judicial review when an applicant can only show an appearance or apprehension of a violation of the principles of natural justice or fairness (unless it relates to bias); the applicant must establish an actual violation or breach. The only exception to the discretion of the courts occurs when it is shown that there has been an unlawful detention. An individual has a right to be released from an unlawful detention.

(d) What are typical questions on a judicial review?

On a judicial review, the court does not determine whether the judge(s) would have made a different decision or even whether the administrative tribunal made the best decision. The court also does not try to ensure consistency between different decisions of the same administrative tribunal. The job of the court is not to second-guess the decision made by the administrative tribunal. The court only needs to determine whether the administrative tribunal had the authority to initiate an inquiry on a particular subject and whether it exercised that authority in a reasonable and fair manner.

The following are examples of typical questions on a judicial review:

---

[7] Section 18.5 of the *Federal Court Act* provides that judicial review cannot occur when there is a right to appeal in a federal statute. There is no discretion in the Federal Court to refuse or grant judicial review, judicial review must be refused.

[8] For example, the *Judicial Review Procedure Acts* in British Columbia and Ontario provide that judicial review can be refused when the sole ground for relief is a defect in form or a technical irregularity and the court finds that no substantial wrong or miscarriage of justice has occurred.

1. Did the administrative tribunal have the authority to initiate an inquiry on the particular subject matter?
2. Did the administrative tribunal exercise its authority unfairly by not following proper procedures?
3. Did the administrative tribunal exercise its authority for improper purposes?
4. Did the administrative tribunal exercise its authority in an arbitrary or discriminatory manner?
5. Did the administrative tribunal refuse to exercise its authority by strictly following its general policies?
6. Did the administrative tribunal fail to take into account relevant considerations?
7. Did the administrative tribunal take into account irrelevant considerations?
8. Did someone else make the decision instead of the administrative tribunal?

(e) Do courts defer to the decisions of administrative tribunals?

Over the years, the extent to which courts will substitute their opinion for the opinion of the administrative tribunal on judicial review has changed considerably. Traditionally, the courts often intervened and substituted their opinion for the opinion of the administrative tribunal. In contrast, the more recent trend is for the courts to "defer" or respect the decision of the administrative tribunal especially dealing with matters where the courts recognize that the administrative tribunal has more expertise. In a case where the courts determine that it is appropriate to defer to the administrative tribunal, the courts will usually not intervene unless the decision of the administrative tribunal is "patently unreasonable" or clearly irrational. This is often described as "curial deference".[9]

In determining whether the administrative tribunal has greater expertise that will require the courts to defer to the administrative tribunal, the courts use a "pragmatic and functional" approach. This approach helps the court decide who is in the best position to make the decision.

The courts have determined that the pragmatic and functional approach requires that the reviewing court look at three main criteria: the nature of the issue or problem that is before the administrative tribunal, the purpose and wording of the governing statute, and the characteristics of the administrative tribunal.

In terms of the issue or the problem, the courts have indicated that the factors to be considered include things such as:

1. Does the problem fall within the express or implied powers of the administrative tribunal?
2. Does the problem require specialized knowledge or experience?

---

[9] In contrast, when a court determines that no deference should be given to the decision of the administrative tribunal, the court will intervene when the court does not agree with the decision under review. This means that the administrative tribunal must be "correct" in its decision, otherwise, the court will intervene.

3. Would it be best to decide the question in a context-specific setting or is it a question of general application that applies to many cases?
4. Does the problem have only one correct answer or are there a variety of possible and reasonable answers?
5. Are there reasons to think that a court would be better suited to deal with the problem?
6. Does it involve a question of constitutional interpretation?

In terms of the governing statute, the courts have stated that the factors to be considered include the following:

1. What is the purpose of the administrative tribunal?
2. What is the scope of the powers of the administrative tribunal (*i.e.*, policy-making) and are these powers set out in broad or narrow terms in the governing statute?
3. Whether the language of the governing statute suggests more or less deference should be given to the administrative tribunal, such as whether the governing statute has a privative clause?

In terms of the administrative tribunal, the courts have indicated that the factors to be considered include things such as:

1. Does the administrative tribunal have expertise — specialized knowledge or extensive experience?
2. Does the administrative tribunal have a developed body of cases that guides it and functions as precedents in making decisions in the future?
3. How are members selected or appointed to the administrative tribunal and how do they participate in the decision-making process?

For example, the courts will often defer to the decision of the administrative tribunal when the governing statute contains a section which prohibits or prevents a court from reviewing the decision of the administrative tribunal. This occurs when the governing statute has a privative clause. An example of a privative clause can be found in Ontario's *Labour Relations Act, 1995*:[10]

> 114(1) The Board has exclusive jurisdiction to exercise the powers conferred upon it by or under this Act and to determine all questions of fact or law that arise in any matter before it, and the action or decision of the Board thereon is final and conclusive for all purposes, but nevertheless the Board may at any time, if it considers it advisable to do so, reconsider any decision, order, direction, declaration or ruling made by it and vary or revoke any such decision, order, direction, declaration or ruling.
>
> . . . . .
>
> 116. No decision, order, direction, declaration or ruling of the Board shall be questioned or reviewed in any court, and no order shall be made or process entered, or proceedings taken in any court, whether by way of injunction, declaratory judg-

---

[10] S.O. 1995, c. 1, Sch. A, ss. 114(1) and 116.

ment, certiorari, mandamus, prohibition, quo warranto, or otherwise, to question, review, prohibit or restrain the Board or any of its proceedings.

The courts will also defer to the decision of the administrative tribunal when the courts determine that the administrative tribunal has more expertise than the courts on a particular subject. This will involve considering the expertise of the administrative tribunal, the expertise of the court in comparison with the administrative tribunal, and the relationship of the issue to be decided by the administrative tribunal to the administrative tribunal's expertise. For example, the courts have consistently held that administrative tribunals conducting professional discipline hearings have expertise in determining what is and what is not professional misconduct, and, consequently, defer to the decision of the administrative tribunal on that issue. Nevertheless, even when there is a strong privative clause or it is determined that the administrative tribunal has more expertise, the courts may decide to intervene.

In contrast, in certain circumstances, the courts will not defer to the decision of the administrative tribunal.[11] For example, the courts will often not give deference when there is a full right of appeal in the governing statute. Also, the courts will not give deference to the decision of an administrative tribunal on issues about the *Canadian Charter of Rights and Freedoms*.[12] In addition, when it comes to determining whether the administrative tribunal followed the proper procedures,[13] the courts will not give deference to the administrative tribunal.

The courts have determined that the same criteria which are used in the "pragmatic and functional" approach to determine whether deference should be shown to an administrative tribunal on judicial review should also be used to determine whether deference should be shown to an administrative tribunal on an appeal. The criteria that should be considered to determine whether deference should be shown on an appeal are: the nature of the issue or problem that is before the administrative tribunal, the purpose and wording of the governing statute, and the expertise of the administrative tribunal. If it is determined that the adminis-

---

[11] When a court determines that no deference should be given to the decision of the administrative tribunal, the court will intervene when the court does not agree with the decision under review. This means that the administrative tribunal must be "correct" in its decision, otherwise, the court will intervene.

[12] Part I of the *Constitution Act, 1982*, being Schedule B of the *Canada Act 1982* (U.K.), 1982, c. 11.

[13] As a result of the Supreme Court of Canada's decision in *Baker v. Canada (Minister of Citizenship and Immigration)* (1999), 174 D.L.R. (4th) 193, [1999] 2 S.C.R. 817, 14 Admin. L.R. (3d) 173, 1 Imm. L.R. (3d) 1, 243 N.R. 22, there appears to be a move towards giving more deference to the decisions made by administrative tribunals on procedural matters. The court indicated that the choice of procedures made by the administrative tribunal should be respected when the statute leaves to the decision-maker the ability to choose its own procedures or when the administrative tribunal has an expertise in determining what procedures are appropriate in the circumstances. It will be interesting to see how future courts will approach the decisions made by administrative tribunals on procedural matters.

trative tribunal on an appeal is entitled to deference, the court cannot intervene unless the decision of the administrative tribunal is unreasonable or clearly wrong. The unreasonable or clearly wrong standard is not equivalent to the patently unreasonable or clearly irrational standard that is applicable on judicial review. The patently unreasonable or clearly irrational standard gives more deference to the decision of an administrative tribunal than the unreasonable or clearly wrong standard. If the defect is immediately apparent or obvious, the administrative tribunal's decision is patently unreasonable. In contrast, if it takes significant searching or testing to find the defect in the decision, the decision is unreasonable. The Supreme Court of Canada in *Canada (Director of Investigation and Research) v. Southam Inc.*[14] described the unreasonable standard as follows:

> In my view, considering all of the factors I have canvassed, what is dictated is a standard more deferential than correctness but less deferential than "not patently unreasonable" . . . Because there are indications both ways, the proper standard of review falls somewhere between the ends of the spectrum.
>
> . . . . .
>
> For that reason alone, review of the decision of a tribunal should often be on a standard more deferential than correctness. Accordingly, a third standard is needed.
>
> I conclude that the third standard should be whether the decision of the Tribunal is unreasonable. This test is to be distinguished from the most deferential standard of review, which requires courts to consider whether a tribunal's decision is patently unreasonable.
>
> . . . . .
>
> Even as a matter of semantics, the closeness of the "clearly wrong" test to the standard of reasonableness *simpliciter* is obvious. It is true that many things are wrong that are not unreasonable; but when "clearly" is added to "wrong", the meaning is brought much nearer to that of "unreasonable". Consequently, the clearly wrong test represents a striking out from the correctness test in the direction of deference. But the clearly wrong test does not go so far as the standard of patent unreasonableness. For if many things are wrong that are not unreasonable, then many things are clearly wrong that are not patently unreasonable (on the assumption that "clearly" and "patently" are close synonyms). It follows, then, that the clearly wrong test, like the standard of reasonableness *simpliciter*, falls on the *continuum* between correctness and the standard of patent unreasonableness.

The courts have also determined that the same spectrum of standards that applies to appeals (as set above in the *Southam* case) also applies to applications for judicial review. This was recently confirmed by the Supreme Court of Canada in *Pushpanathan v. Canada (Minister of Citizenship and Immigration)*,[15] a case involving an application for judicial review:

---

[14] (1997), 144 D.L.R. (4th) 1 at pp. 18-21, [1997] 1 S.C.R. 748, 50 Admin. L.R. (2d) 199, 71 C.P.R. (3d) 417, 209 N.R. 20.

[15] (1998), 160 D.L.R. (4th) 193 at p. 209, [1998] 1 S.C.R. 982, 11 Admin. L.R. (3d) 1, 43 Imm. L.R. (2d) 117, 226 N.R. 201, supplementary reasons [1998] 1 S.C.R. 1222, 11 Admin. L.R. (3d) 130.

This more nuanced approach in determining legislative intent is also reflected in the range of possible standards of review. Traditionally, the "correctness" standard and the "patent unreasonableness" standard were the only two approaches available to a reviewing court. But in *Canada (Director of Investigation and Research)* v. *Southam Inc.*, [1997] 1 S.C.R. 748, 144 D.L.R. (4th) 1, a "reasonableness *simpliciter*" standard was applied as the most accurate reflection of the competence intended to be conferred on the tribunal by the legislator. Indeed, the Court there described the range of standards available as a "spectrum" with a "more exacting end" and a "more deferential end" (para. 30).

Whether this spectrum of standards applies to applications for judicial review when the principles of natural justice or fairness have been violated by not following proper procedures is not clear.

(f) What are the remedies available on a judicial review?

The remedies that are available on a judicial review are unique to administrative law. In private law, if an individual's rights are affected, an action can be brought for damages against the individual(s) causing the damage. For example, when a company fires an employee without giving him or her any notice and without any valid grounds, the employee can sue his or her employer for wrongful dismissal and collect money as damages. In contrast, in administrative law, if the court concludes that an administrative tribunal has failed to comply with the procedural and/or substantive principles of administrative law, the affected individual will generally not be able to get a money award unless he or she brings a separate action for damages.[16]

As a general rule, since the court on a judicial review does not have the authority to determine whether the administrative tribunal made the best decision, it cannot substitute its own decision for the decision of the administrative tribunal. The remedies that are available to a court on a judicial review tend to require the administrative tribunal to do something or to stop it from doing something rather than taking over the entire process.

The remedies that are available are as follows:[17]

- Prohibition — preventing an administrative tribunal from doing something
- *Mandamus* — forcing an administrative tribunal to do something when it has a duty to act but it refuses to act
- *Certiorari* — reviewing and then quashing or setting aside a decision of an administrative tribunal

---

[16] The Alberta *Rules of Court*, Alta. Reg. 390/68, specifically provide that an action for damages cannot be joined with an application for judicial review.

[17] Quebec and the federal Parliament have their own remedies that are set out in their respective statutes. For example, the remedy of évocation in Quebec is found in article 846 of the *Code of Civil Procedure* and it is basically a combination of *certiorari* and prohibition. The federal remedies are set out in ss. 18, 18.1, 18.2, 18.3 and 28 of the *Federal Court Act*.

- *Habeas Corpus* —granting release from an unlawful detention[18]
- *Quo Warranto* — challenging the right of an elected official to hold public office or an official's right to exercise the functions of that office
- Declaration — seeking a ruling about the validity of an action or decision of an administrative tribunal *or* the meaning of a particular section in the governing statute to determine a person's legal rights, duties or status, or the authority of the administrative tribunal
- Injunction — preventing or stopping a violation of the law *or* compelling the administrative tribunal to act lawfully

(2) Appeals

Judicial review is only one of the ways that decisions of administrative tribunals can be reviewed. In some cases, a simpler and preferable method of reviewing the decisions of administrative tribunals is by an appeal.

(a) Does a person have a "right" to appeal?

There is no automatic right to appeal. Whether there is a right to appeal depends on the administrative tribunal's governing statute or any other statute which is applicable to the administrative tribunal. If the governing statute provides for an appeal to be made to a court from the administrative tribunal's decision, then a party can appeal. The governing statute will also set out the procedure to be followed, the scope of the appeal, and the remedies or powers of the court that are available on the appeal. If the governing statute does not provide for an appeal to be made to a court, then the only way to have a court review the decision of the administrative tribunal is by judicial review.

Where a right to appeal exists in the governing statute, the general rule is that a party must first appeal the decision of the administrative tribunal before seeking a remedy by judicial review. Courts have consistently applied this general rule and have dismissed applications for judicial review brought by a party who has not exhausted his or her right to appeal under the administrative tribunal's governing statute.

In the case of *Howe v. Institute of Chartered Accountants of Ontario*,[19] a chartered accountant was charged with breaches of the Institute's Rules of Professional Conduct. Another accountant, who had been hired by the Institute to conduct an investigation into the charges, prepared a report of his findings. The investigator was going to be a witness at the hearing of the Institute's

---

[18] The provincial Superior or Supreme Courts not the Federal Court of Canada have the authority over the remedy of *habeas corpus* for federal administrative tribunals.

[19] (1994), 118 D.L.R. (4th) 129, 19 O.R. (3d) 483, 74 O.A.C. 26, 27 Admin. L.R. (2d) 118 (C.A.), leave to appeal to S.C.C. refused 119 D.L.R. (4th) vi, 85 O.A.C. 320*n*, 186 N.R. 78*n*.

Discipline Committee. The accountant who was charged with professional misconduct tried to get a copy of the report from the Institute before the hearing began. The Chair of the Discipline Committee refused to give the accountant a copy of the report. The accountant brought an application for judicial review to the court.

In his application for judicial review, the accountant asked for an order setting aside the decision of the Chair of the Discipline Committee and an order in the nature of *mandamus* requiring the Institute to provide him with a copy of the report. The Court of Appeal dismissed the application for judicial review as being premature because the accountant would have a right to appeal at the end of the hearing of the Discipline Committee. The Court of Appeal restated the well-established principle that courts should not interfere with preliminary rulings of administrative tribunals where a right to appeal exists.

Courts are reluctant to consider judicial review applications when a right to appeal exists because it is helpful for them to have the decision of the administrative tribunal, which has specialized expertise, before reviewing the case. Also, judicial review applications would waste court time and delay hearings before the Discipline Committees of administrative tribunals. In addition, judicial review applications may not be necessary if the administrative tribunal makes a decision that is satisfactory to all parties or at least to the party who was seeking judicial review.

(b) What is the scope of an appeal?

One of the main reasons that an appeal is preferable to judicial review is that the court's scope of review is generally much broader. The governing statute of the administrative tribunal sets out the court's scope of review on an appeal. Therefore, the scope of review varies from one administrative tribunal to another.

Generally, the scope of review can be classified in three broad categories:

1. Appeal *de novo* — provides for a new hearing and requires that the court make a decision based on the evidence that is brought before it.
2. Appeal on questions of fact and law[20] — provides for a broad review of all aspects of the decision of the administrative tribunal, including questions of fact and law.

---

[20] In *Canada (Director of Investigation and Research) v. Southam Inc.*, *supra*, footnote 10, at p. 12, the Supreme Court of Canada looked at the problems of making distinctions between questions of law and fact and then defined them as follows:

Briefly stated, questions of law are questions about what the correct legal test is; questions of fact are questions about what actually took place between the parties; and questions of mixed law and fact are questions about whether the facts satisfy the legal tests. A simple example will illustrate these concepts. In the law of tort, the question what "negligence" means is a question of law. The question whether the defendant did this or that is a question of fact. And, once it has been decided that

3. Appeal on questions of law — provides for a limited review of the decision of the administrative tribunal on questions of law only.

(c) What powers do courts have on an appeal?

The governing statute also sets out the powers of the court on an appeal. Therefore, the powers of the court on an appeal vary from one administrative tribunal to another. In some cases, the governing statute gives the court general powers by giving the court on an appeal all the powers of the administrative tribunal that made the decision. In other cases, the governing statute gives the court specific powers by permitting the court on an appeal to substitute its own decision for the decision of the administrative tribunal.

(3) Rehearing/Reopening/Reconsideration by Administrative Tribunals of their Decisions

Some governing statutes provide for a "rehearing" of the decisions of an administrative tribunal by the administrative tribunal itself, either on the initiative of the administrative tribunal or on the application of a party. For example, the governing statute may state that "the Committee may rehear any application before deciding it". Other governing statutes provide for a "reopening" or a "reconsideration" of the decisions of an administrative tribunal. The specific section in the governing statute must be read and interpreted very carefully because the scope may be different depending on the wording of the section and whether it permits a rehearing, reopening or reconsideration. For example, the scope of a rehearing may be limited to the situation where new facts have come out since the hearing or where facts have been discovered which could not have been determined at the time of the hearing. In other statutes, the scope of the rehearing may be quite broad if it provides for a fresh hearing. Also, the words "reopening" or "reconsideration" in contrast to the word "rehearing" may mean that the administrative tribunal is limited to hearing only certain evidence or arguments. Nevertheless, the courts are aware of the uniqueness of this power and tend to interpret it widely rather than on a narrow basis in order to maintain the integrity of the administrative process and to prevent injustice.

This power to rehear, reopen or reconsider is one of the ways that administrative tribunals differ from courts. Once a court has made a decision, it cannot conduct a rehearing, reopening or reconsideration. The only available option is to bring an appeal.

Administrative tribunals are given the power to rehear, reopen or reconsider for three main reasons. First, there is no automatic right to appeal the decisions of an administrative tribunal. A party can only bring an appeal if the governing statute provides for an appeal. Also, when an appeal is permitted, it may not

---

the applicable standard is one of negligence, the question whether the defendant satisfied the appropriate standard of care is a question of mixed law and fact.

extend to questions of fact, it may be limited to questions of law. Therefore, a rehearing, reopening or a reconsideration provides an administrative tribunal with a quick and informal way to correct errors made by the administrative tribunal. Second, courts have the discretion to decide whether to grant judicial review in a particular case. In exercising this discretion, the courts will consider whether the administrative tribunal had the power to rehear, reopen or reconsider, and if so, whether the applicant asked the administrative tribunal for a rehearing, reopening or reconsideration before seeking judicial review. Third, administrative tribunals must be flexible and respond to changes that occur which impact on their mandate or objective.

Even if an administrative tribunal is not given an express power in its governing statute to rehear, reopen or reconsider, there are limited circumstances where an administrative tribunal still has the power. The most common example is where there is a clear typing or clerical error in the decision of the administrative tribunal. For example, in Ontario, s. 21.1 of the *Statutory Powers Procedure Act*[21] (the "SPPA") allows an administrative tribunal to correct a typographical error, error of calculation, or similar error made in its decision. Also, s. 21.2 of the SPPA allows an administrative tribunal to review a decision and confirm, vary, suspend or cancel the decision but the review must take place within a reasonable time after the decision was made. The SPPA only gives an administrative tribunal the authority to review a decision if the administrative tribunal has made rules under s. 25.1 of the Act dealing with the power to review.

---

[21] R.S.O. 1990, c. S.22.

6

Canadian Charter of Rights
and Freedoms

(1) Introduction

The *Canadian Charter of Rights and Freedoms*[1] (the "Charter") protects the rights and freedoms of individuals such as: the right to vote; the right to enter, remain in and leave Canada; the right not to be denied reasonable bail without just cause; and the right to have their children receive primary and secondary school instruction in the same language. As a result, it appears that the Charter is addressed mostly at and applies only to the federal Parliament and provincial legislatures and the courts but not to administrative tribunals. In reality, the Charter contains other rights and freedoms that do apply to federal and provincial administrative tribunals. Moreover, even though only certain sections of the Charter apply to administrative tribunals, the Charter supplements and can even overrule the principles of administrative law that are contained in the legislation and the common law when there is an inconsistency.[2]

(2) What Sections of the Charter Apply to Administrative Tribunals?

(a) Expression — s. 2(b)

Section 2(*b*) of the Charter guarantees to everyone: "freedom of thought, belief, opinion and expression, including freedom of the press and other media of communication".

This section guarantees that freedom of expression includes "freedom of the press and other media of communication". Even though the Supreme Court of

---

[1] Part I of the *Constitution Act, 1982*, being Schedule B of the *Canada Act 1982* (U.K.), 1982, c. 11.

[2] The Charter can overrule the principles of administrative law contained in legislation and the common law because of s. 52 which indicates that the Charter is the supreme law of Canada. When there is an inconsistency between the Charter and either a statute or the common law, the Charter takes precedence.

Canada has indicated that this guarantee requires the courts to be open to the public, the Supreme Court of Canada has not conclusively stated that s. 2(*b*) applies to administrative tribunals.[3] Nevertheless, this section has the potential to require that hearings before administrative tribunals be open to the public and that any power to limit access or to hold hearings or portions of hearings in private must be specifically granted by the governing legislation or other applicable legislation. In addition, even if the governing legislation or other applicable legislation specifically grants this power, the administrative tribunal may decide that s. 2(*b*) has been violated and the violation is not justified if the particular section places a complete ban on access by a requirement that all hearings be closed to the public.

(b) Fundamental justice — s. 7

Section 7 of the Charter guarantees that: "Everyone has the right to life, liberty and security of the person and the right not to be deprived thereof except in accordance with the principles of fundamental justice."

As a starting point, this section can only apply to administrative tribunals which deal with the "life, liberty and security of the person". In regard to the term "life", there are probably no current administrative tribunals who make decisions dealing with questions of life.

In regard to the term "liberty", it is important to determine what is included in liberty. The courts have determined that "liberty" deals with the physical liberty of a person. There are many administrative tribunals which make decisions regarding a person's physical "liberty" such as parole boards and prison disciplinary tribunals. However, other administrative tribunals that can only impose a fine as a penalty do not deprive a person of his or her physical liberty. Even though the Supreme Court of Canada has determined that liberty is no longer restricted to protecting the physical liberty of a person, the Supreme Court of Canada has refused to extend liberty to include economic rights, such as the right to carry on a trade or to practise a profession. Nevertheless, there has been inconsistency among the provinces and territories because there are some courts which have decided that s. 7 applies to restrictions on the economic liberty of professions such as restrictions on the practice of medicine while other courts have indicated that s. 7 does not apply.

In terms of "security of the person", it is also important to determine what is included in this phrase. Similar to the way that the courts have defined "liberty",

---

[3] Interestingly, the courts in two fairly recent decisions in Ontario and Prince Edward Island have indicated that s. 2(*b*) of the Charter applies to administrative tribunals. In both cases, the courts determined that a requirement in the governing legislation that police discipline hearings be closed to the public violated s. 2(*b*) of the Charter. See *Southam Inc. v. Canada (Attorney General)* (1997), 154 D.L.R. (4th) 370, 47 C.R.R. (2d) 210, 36 O.R. (3d) 721 (Gen. Div.), and *Canadian Broadcasting Corp. v. Summerside (City)* (1999), 170 D.L.R. (4th) 731, 173 Nfld. & P.E.I.R. 56, 61 C.R.R. (2d) 311 (P.E.I.S.C.).

the courts have determined that "security of the person" relates to a person's physical health and safety. This means that administrative tribunals which make decisions dealing with the physical well being of an individual, including the possibility of danger to a person's life or liberty, can be considered to be making determinations that affect the security of the person. More recently, the courts have also determined that "security of the person" relates to a person's psychological integrity or mental health.

Once it is determined that an administrative tribunal has made a decision that deprives the life or liberty or security of a person, the next step is to determine whether that decision has been made according to or in violation of the principles of fundamental justice. The Supreme Court of Canada has not given an exhaustive or even a precise definition of what is considered to be fundamental justice, but it has determined that fundamental justice covers substantive justice as well as natural justice or procedural fairness.[4] As a result, it is unclear what the courts will consider to be included in the principles of fundamental justice. Nevertheless, if it is determined that the decision by the administrative tribunal was not made according to the principles of fundamental justice, then the person's rights under s. 7 of the Charter have been violated.

(c) Unreasonable search or seizure — s. 8

Section 8 of the Charter guarantees that: "Everyone has the right to be secure against unreasonable search or seizure."

Even though many people would probably think that the words "search or seizure" would only apply to police officers during a criminal investigation, the meaning of the words is broad enough to include many of the acts that are engaged in by administrative tribunals in the course of their inspections, audits and investigations. In order to determine whether an administrative tribunal has violated a person's rights under s. 8, a court will need to examine these acts very closely to determine whether there has been a search or seizure and whether it is reasonable or unreasonable. The court will need to determine whether the act or acts are authorized by the governing statute or some other applicable statute, whether a legitimate right or reasonable expectation of privacy has been violated, whether there were appropriate procedural safeguards in authorizing the search or seizure, and whether the search or seizure was done in a reasonable way.

The Supreme Court of Canada has indicated that a less strenuous and more flexible approach is required when examining and evaluating inspections, audits

---

[4] Since the principles of fundamental justice include natural justice and procedural fairness, this probably means that the procedural protections required by the common law will be included in the principles of fundamental justice. For example, the Supreme Court of Canada has determined that the principles of fundamental justice require that a fair hearing be provided by the administrative tribunal. However, in order for s. 7 to be triggered, the administrative tribunal must make a decision that deprives the life, liberty or security of the person; it is not enough that an administrative tribunal has made a decision that is not according to the principles of fundamental justice.

and investigations by administrative tribunals to determine whether a person's rights under s. 8 have been violated.[5]

(d) Arbitrary detention or imprisonment — s. 9

Section 9 of the Charter guarantees that: "Everyone has the right not to be arbitrarily detained or imprisoned."

Section 9 only applies if a person has been detained or imprisoned. Many people would probably think that administrative tribunals do not detain or imprison individuals. However, the Supreme Court of Canada has given a very wide meaning to the word detention to include circumstances where a person feels that he or she is not free to leave at any time. Therefore, s. 9 may apply to an administrative tribunal which sends out investigators or inspectors to question individuals especially if the person being questioned feels that he or she is not free to leave at any point during the questioning process. In order to determine whether a detention by an administrative tribunal is arbitrary and violates a person's rights under s. 9 of the Charter, the court will need to determine whether the detention is authorized by the governing statute or some other applicable statute, whether there are adequate standards or criteria for the detention, and whether it is reasonable given the facts and circumstances of the case.

(e) Right to counsel — s. 10(b)

Section 10(*b*) guarantees that: "Everyone has the right on arrest or detention . . . to retain and instruct counsel without delay and to be informed of that right".

Section 10(*b*) only applies if a person has been arrested or detained. An arrest or detention involves some form of compulsion or coercion. As indicated above, the Supreme Court of Canada has given a very broad meaning to the word detention to include situations where an individual has the impression that he or she is not free to leave at any time. Therefore, if a person voluntarily cooperated with an administrative tribunal's investigator or inspector by inviting the investigator or inspector into his or her home and answering questions without feeling that he or she is not free to stop the questioning, s. 10(*b*) will not apply.[6] However, s.

---

[5] *British Columbia Securities Commission v. Branch* (1995), 123 D.L.R. (4th) 462, [1995] 2 S.C.R. 3, [1995] 5 W.W.R. 129, 99 W.A.C. 1, 4 B.C.L.R. (3d) 1, 97 C.C.C. (3d) 505, 38 C.R. (4th) 133, 27 C.R.R. (2d) 189, 180 N.R. 241.

[6] The court in a fairly recent decision in Ontario has indicated that a physiotherapist was not detained or deprived of access to counsel when she made a statement to the investigator for the College of Physiotherapists of Ontario during an investigation into allegations of professional misconduct being made against her: *Melunsky v. College of Physiotherapists of Ontario* (1999), 85 A.C.W.S. (3d) 458 (Ont. Div .Ct.). In this case, the statement to the investigator was given in the physiotherapist's home after the physiotherapist had invited the investigator into her home at a set time to review a patient chart as part of the investigation. In coming to a decision that there was no detention, the Discipline Committee had relied on, among other things, the fact that the physiotherapist controlled the time and location of the interview and she had stipulated to the investigator that she had no need for legal advice at that point in time.

10(*b*) may apply to an administrative tribunal which sends out investigators or inspectors to question individuals if the person being questioned feels that he or she is not free to leave at any point during the questioning process or feels that that he or she is not free to stop the questioning process.

Once it has been determined that a detention has occurred, the next step is to decide whether a person's right to counsel has been violated. Given the fact that there is very little case law on s. 10(*b*) and administrative tribunals, it is not clear what factors will need to be considered. It is unclear whether all or any of the factors which apply in a criminal law case will also apply when considering whether an administrative tribunal has violated a person's s. 10(*b*) rights.

(f) Rights on being charged with an offence — s. 11

Section 11 of the Charter guarantees that:

11. Any person charged with an offence has the right
   (*a*) to be informed without unreasonable delay of the specific offence;
   (*b*) to be tried within a reasonable time;
   (*c*) not to be compelled to be a witness in proceedings against that person in respect of the offence;
   (*d*) to be presumed innocent until proven guilty according to law in a fair and public hearing by an independent and impartial tribunal;
   (*e*) not to be denied reasonable bail without just cause;
   (*f*) except in the case of an offence under military law tried before a military tribunal, to the benefit of trial by jury where the maximum punishment for the offence is imprisonment for five years or a more severe punishment;
   (*g*) not to be found guilty on account of any act or omission unless, at the time of the act or omission, it constituted an offence under Canadian or international law or was criminal according to the general principles of law recognized by the community of nations;
   (*h*) if finally acquitted of the offence, not to be tried for it again and, if finally found guilty and punished for the offence, not to be tried or punished for it again; and
   (*i*) if found guilty of the offence and if the punishment for the offence has been varied between the time of commission and the time of sentencing, to the benefit of the lesser punishment.

This section guarantees legal rights to "any person charged with an offence". If you look at the list of legal rights that are guaranteed, it is quite evident that they are comprehensive. Yet, they have limited application to administrative tribunals because administrative tribunals do not deal with "offences" because the Supreme Court of Canada has given the word "offence" a very limited meaning. In addition, the Supreme Court[7] has limited the rights guaranteed by s. 11 to

---

[7] In *Blencoe v. British Columbia (Human Rights Commission)* (2000), 190 D.L.R. (4th) 513, [2000] 2 S.C.R. 307, [2000] 10 W.W.R. 567, 231 W.A.C. 161, 81 B.C.L.R. (3d) 1, 23 Admin. L.R. (3d) 175, 3 C.C.E.L. (3d) 165, 38 C.H.R.R. D/153, 2000 C.L.L.C. ¶230-040, 77 C.R.R. (2d) 189, 260 N.R. 1, 2000 SCC 44, the Supreme Court of Canada recently reaffirmed that s. 11(*b*) of the Charter is restricted to pending criminal cases and has no application in administrative proceedings.

criminal proceedings or proceedings where a conviction can lead to imprisonment or a substantial fine. Therefore, the courts have determined that s. 11 does not apply to administrative tribunals conducting professional discipline hearings. The courts have also determined that it does not apply to administrative tribunals conducting discipline hearings against police officers except where a negative finding may lead to imprisonment.

(g) Cruel and unusual treatment or punishment — s. 12

Section 12 of the Charter guarantees that: "Everyone has the right not to be subjected to any cruel and unusual treatment or punishment."

Section 12 prohibits any cruel and unusual treatment or punishment. This means that unless a decision by an administrative tribunal amounts to treatment or punishment, s. 12 does not apply. Whether s. 12 applies to administrative tribunals is unclear because there is very little case law.[8]

(h) Self-incrimination — s. 13

Section 13 of the Charter guarantees that: "A witness who testifies in any proceedings has the right not to have any incriminating evidence so given used to incriminate that witness in any other proceedings, except in a prosecution for perjury or for the giving of contradictory evidence".

This section has very little, if any, application to a hearing by an administrative tribunal. For example, it does not prohibit an administrative tribunal from requiring a person to testify at a hearing even if that person may be prosecuted in the future in a criminal court in regard to the same facts. As another example, it is unclear whether this section protects a person from his or her evidence in a civil or criminal trial being used against him or her when he or she appears before an administrative tribunal.[9]

---

[8] In one case, *Isabey v. Manitoba Health Services Commission* (1986), 28 D.L.R. (4th) 735, [1986] 4 W.W.R. 310, 38 Man. R. (2d) 456 (C.A.), leave to appeal to S.C.C. refused, [1986] 6 W.W.R. lxv, 45 Man. R. (2d) 240*n*, the Manitoba Court of Appeal determined that s. 12 did not apply to a Medical Review Committee when it ordered a doctor to reimburse the Manitoba Health Services Commission for excess payments in the amount of $49,070.45 that he had received after a review of his medical practice determined that he had departed from the established pattern of medical practice.

[9] The British Columbia Court of Appeal in *Donald v. Law Society of British Columbia* (1983), 2 D.L.R. (4th) 385, [1984] 2 W.W.R. 46, 48 B.C.L.R. 210, 7 C.R.R. 305 (C.A.), leave to appeal to S.C.C. refused 55 N.R. 237*n*, determined that s. 13 prevented a transcript of the evidence that had been given by a lawyer as a witness in a civil trial from being used against that lawyer in professional discipline proceedings. In contrast, the Saskatchewan Court of Appeal in *Knutson v. Saskatchewan Registered Nurses Assn.* (1990), 75 D.L.R. (4th) 723, [1991] 2 W.W.R. 327, 90 Sask. R. 120, 46 Admin. L.R. 235, 4 C.R.R. (2d) 168 (C.A.), determined that s. 13 did not prevent a transcript of the evidence that had been given by a nurse in a criminal trial for theft from being used against that nurse in professional discipline proceedings.

However, this section does protect a person from his or her evidence at the administrative tribunal hearing being used against him or her if he or she appears before a court or another administrative tribunal in a subsequent proceeding and the court or administrative tribunal who conducts the subsequent proceeding determines that s. 13 applies. In order to avoid a violation of s. 13 in that situation, safeguards can be put in place such as sealing the transcript of the evidence of the administrative tribunal hearing until the conclusion of the subsequent proceeding. Another possible safeguard is requiring the parties to the administrative tribunal hearing, their counsel or agent, and their witnesses to sign an undertaking or agreement that they will not disclose the oral testimony or show the documentary evidence to anyone until the conclusion of the subsequent proceeding.

(i) Assistance of an interpreter — s. 14

Section 14 of the Charter guarantees that: "A party or witness in any proceedings who does not understand or speak the language in which the proceedings are conducted or who is deaf has the right to the assistance of an interpreter."

Since a hearing before an administrative tribunal is considered a "proceeding", the right to the assistance of an interpreter which is guaranteed by s. 14 would apply to hearings before administrative tribunals.[10] Whether this right exists only at the hearing before an administrative tribunal or also applies to the investigation stage of the proceedings of an administrative tribunal is unclear.

(j) Equality — s. 15(1)

Section 15(1) of the Charter guarantees that:

> 15(1) Every individual is equal before and under the law and has the right to the equal protection and equal benefit of the law without discrimination and, in particular, without discrimination based on race, national or ethnic origin, colour, religion, sex, age or mental or physical disability.

This section is usually used to attack statutes, regulations and by-laws of administrative tribunals which make distinctions between individuals or groups. However, a person's s. 15 rights will not be violated unless it is shown that these distinctions are discriminatory. Discrimination occurs where a distinction, whether intentional or not, is based on grounds[11] relating to personal characteristics of the individual or group which has the effect of imposing burdens, obligations or disadvantages not imposed upon others or limiting access to opportunities, benefits and advantages available to other members of society.

---

[10] For instance, the Ontario Court of Appeal in *Roy v. Hackett* (1987), 45 D.L.R. (4th) 415, 62 O.R. (2d) 365, 23 O.A.C. 382, has indicated that s. 14 of the Charter applies to proceedings before arbitration boards.

[11] The grounds of discrimination must be listed in s. 15 (race, national or ethnic origin, colour, religion, sex, age or mental or physical disability) or analogous to the ones listed in s. 15. For example, the Supreme Court of Canada has determined that marital status, sexual orientation and citizenship status are analogous grounds of discrimination.

Therefore, it is clear that a person's s. 15 rights would be violated if an administrative tribunal's legislation limited or withheld access to opportunities, benefits or advantages to that person but gave them to others on the basis of race, national or ethnic origin, colour, religion, sex, age, mental or physical disability, marital status, sexual orientation or citizenship status. Similarly, it is also clear that a person's s. 15 rights would be violated if an administrative tribunal's legislation imposed burdens, obligations or disadvantages on that person which were not imposed on others on the basis of race, national or ethnic origin, colour, religion, sex, age, mental or physical disability, marital status, sexual orientation or citizenship status.

(3) Can Administrative Tribunals Decide Charter Issues?

Since the sections of the Charter which might apply to administrative tribunals have been identified, it is necessary for an administrative tribunal to consider the important and practical question of whether that particular administrative tribunal can decide a Charter issue that is raised by someone appearing before that administrative tribunal.

The first thing to consider is s. 52(1) of the *Constitution Act, 1982*:

> 52(1) The Constitution of Canada is the supreme law of Canada, and any law that is inconsistent with the provisions of the Constitution is, to the extent of the inconsistency, of no force or effect.

This section does not give an administrative tribunal the power to decide Charter issues. The power of an administrative tribunal to decide Charter issues comes from the wording of its governing statute. This requires considering, among other things, the wording of the administrative tribunal's governing statute to determine whether the administrative tribunal has an express or even an implied power to interpret and apply the law.

Instead, this section sets out the fundamental principle that the Constitution must overrule any other law and that anyone who is required to interpret and apply the law must place the Constitution at the top in terms of priority. Therefore, this section applies not only to courts but also to anyone else who interprets and applies laws. As a result, it should mean that any administrative tribunal who interprets and applies the law must apply the Constitution, including the Charter, as the supreme law of Canada.

The Supreme Court of Canada has recognized that an administrative tribunal must apply the Charter as the supreme law of Canada. For example, the Supreme Court of Canada in *Douglas/Kwantlen Faculty Assn. v. Douglas College*[12] stated: "A tribunal must respect the Constitution so that if it finds invalid a law it is called upon to apply, it is bound to treat it as having no force or effect." The prac-

---

[12] (1990), 77 D.L.R. (4th) 94 at p. 117, [1990] 3 S.C.R. 570, [1991] 1 W.W.R. 643, 52 B.C.L.R. (2d) 68, 50 Admin. L.R. 69, 13 C.H.R.R. D/403, 91 C.L.L.C. ¶17,002, 2 C.R.R. (2d) 157, 118 N.R. 340.

tical effect of this is that administrative tribunals must apply all the relevant law including the Charter when interpreting and applying their governing legislation or any other applicable legislation. If an administrative tribunal then determines that a particular section in their governing legislation or any other applicable legislation violates the Charter and that this violation cannot be justified, it must treat that section as having no legal force or effect. The effect of this determination would be that an administrative tribunal has to decide the case as if the particular section did not exist. This can have a tremendous impact on an administrative tribunal especially if the particular section that has been determined to be invalid is the section in the governing statute that gives the administrative tribunal the authority to initiate an inquiry. This means that the administrative tribunal could not continue the inquiry because the administrative tribunal has lost the authority to proceed with the inquiry.

The exception[13] to the requirement that an administrative tribunal must apply the Charter will occur if the particular administrative tribunal does not have the express or implied power or authority to interpret and apply the law.[14] This means that the administrative tribunal must apply the particular section in their governing legislation or any other applicable legislation to the circumstances of the case even though that section violates the Charter. This results in the administrative tribunal having to make a decision as if the Charter did not exist.

In addition to s. 52(1) of the *Constitution Act, 1982*, s. 24(1) of the Charter must also be considered:

---

[13] As an additional exception, but a rare one, an administrative tribunal would not be required to apply the Charter if the governing statute specifically indicates that the administrative tribunal cannot determine the constitutionality of the sections of the governing statute. For example, s. 40.2 of the *Immigration Act*, R.S.C. 1985, c. I-2, states: "An adjudicator does not have jurisdiction to determine the constitutionality of sections 39 to 40.1."

[14] The Supreme Court of Canada in cases such as *Douglas/Kwantlen Faculty Assn. v. Douglas College, supra*, footnote 12, and *Cuddy Chicks Ltd. v. Ontario (Labour Relations Board)* (1991), 81 D.L.R. (4th) 121, [1991] 2 S.C.R. 5, 3 O.R. (3d) 128*n*, 47 O.A.C. 271, 50 Admin. L.R. 44, 91 C.L.L.C. ¶14,024, 4 C.R.R. (2d) 1, [1991] O.L.R.B. Rep. 790, 122 N.R. 361, has determined that an administrative tribunal has an express power in its governing statute to interpret and apply the law when the governing statute gives an administrative tribunal the express power to decide questions of law by the use of words such as: "interpret and apply any Act intended to regulate employment", "determine all questions of fact or law that arise in any matter before it". In both cases, this express power gave these administrative tribunals the power to decide a Charter issue. In contrast, the Supreme Court of Canada in *Cooper v. Canada (Human Rights Commission)* (1996), 140 D.L.R. (4th) 193, [1996] 3 S.C.R. 854, 43 Admin. L.R. (2d) 155, 26 C.C.E.L. (2d) 1, 27 C.H.R.R. D/173, 96 C.L.L.C. ¶230-056, 40 C.R.R. (2d) 81, 204 N.R. 1, indicated that an administrative tribunal does not have the express power to decide questions of law when the governing statute uses the words "interpret and apply its enabling statute". In this case, this lack of an express power was one of the factors that was considered by the court in determining that the administrative tribunals in this case did not have the power to decide a Charter issue.

24(1) Anyone whose rights or freedoms, as guaranteed by this Charter, have been infringed or denied may apply to a court of competent jurisdiction to obtain such remedy as the court considers appropriate and just in the circumstances.

Similar to s. 52(1), this section does not give an administrative tribunal the power to decide Charter issues. Instead, it authorizes a court of competent jurisdiction to grant a remedy when a Charter right or freedom has been breached. In considering this section, the meaning of the word "court" in the phrase "court of competent jurisdiction" must be determined. Many people would probably automatically assume that this would not include anything other than a traditional court. However, it is important to realize that the French version of s. 24(1) uses the word "tribunal" and this is defined more broadly than the word "court". As a result, it would make sense that any inconsistency between the French and English versions should be determined in favour of the broader interpretation. Nevertheless, it is unclear what an administrative tribunal should do in a particular case because there is limited case law on this and it has been indecisive.

Even if it is determined that a particular administrative tribunal is considered to be a "court", the next question to be determined is whether it is "of competent jurisdiction". The Supreme Court of Canada has interpreted this phrase to mean that the court or administrative tribunal[15] must have jurisdiction or power over the parties, over the subject matter, and over the remedy that is being requested. This means that an administrative tribunal can only apply the Charter under s. 24(1) if: a problem with a Charter issue occurs in a case that is properly before the administrative tribunal, the Charter issue is directly relevant to deciding the case before the administrative tribunal, and the remedy that is requested can be granted by the administrative tribunal.

Once it is determined that s. 24(1) is applicable to a particular administrative tribunal because it is a "court of competent jurisdiction", it is important to be aware that this subsection places limits on the type of remedies that can be

---

[15] The Supreme Court of Canada in *Weber v. Ontario Hydro* (1995), 125 D.L.R. (4th) 583, [1995] 2 S.C.R. 929, 24 O.R. (3d) 358n, 82 O.A.C. 321, 30 Admin. L.R. (2d) 1, 12 C.C.E.L. (2d) 1, 24 C.C.L.T. (2d) 217, 95 C.L.L.C. ¶210-027, 30 C.R.R. (2d) 1, 183 N.R. 241, determined that an administrative tribunal is a court of competent jurisdiction if its governing statute gives it power over: the parties, the subject matter and the Charter remedy that is being sought. In that case, the court determined that a board of arbitration under the collective agreement was a court of competent jurisdiction because it had jurisdiction over the parties, the subject matter and the Charter remedy. In contrast, in *Mooring v. Canada (National Parole Board)* (1996), 132 D.L.R. (4th) 56, [1996] 1 S.C.R. 75, [1996] 3 W.W.R. 305, 115 W.A.C. 1, 20 B.C.L.R. (3d) 1, 38 Admin. L.R. (2d) 149, 104 C.C.C. (3d) 97, 45 C.R. (4th) 265, 33 C.R.R. (2d) 189, 192 N.R. 161, the Supreme Court determined that the National Parole Board was not a court of competent jurisdiction because even though it had power over the parties and the subject matter, it did not have power to grant the Charter remedy that was being sought. This means that an administrative tribunal will not be considered to be a court of competent jurisdiction unless it has power or jurisdiction over all of the three criteria: the parties, the subject matter and the Charter remedy.

granted. This subsection authorizes the granting of "such remedy as the court considers appropriate and just in the circumstances". The courts have interpreted this as meaning that the Charter does not give additional or new remedy powers to the courts. As a result, if an administrative tribunal is determined to be a court of competent jurisdiction, the administrative tribunal is also not given any additional or new remedy powers. This means that administrative tribunals are not given the authority to grant remedies that it has no authority to grant such as issuing a formal declaration regarding the validity of a particular section in its governing statute.

The Supreme Court of Canada has made it clear that neither s. 52(1) of the *Constitution Act, 1982* nor s. 24(1) of the Charter give an administrative tribunal the power to decide Charter issues. The Supreme Court of Canada has also made it clear that an express or an implied power to interpret and apply the law in the administrative tribunal's governing statute is an important determinant of whether an administrative tribunal has the power to decide Charter issues, but, there are also other factors which need to be examined. The Ontario Workers' Compensation Appeal Tribunal,[16] in a case which involved determining whether it had authority to determine the constitutional validity of the *Workers' Compensation Act*,[17] reviewed the Supreme Court of Canada cases[18] on this issue. From this review, it identified a list of factors to be considered in determining whether an administrative tribunal can decide a Charter issue:[19]

1. Is the administrative tribunal granted authority to provide a "final and conclusive" settlement of a dispute?
2. In accomplishing its ordinary tasks, is the administrative tribunal explicitly or implicitly empowered to determine questions of law — to interpret and apply any Act bearing on the issues before it?
3. How strongly do considerations of "practicality and convenience" argue against the administrative tribunal having the jurisdiction to deal with the Charter challenge when compared to the advantages of the administrative tribunal being seen to have that jurisdiction?
4. Is the administrative tribunal's caseload primarily involved only in fact-finding or is its work more adjudicative in nature? Does its usual business involve the resolution of issues concerning the outcome of applying complex legislative rules or regulations to findings of fact?

---

[16] The name of the Workers' Compensation Appeal Tribunal has been changed to the Workplace Safety and Insurance Appeals Tribunal.

[17] The name of the *Workers' Compensation Act* has been changed to the *Workplace Safety and Insurance Act, 1997*, S.O. 1997, c. 16, Sch. A.

[18] *Douglas/Kwantlen Faculty Assn. v. Douglas College, supra,* footnote 12; *Cuddy Chicks Ltd. v. Ontario (Labour Relations Board), supra,* footnote 14, and *Tétreault-Gadoury v. Canada (Employment & Immigration Commission)* (1991), 81 D.L.R. (4th) 358, [1991] 2 S.C.R. 22, 50 Admin. L.R. 1, 36 C.C.E.L. 117, 43 C.R.R. (2d) 12, 126 N.R. 1.

[19] *Decision No. 534/90* (1992), 23 W.C.A.T.R. 121 at pp. 131-2 (W.C.A.T.).

5. Is the interpretation and application of the Charter "vastly different" from the administrative tribunal's ordinary responsibilities?
6. Do the remedies ordinarily available to the administrative tribunal come naturally into play and would they be effective if identification of a Charter violation were seen to make a section of a statute of no force or effect?
7. Will the assertion before the administrative tribunal of the Charter rights provide parties with a speedy determination of those rights?
8. Does the administrative tribunal have a "specialized competence" or "calibre" that would allow it to make an especially valuable contribution to the constitutional interpretation?
9. Would the experience of the administrative tribunal be highly relevant to the Charter challenge, "particularly at the s. 1 stage where policy concerns prevail"?
10. Is it apparent that "at the end of the day the legal process will be better served" if the administrative tribunal "makes an initial determination of the jurisdictional issue arising from the constitutional challenge"?
11. Is there an alternative administrative tribunal with better credentials for dealing with the Charter challenge?
12. Does the applicant have other options outside the court system for pursuing the Charter challenge?

(4) Examples of Charter Challenges to the Decisions of Administrative Tribunals

Administrative tribunals, like the federal and provincial governments and its various government departments, must not violate the rights and freedoms that are protected by the Charter. Nevertheless, allegations of Charter violations often form the basis of an appeal or an application for judicial review of the actions and decisions of administrative tribunals.

In *Taylor v. Institute of Chartered Accountants of Saskatchewan*,[20] a chartered accountant who was admitted into the Institute of Chartered Accountants of Ontario on the basis of having passed the examination of the American Institute of Certified Public Accountants, was refused admission into the Institute of Chartered Accountants of Saskatchewan. Upon reviewing the chartered accountant's application, the Institute of Chartered Accountants of Saskatchewan determined that the chartered accountant was required to pass the Uniform Final Examination, a national examination used across Canada, in order to fulfill the requirements for qualification as a member in the Institute's by-laws. The chartered accountant asked the court to review the Institute's decision. He argued that the decision violated his right to pursue the gaining of a livelihood in any province (s. 6 of the Charter), his right to life, liberty and security of the person

---

[20] (1989), 59 D.L.R. (4th) 656, 75 Sask. R. 153, 44 C.R.R. 311 (C.A.).

112

(s. 7 of the Charter), and his right to equality before and under the law and equal protection and benefit of the law without discrimination (s. 15(1) of the Charter).

The Saskatchewan Court of Appeal determined that none of these sections of the Charter were violated by the Institute's decision. The court found that s. 6 does not prevent the provinces from regulating the professions, and thus, does not give the chartered accountant the right to admission in one provincial Institute just because he has been previously admitted into another provincial Institute. The court found that even if the chartered accountant was deprived of his right to liberty, there was no violation of his s. 7 rights because he was not denied the principles of fundamental justice. The discretion given to the Institute to make a decision regarding admission to membership and the actual exercise of the discretion by the Institute in refusing admission to the chartered accountant does not violate the principles of fundamental justice. The court also found that the decision was not discriminatory and did not violate his s. 15 rights because he was not refused membership due to any personal characteristic, rather he had not taken and passed the Uniform Final Examination.

In *Johnstone v. Law Society of British Columbia*,[21] a lawyer had been charged with professional misconduct arising from his conduct in a particular criminal case and the subsequent assessment of his account in that case. At the Discipline Committee hearing, the lawyer was asked whether the evidence that he gave on the assessment of his account was true. He stated that the evidence was true when it was given but was now incorrect. Counsel for the lawyer objected to the admission of the transcripts of the evidence of the lawyer from the hearing before the court Registrar on the assessment of his account. The Discipline Committee admitted the transcripts on the issue of credibility. The Discipline Committee found the lawyer to be guilty of professional misconduct. The lawyer appealed the conviction arguing that his right to be protected against self-incrimination in s. 13 of the Charter was violated.

The British Columbia Court of Appeal determined that the lawyer's rights under s. 13 were violated. The court indicated that s. 13 should not be restricted to criminal proceedings and should be given a broader meaning so that it could be extended to any proceeding where an individual is exposed to a criminal charge, penalty or forfeiture as a result of having testified in earlier proceedings. The court went on to indicate that the Discipline Committee used some of the evidence given by the lawyer at the hearing before the Registrar as admissions rather than to determine credibility and then made findings of fact based on these admissions which incriminated the lawyer. Nevertheless, the court still dismissed the appeal because even without the evidence given by the lawyer when he appeared before the Registrar on the assessment proceedings, there was enough other admissible evidence to establish that he was guilty of professional misconduct.

---

[21] (1987), 40 D.L.R. (4th) 550, [1987] 5 W.W.R. 637, 15 B.C.L.R. (2d) 1 (C.A.).

Appendix A

Glossary

Act — A bill that has gone through all the legislative stages and has now become law. It is also commonly referred to as a statute.

action — A legal proceeding that results in a trial. In administrative law, it is used for getting a money award or damages against an administrative tribunal.

adjudication — The process of making a decision after a hearing.

agent — A person who has obtained the authority to act for another person. In administrative law, this is commonly used to refer to a representative who is not a lawyer.

appeal — This is one of the methods of reviewing the decisions of administrative tribunals. The review, depending on the wording of the governing statute, can be conducted by a higher-level decision-maker within the administrative tribunal or by a court.

application — A legal proceeding that is used in administrative law for judicial review of the actions and decisions of administrative tribunals. The evidence for an application is usually given in an affidavit or sworn statement.

application for judicial review — This is the document that initiates judicial review. However, for some provinces and territories, a variety of different documents such as a petition or notice of motion initiates judicial review.

arbitration — A form of alternative dispute resolution where an independent, neutral third person or arbitrator is appointed to hear a dispute and then make a final and binding decision called an award. The parties to the dispute choose the arbitrator and the procedure for the arbitration.

biased — A term used to describe a decision-maker that is not impartial when making a decision.

bill — A term used to describe draft or proposed legislation when it is introduced in the federal Parliament or a provincial legislature and it goes thorough the legislative stages until it becomes law.

civil law — A body of law that is codified or systematized by putting all the law in one or more documents called a Code. It is also the body of law which deals

115

with the private rights of individuals as opposed to criminal law which deals with the public rights of individuals.

codify — A process where legal principles are systematically put into a statute with little or no change.

common law — A body of law, based on the past decisions of judges, which acts as a guide for judges in deciding future cases. It is also commonly referred to as case law.

correctness — This is one of the three standards of review used by the courts to review the actions or decisions of administrative tribunals. It is the standard that gives no deference to the administrative tribunal. This standard only requires the court to determine whether the action or decision was right or wrong.

counsel — This is a more formal term to describe a lawyer who represents a person or organization before an administrative tribunal.

deference — This term means respect by a court for the actions or decisions of an administrative tribunal so that on an application for judicial review, the applicant will need to show a very strong case before the court will intervene.

directly affected — A person whose legal interests are or will be influenced or changed by the actions or decision(s) of an administrative tribunal. This type of person must be provided with adequate notice of the allegations or charges being made against him or her and the proposed action, before a hearing takes place by an administrative tribunal. Also, this type of person is usually considered as automatically having the standing to seek judicial review of the actions or decision(s) of an administrative tribunal.

discretion — The power of an administrative tribunal or a court to act or make decisions. In exercising this power, the administrative tribunal or court has a choice about how it will act or make decisions. In the governing statute, a power to act or make decisions is usually expressed by using the word "may".

equity — A body of law, developed in England because the common law courts had become rigid and inflexible, which involved applying principles of fairness and justice when deciding a legal dispute.

exhibit — A document or object that is presented as evidence in a proceeding before an administrative tribunal or a court.

fairness — In the past, this term described the procedural requirements of an administrative tribunal when it was exercising an administrative function. Since the courts have moved away from distinguishing between fairness and natural justice, this term now describes the procedural requirements of an administrative tribunal regardless of its function. The two basic components of fairness or natural justice are the right to be heard and the right to an impartial or unbiased decision-maker.

fundamental justice — The expected standard of an administrative tribunal or a court when it makes a decision that deprives the life or liberty or security of a person under s. 7 of the Charter. This standard has procedural and substantive elements.

hearsay — A statement offered as proof by a witness of something he or she did not personally observe but was told about by someone else. It is a second-hand report of a conversation or an event that has occurred. It is admissible at a hearing to which the *Statutory Powers Procedure Act* ("SPPA") applies but it is inadmissible in a court. Certain statutes which create administrative tribunals to which the SPPA applies, expressly stipulate that the rules of evidence applicable in a court apply to the hearing rather than the rules under the SPPA. For hearings held by those administrative tribunals, hearsay evidence would not be admitted.

intra vires — A Latin phrase which means that an administrative tribunal has acted within the authority granted to it by the governing statute. It is the opposite of the Latin phrase of *ultra vires*. It also refers to a provincial legislature or the federal Parliament when it passes a law on a subject matter within the authority granted to it by the Constitution.

judicial or quasi-judicial — The authority of a court or administrative tribunal to make a decision about a person's rights. In administrative law, traditionally, the principles of natural justice only applied to an administrative tribunal that could be classified as judicial or quasi-judicial.

judicial review — This is a method used by the courts to review the actions and decisions of administrative tribunals.

jurisdiction — The authority of a court or an administrative tribunal. The authority of an administrative tribunal is located in the statute which establishes that administrative tribunal — the enabling or governing statute. It also refers to the authority of the provincial legislatures and the federal Parliament to pass laws within certain prescribed areas.

natural justice — In the past, this term described the procedural requirements of an administrative tribunal when it was exercising a judicial or quasi-judicial function. Since the courts have moved away from distinguishing between natural justice and fairness, this term now describes the procedural requirements of an administrative tribunal regardless of its function. The two basic components of natural justice or fairness are the right to be heard and the right to an impartial or unbiased decision-maker.

patently unreasonable — This is one of the three standards of review used by the courts to review the actions or decisions of administrative tribunals. It is the standard that gives the most deference to the administrative tribunal. This standard requires the court to determine whether the action or decision was clearly irrational.

precedent — An earlier decision which is similar in facts to the current case.

privative clause — A section or sections in an administrative tribunal's governing statute which attempts to prohibit or prevent the courts from reviewing the actions and decisions of that administrative tribunal.

public interest standing — This form of standing to seek judicial review is given by the courts to an individual or group who does not meet the normal requirement for standing of being a party or directly affected by the actions or decision(s) of an administrative tribunal.

standing — A term used to describe the individuals or groups who have a legal right to seek judicial review.

stare decisis — A Latin phrase which describes a process where judges must follow previous decisions or precedents if the facts are similar.

statute — A bill that has gone through all the legislative stages and has now become law. It is also commonly referred to as an Act.

ultra vires — A Latin phrase which means that an administrative tribunal has acted outside of or beyond the authority granted to it by the governing statute. It is the opposite of the Latin phrase of *intra vires*. It also refers to a provincial legislature or the federal Parliament when it passes a law on a subject matter beyond or outside the authority granted to it by the Constitution. The law becomes invalid and has no legal force or effect.

unreasonable — This term, also sometimes referred to as reasonableness *simpliciter*, is one of the three standards of review used by the courts to review the actions or decisions of administrative tribunals. It is the middle standard, it is commonly used in appeals, and it gives some deference to the administrative tribunal. This standard requires the court to determine whether the action or decision was clearly wrong. This term is also used to describe the type of search or seizure which violates a person's rights under s. 8 of the Charter or the type of delay which violates a person's rights under s. 11 of the Charter.

void — A term used to describe a decision that is invalid and has no legal force or effect.

Appendix B

Ontario
Statutory Powers Procedure Act
R.S.O. 1990, c. S.22

Amendments

Amended 1993, c. 27, Sch.; deemed in force December 31, 1991
Amended 1994, c. 27, s. 56(1) to (44); proclaimed in force April 1, 1995
Amended 1997, c. 23, s. 13; in force November 28, 1997
Amended 1999, c. 12, Sch. B, s. 16; proclaimed in force February 14, 2000

1. (1) **Definitions.**— In this Act,

"electronic hearing" means a hearing held by conference telephone or some other form of electronic technology allowing persons to hear one another;

"hearing" means a hearing in any proceeding;

"licence" includes any permit, certificate, approval, registration or similar form of permission required by law;

"municipality" has the same meaning as in the *Municipal Affairs Act*, and includes a district, metropolitan and regional municipality and their local boards;

"oral hearing" means a hearing at which the parties or their counsel or agents attend before the tribunal in person;

"proceeding" means a proceeding to which this Act applies;

"statutory power of decision" means a power or right, conferred by or under a statute, to make a decision deciding or prescribing,

    (a) the legal rights, powers, privileges, immunities, duties or liabilities of any person or party, or

    (b) the eligibility of any person or party to receive, or to the continuation of, a benefit or licence, whether the person is legally entitled thereto or not;

"tribunal" means one or more persons, whether or not incorporated and however described, upon which a statutory power of decision is conferred by or under a statute.

"written hearing" means a hearing held by means of the exchange of documents, whether in written form or by electronic means. 1994, c. 27, s. 56(1) to (3).

(2) **Meaning of "person" extended.**— A municipality, an unincorporated association of employers, a trade union or council of trade unions who may be a party to a proceeding in the exercise of a statutory power of decision under the statute conferring the power shall be deemed to be a person for the purpose of any provision of this Act or of any rule made under this Act that applies to parties.

2. Interpretation.— This Act, and any rule made by a tribunal under section 25.1, shall be liberally construed to secure the just, most expeditious and cost-effective determination of every proceeding on its merits. 1999, c. 12, Sch. B, s. 16(1).

3. (1) Application of Act.— Subject to subsection (2), this Act applies to a proceeding by a tribunal in the exercise of a statutory power of decision conferred by or under an Act of the Legislature, where the tribunal is required by or under such Act or otherwise by law to hold or to afford to the parties to the proceeding an opportunity for a hearing before making a decision. 1994, c. 27, s. 56(5).

(2) **Where Act does not apply.**— This Act does not apply to a proceeding,
    (a) before the Assembly or any committee of the Assembly;
    (b) in or before,
        (i) the Court of Appeal,
        (ii) the Ontario Court (General Division) [Superior Court of Justice],
        (iii) the Ontario Court (Provincial Division) [Ontario Court of Justice],
        (iv) the Unified Family Court,
        (v) the Small Claims Court, or
        (vi) a justice of the peace;
    (c) to which the Rules of Civil Procedure apply;
    (d) before an arbitrator to which the *Arbitrations Act* or the *Labour Relations Act* applies;
    (e) at a coroner's inquest;
    (f) of a commission appointed under the *Public Inquiries Act*;
    (g) of one or more persons required to make an investigation and to make a report, with or without recommendations, where the report is for the information or advice of the person to whom it is made and does not in any way legally bind or limit that person in any decision he or she may have power to make; or
    (h) of a tribunal empowered to make regulations, rules or by-laws in so far as its power to make regulations, rules or by-laws is concerned. 1994, c. 27, s. 56(6).

4. (1) Waiver of procedural requirement.— Any procedural requirement of this Act, or of another Act or a regulation that applies to a proceeding, may be waived with the consent of the parties and the tribunal. 1994, c. 27, s. 56(7), part; 1997, c. 23, s. 13(1).

(2) **Same, rules.**— Any provision of a tribunal's rules made under section 25.1 may be waived in accordance with the rules. 1994, c. 27, s. 56(7), part.

4.1 Disposition without hearing.— If the parties consent, a proceeding may be disposed of by a decision of the tribunal given without a hearing, unless another Act or a regulation that applies to the proceeding provides otherwise. 1994, c. 27, s. 56(7), part; 1997, c. 23, s. 13(2).

4.2 (1) Panels, certain matters.— A procedural or interlocutory matter in a proceeding may be heard and determined by a panel consisting of one or more members of the tribunal, as assigned by the chair of the tribunal. 1994, c. 27, s. 56(8), part.

(2) **Assignments.**— In assigning members of the tribunal to a panel, the chair shall take into consideration any requirement imposed by another Act or a regulation that applies to the proceeding that the tribunal be representative of specific interests. 1994, c. 27, s. 56(8), part; 1997, c. 23, s. 13(3).

(3) **Decision of panel.**— The decision of a majority of the members of a panel, or their unanimous decision in the case of a two-member panel, is the tribunal's decision. 1994, c. 27, s. 56(8), part.

4.2.1 (1) Panel of one.— The chair of a tribunal may decide that a proceeding be heard by a panel of one person and assign the person to hear the proceeding unless there is a statutory requirement in another Act that the proceeding be heard by a panel of more than one person.

(2) **Reduction in number of panel members.**— Where there is a statutory requirement in another Act that a proceeding be heard by a panel of a specified number of persons, the chair of the tribunal may assign to the panel one person or any lesser number of persons than the number specified in the other Act if all parties to the proceeding consent. 1999, c. 12, Sch. B, s. 16(2).

4.3 Expiry of term.— If the term of office of a member of a tribunal who has participated in a hearing expires before a decision is given, the term shall be deemed to continue, but only for the purpose of participating in the decision and for no other purpose. 1994, c. 27, s. 56(9), part; 1997, c. 23, s. 13(4).

4.4 (1) Incapacity of member.— If a member of a tribunal who has participated in a hearing becomes unable, for any reason, to complete the hearing or to participate in the decision, the remaining member or members may complete the hearing and give a decision. 1994, c. 27, s. 56(9), part.

(2) **Other Acts and regulations.**— Subsection (1) does not apply if another Act or a regulation specifically deals with the issue of what takes place in the circumstances described in subsection (1). 1994, c. 27, s. 56(9), part; 1997, c. 23, s. 13(5).

4.5 (1) **Decision not to process commencement of proceeding.**— Subject to subsection (3), upon receiving documents relating to the commencement of a proceeding, a tribunal or its administrative staff may decide not to process the documents relating to the commencement of the proceeding if,

    (a) the documents are incomplete;

    (b) the documents are received after the time required for commencing the proceeding has elapsed;

    (c) the fee required for commencing the proceeding is not paid; or

    (d) there is some other technical defect in the commencement of the proceeding.

(2) **Notice.**— A tribunal or its administrative staff shall give the party who commences a proceeding notice of its decision under subsection (1) and shall set out in the notice the reasons for the decision and the requirements for resuming the processing of the documents.

(3) **Rules under s. 25.1.**— A tribunal or its administrative staff shall not make a decision under subsection (1) unless the tribunal has made rules under section 25.1 respecting the making of such decisions and those rules shall set out,

    (a) any of the grounds referred to in subsection (1) upon which the tribunal or its administrative staff may decide not to process the documents relating to the commencement of a proceeding; and

    (b) the requirements for the processing of the documents to be resumed.

(4) **Continuance of provisions in other statutes.**— Despite section 32, nothing in this section shall prevent a tribunal or its administrative staff from deciding not to process documents relating to the commencement of a proceeding on grounds that differ from those referred to in subsection (1) or without complying with subsection (2) or (3) if the tribunal or its staff does so in accordance with the provisions of an Act that are in force on the day this section comes into force. 1999, c. 12, Sch. B, s. 16(3), part.

4.6 (1) **Dismissal of proceeding without hearing.**— Subject to subsections (5) and (6), a tribunal may dismiss a proceeding without a hearing if,

    (a) the proceeding is frivolous, vexatious or is commenced in bad faith;

    (b) the proceeding relates to matters that are outside the jurisdiction of the tribunal; or

    (c) some aspect of the statutory requirements for bringing the proceeding has not been met.

(2) **Notice.**— Before dismissing a proceeding under this section, a tribunal shall give notice of its intention to dismiss the proceeding to,

    (a) all parties to the proceeding if the proceeding is being dismissed for reasons referred to in clause (1)(b); or

    (b) the party who commences the proceeding if the proceeding is being dismissed for any other reason.

(3) **Same.**— The notice of intention to dismiss a proceeding shall set out the reasons for the dismissal and inform the parties of their right to make written submissions to the tribunal with respect to the dismissal within the time specified in the notice.

(4) **Right to make submissions.**— A party who receives a notice under subsection (2) may make written submissions to the tribunal with respect to the dismissal within the time specified in the notice.

(5) **Dismissal.**— A tribunal shall not dismiss a proceeding under this section until it has given notice under subsection (2) and considered any submissions made under subsection (4).

(6) **Rules.**— A tribunal shall not dismiss a proceeding under this section unless it has made rules under section 25.1 respecting the early dismissal of proceedings and those rules shall include,
  (a) any of the grounds referred to in subsection (1) upon which a proceeding may be dismissed;
  (b) the right of the parties who are entitled to receive notice under subsection (2) to make submissions with respect to the dismissal; and
  (c) the time within which the submissions must be made.

(7) **Continuance of provisions in other statutes.**— Despite section 32, nothing in this section shall prevent a tribunal from dismissing a proceeding on grounds other than those referred to in subsection (1) or without complying with subsections (2) to (6) if the tribunal dismisses the proceeding in accordance with the provisions of an Act that are in force on the day this section comes into force. 1999, c. 12, Sch. B, s. 16(3), part.

4.7 Classifying proceedings.— A tribunal may make rules under section 25.1 classifying the types of proceedings that come before it and setting guidelines as to the procedural steps or processes (such as preliminary motions, pre-hearing conferences, alternative dispute resolution mechanisms, expedited hearings) that apply to each type of proceeding and the circumstances in which other procedures may apply. 1999, c. 12, Sch. B, s. 16(3), part.

4.8 (1) Alternative dispute resolution.— A tribunal may direct the parties to a proceeding to participate in an alternative dispute resolution mechanism for the purposes of resolving the proceeding or an issue arising in the proceeding if,
  (a) it has made rules under section 25.1 respecting the use of alternative dispute resolution mechanisms; and
  (b) all parties consent to participating in the alternative dispute resolution mechanism.

(2) **Definition.**— In this section,
"alternative dispute resolution mechanism" includes mediation, conciliation, negotiation or any other means of facilitating the resolution of issues in dispute.

(3) **Rules.**— A rule under section 25.1 respecting the use of alternative dispute resolution mechanisms shall include procedural guidelines to deal with the following:

1. The circumstances in which a settlement achieved by means of an alternative dispute resolution mechanism must be reviewed and approved by the tribunal.
2. Any requirement, statutory or otherwise, that there be an order by the tribunal.

(4) **Mandatory alternative dispute resolution.**— A rule under subsection (3) may provide that participation in an alternative dispute resolution mechanism is mandatory or that it is mandatory in certain specified circumstances.

(5) **Person appointed to mediate, etc.**— A rule under subsection (3) may provide that a person appointed to mediate, conciliate, negotiate or help resolve a matter by means of an alternative dispute resolution mechanism be a member of the tribunal or a person independent of the tribunal. However, a member of the tribunal who is so appointed with respect to a matter in a proceeding shall not subsequently hear the matter if it comes before the tribunal unless the parties consent.

(6) **Continuance of provisions in other statutes.**— Despite section 32, nothing in this section shall prevent a tribunal from directing parties to a proceeding to participate in an alternative dispute resolution mechanism even though the requirements of subsections (1) to (5) have not been met if the tribunal does so in accordance with the provisions of an Act that are in force on the day this section comes into force.1999, c. 12, Sch. B, s. 16(3), part.

4.9 (1) **Mediators, etc., not compellable.**— No person employed as a mediator, conciliator or negotiator or otherwise appointed to facilitate the resolution of a matter before a tribunal by means of an alternative dispute resolution mechanism shall be compelled to give testimony or produce documents in a proceeding before the tribunal or in a civil proceeding with respect to matters that come to his or her knowledge in the course of exercising his or her duties under this or any other Act.

(2) **Evidence in civil proceedings.**— No notes or records kept by a mediator, conciliator or negotiator or by any other person appointed to facilitate the resolution of a matter before a tribunal by means of an alternative dispute resolution mechanism under this or any other Act are admissible in a civil proceeding. 1999, c. 12, Sch. B, s. 16(3), part.

5. Parties.— The parties to a proceeding shall be the persons specified as parties by or under the statute under which the proceeding arises or, if not so specified, persons entitled by law to be parties to the proceeding.

5.1 (1) **Written hearings.**— A tribunal whose rules made under section 25.1 deal with written hearings may hold a written hearing in a proceeding. 1994, c. 27, s. 56(10), part; 1997, c. 23, s. 13(6).

(2) **Exception.**— The tribunal shall not hold a written hearing if a party satisfies the tribunal that there is good reason for not doing so. 1994, c. 27, s. 56(10), part; 1999, c. 12, Sch. B, s. 16(4).

(2.1) **Same.**— Subsection (2) does not apply if the only purpose of the hearing is to deal with procedural matters. 1999, c. 12, Sch. B, s. 16(4).

(3) **Documents.**— In a written hearing, all the parties are entitled to receive every document that the tribunal receives in the proceeding. 1994, c. 27, s. 56(10), part.

5.2 (1) **Electronic hearings.**— A tribunal whose rules made under section 25.1 deal with electronic hearings may hold an electronic hearing in a proceeding. 1994, c. 27, s. 56(10), part; 1997, c. 23, s. 13(7).

(2) **Exception.**— The tribunal shall not hold an electronic hearing if a party satisfies the tribunal that holding an electronic rather than an oral hearing is likely to cause the party significant prejudice.

(3) **Same.**— Subsection (2) does not apply if the only purpose of the hearing is to deal with procedural matters.

(4) **Participants to be able to hear one another.**— In an electronic hearing, all the parties and the members of the tribunal participating in the hearing must be able to hear one another and any witnesses throughout the hearing. 1994, c. 27, s. 56(10), part.

5.2.1 Different kinds of hearings in one proceeding.— A tribunal may, in a proceeding, hold any combination of written, electronic and oral hearings. 1997, c. 23, s. 13(8).

5.3 (1) **Pre-hearing conferences.**— If the tribunal's rules made under section 25.1 deal with pre-hearing conferences, the tribunal may direct the parties to participate in a pre-hearing conference to consider,
    (a) the settlement of any or all of the issues;
    (b) the simplification of the issues;
    (c) facts or evidence that may be agreed upon;
    (d) the dates by which any steps in the proceeding are to be taken or begun;
    (e) the estimated duration of the hearing; and
    (f) any other matter that may assist in the just and most expeditious disposition of the proceeding. 1994, c. 27, s. 56(11), part; 1997, c. 23, s. 13(9).

(1.1) **Other Acts and regulations.**— The tribunal's power to direct the parties to participate in a pre-hearing conference is subject to any other Act or regulation that applies to the proceeding. 1997, c. 23, s. 13(10), part.

(2) **Who presides.**— The chair of the tribunal may designate a member of the tribunal or any other person to preside at the pre-hearing conference.

(3) **Orders.**— A member who presides at a pre-hearing conference may make such orders as he or she considers necessary or advisable with respect to the conduct of the proceeding, including adding parties.

(4) **Disqualification.**— A member who presides at a pre-hearing conference at which the parties attempt to settle issues shall not preside at the hearing of the proceeding unless the parties consent. 1994, c. 27, s. 56(11), part.

(5) **Application of s. 5.2.**— Section 5.2 applies to a pre-hearing conference, with necessary modifications. 1997, c. 23, s. 13(10), part.

5.4 (1) **Disclosure.**— If the tribunal's rules made under section 25.1 deal with disclosure, the tribunal may, at any stage of the proceeding before all hearings are complete, make orders for,
   (a) the exchange of documents;
   (b) the oral or written examination of a party;
   (c) the exchange of witness statements and reports of expert witnesses;
   (d) the provision of particulars;
   (e) any other form of disclosure. 1994, c. 27, s. 56(12), part; 1997, c. 23, s. 13(11).

(1.1) **Other Acts and regulations.**— The tribunal's power to make orders for disclosure is subject to any other Act or regulation that applies to the proceeding. 1997, c. 23, s. 13(12).

(2) **Exception, privileged information.**— Subsection (1) does not authorize the making of an order requiring disclosure of privileged information. 1994, c. 27, s. 56(12), part.

6. (1) **Notice of hearing.**— The parties to a proceeding shall be given reasonable notice of the hearing by the tribunal.

(2) **Statutory authority.**— A notice of a hearing shall include a reference to the statutory authority under which the hearing will be held. 1994, c. 27, s. 56(13), part.

(3) **Oral hearing.**— A notice of an oral hearing shall include,
   (a) a statement of the time, place and purpose of the hearing; and
   (b) a statement that if the party notified does not attend at the hearing, the tribunal may proceed in the party's absence and the party will not be entitled to any further notice in the proceeding. 1994, c. 27, s. 56(13), part.

(4) **Written hearing.**— A notice of a written hearing shall include,
   (a) a statement of the date and purpose of the hearing, and details about the manner in which the hearing will be held;

(b) a statement that the hearing shall not be held as a written hearing if the party satisfies the tribunal that there is good reason for not holding a written hearing (in which case the tribunal is required to hold it as an electronic or oral hearing) and an indication of the procedure to be followed for that purpose.

(c) a statement that if the party notified neither acts under clause (b) nor participates in the hearing in accordance with the notice, the tribunal may proceed without the party's participation and the party will not be entitled to any further notice in the proceeding. 1994, c. 27, s. 56(13), part; 1997, c. 23, s. 13(13); 1999, c. 12, Sch. B, s. 16(5).

(5) **Electronic hearing.**— A notice of an electronic hearing shall include,

(a) a statement of the time and purpose of the hearing, and details about the manner in which the hearing will be held;

(b) a statement that the only purpose of the hearing is to deal with procedural matters, if that is the case;

(c) if clause (b) does not apply, a statement that the party notified may, by satisfying the tribunal that holding the hearing as an electronic hearing is likely to cause the party significant prejudice, require the tribunal to hold the hearing as an oral hearing, and an indication of the procedure to be followed for that purpose; and

(d) a statement that if the party notified neither acts under clause (c), if applicable, nor participates in the hearing in accordance with the notice, the tribunal may proceed without the party's participation and the party will not be entitled to any further notice in the proceeding. 1994, c. 27, s. 56(13), part.

7. (1) **Effect of non-attendance at hearing after due notice.**— Where notice of an oral hearing has been given to a party to a proceeding in accordance with this Act and the party does not attend at the hearing, the tribunal may proceed in the absence of the party and the party is not entitled to any further notice in the proceeding. 1994, c. 27, s. 56(14).

(2) **Same, written hearings.**— Where notice of a written hearing has been given to a party to a proceeding in accordance with this Act and the party neither acts under clause 6(4)(b) nor participates in the hearing in accordance with the notice, the tribunal may proceed without the party's participation and the party is not entitled to any further notice in the proceeding.

(3) **Same, electronic hearings.**— Where notice of an electronic hearing has been given to a party to a proceeding in accordance with this Act and the party neither acts under clause 6(5)(c), if applicable, nor participates in the hearing in accordance with the notice, the tribunal may proceed without the party's participation and the party is not entitled to any further notice in the proceeding. 1994, c. 27, s. 56(15).

8. Where character, etc., of a party is in issue.— Where the good character, propriety of conduct or competence of a party is an issue in a proceeding, the party is entitled to be furnished prior to the hearing with reasonable information of any allegations with respect thereto.

9. (1) **Hearings to be public, exceptions.**— An oral hearing shall be open to the public except where the tribunal is of the opinion that,

(a) matters involving public security may be disclosed; or

(b) intimate financial or personal matters or other matters may be disclosed at the hearing of such a nature, having regard to the circumstances, that the desirability of avoiding disclosure thereof in the interests of any person affected or in the public interest outweighs the desirability of adhering to the principle that hearings be open to the public,

in which case the tribunal may hold the hearing in the absence of the public. 1994, c. 27, s. 56(16).

(1.1) **Written hearings.**— In a written hearing, members of the public are entitled to reasonable access to the documents submitted, unless the tribunal is of the opinion that clause (1)(a) or (b) applies.

(1.2) **Electronic hearings.**— An electronic hearing shall be open to the public unless the tribunal is of the opinion that,

(a) it is not practical to hold the hearing in a manner that is open to the public; or

(b) clause (1)(a) or (b) applies. 1994, c. 27, s. 56(17); 1997, c. 23, s. 13(14).

(2) **Maintenance of order at hearings.**— A tribunal may make such orders or give such directions at an oral or electronic hearing as it considers necessary for the maintenance of order at the hearing, and, if any person disobeys or fails to comply with any such order or direction, the tribunal or a member thereof may call for the assistance of any peace officer to enforce the order or direction, and every peace officer so called upon shall take such action as is necessary to enforce the order or direction and may use such force as is reasonably required for that purpose. 1994, c. 27, s. 56(18).

9.1 (1) **Proceedings involving similar questions.**— If two or more proceedings before a tribunal involve the same or similar questions of fact, law or policy, the tribunal may,

(a) combine the proceedings or any part of them, with the consent of the parties;

(b) hear the proceedings at the same time, with the consent of the parties;

(c) hear the proceedings one immediately after the other; or

(d) stay one or more of the proceedings until after the determination of another one of them.

(2) **Exception.**— Subsection (1) does not apply to proceedings to which the *Consolidated Hearings Act* applies. 1994, c. 27, s. 56(19), part.

(3) **Same.**— Clauses (1)(a) and (b) do not apply to a proceeding if,

    (a) any other Act or regulation that applies to the proceeding requires that it be heard in private.

    (b) the tribunal is of the opinion that clause 9(1)(a) or (b) applies to the proceeding. 1994, c. 27, s. 56(19), part; 1997, c. 23, s. 13(15).

(4) **Conflict, consent requirements.**— The consent requirements of clauses (1)(a) and (b) do not apply if another Act or a regulation that applies to the proceedings allows the tribunal to combine them or hear them at the same time without the consent of the parties. 1994, c. 27, s. 56(19), part; 1997, c. 23, s. 13(16).

(5) **Use of same evidence.**— If the parties to the second-named proceeding consent, the tribunal may treat evidence that is admitted in a proceeding as if it were also admitted in another proceeding that is heard at the same time under clause (1)(b). 1994, c. 27, s. 56(19), part.

10. Right to counsel.— A party to a proceeding may be represented by counsel or an agent. 1994, c. 27, s. 56(20), part.

10.1 Examination of witnesses.— A party to a proceeding may, at an oral or electronic hearing,

    (a) call and examine witnesses and present evidence and submissions; and

    (b) conduct cross-examinations of witnesses at the hearing reasonably required for a full and fair disclosure of all matters relevant to the issues in the proceeding. 1994, c. 27, s. 56(20), part.

11. (1) **Rights of witnesses to counsel.**— A witness at an oral or electronic hearing is entitled to be advised by counsel or an agent as to his or her rights but such counsel or agent may take no other part in the hearing without leave of the tribunal. 1994, c. 27, s. 56(21).

(2) **Idem.**— Where an oral hearing is closed to the public, the counsel or agent for a witness is not entitled to be present except when that witness is giving evidence. 1994, c. 27, s. 56(22).

12. (1) **Summonses.**— A tribunal may require any person, including a party, by summons,

    (a) to give evidence on oath or affirmation at an oral or electronic hearing; and

    (b) to produce in evidence at an oral or electronic hearing documents and things specified by the tribunal,

relevant to the subject-matter of the proceeding and admissible at an oral or electronic hearing. 1994, c. 27, s. 56(23).

(2) **Form and service of summons.**— A summons issued under subsection (1) shall be in the prescribed form (in English or French) and,

    (a) where the tribunal consists of one person, shall be signed by him or her;

   (b) where the tribunal consists of more than one person, shall be signed by the chair of the tribunal or in such other manner as documents on behalf of the tribunal may be signed under the statute constituting the tribunal. 1994, c. 27, s. 56(24), part.

(3) **Same.**— The summons shall be served personally on the person summoned. 1994, c. 27, s. 56(24), part.

(3.1) **Fees and allowances.**— The person summoned is entitled to receive the same fees or allowances for attending at or otherwise participating in the hearing as are paid to a person summoned to attend before the Ontario Court (General Division) [Superior Court of Justice]. 1994, c. 27, s. 56(24), part.

(4) **Bench warrant.**— A judge of the Ontario Court (General Division) [Superior Court of Justice] may issue a warrant against a person if the judge is satisfied that,

   (a) a summons was served on the person under this section;

   (b) the person has failed to attend or to remain in attendance at the hearing (in the case of an oral hearing) or has failed otherwise to participate in the hearing (in the case of an electronic hearing) in accordance with the summons; and

   (c) the person's attendance or participation is material to the ends of justice. 1994, c. 27, s. 56(25), part.

(4.1) **Same.**— The warrant shall be in the prescribed form (in English or French), directed to any police officer, and shall require the person to be apprehended anywhere within Ontario, brought before the tribunal forthwith and,

   (a) detained in custody as the judge may order until the person's presence as a witness is no longer required; or

   (b) in the judge's discretion, released on a recognizance, with or without sureties, conditioned for attendance or participation to give evidence. 1994, c. 27, s. 56(25), part.

(5) **Proof of service.**— Service of a summons may be proved by affidavit in an application to have a warrant issued under subsection (4).

(6) **Certificate of facts.**— Where an application to have a warrant issued is made on behalf of a tribunal, the person constituting the tribunal or, if the tribunal consists of more than one person, the chair of the tribunal may certify to the judge the facts relied on to establish that the attendance or other participation of the person summoned is material to the ends of justice, and the judge may accept the certificate as proof of the facts.

(7) **Same.**— Where the application is made by a party to the proceeding, the facts relied on to establish that the attendance or other participation of the person is material to the ends of justice may be proved by the party's affidavit. 1994, c. 27, s. 56(26).

13. (1) **Contempt proceedings.**— Where any person without lawful excuse,

(a) on being duly summoned under section 12 as a witness at a hearing makes default in attending at the hearing; or

(b) being in attendance as a witness at an oral hearing or otherwise participating as a witness at an electronic hearing, refuses to take an oath or to make an affirmation legally required by the tribunal to be taken or made, or to produce any document or thing in his or her power or control legally required by the tribunal to be produced by him or her or to answer any question to which the tribunal may legally require an answer; or

(c) does any other thing that would, if the tribunal had been a court of law having power to commit for contempt, have been contempt of that court,

the tribunal may, of its own motion or on the motion of a party to the proceeding, state a case to the Divisional Court setting out the facts and that court may inquire into the matter and, after hearing any witnesses who may be produced against or on behalf of that person and after hearing any statement that may be offered in defence, punish or take steps for the punishment of that person in like manner as if he or she had been guilty of contempt of the court. 1994, c. 27, s. 56(27).

(2) **Same.**— Subsection (1) also applies to a person who,

(a) having objected under clause 6(4)(b) to a hearing being held as a written hearing, fails without lawful excuse to participate in the oral or electronic hearing of the matter; or

(b) being a party, fails without lawful excuse to attend a pre-hearing conference when so directed by the tribunal. 1997, c. 23, s. 13(17).

14. (1) **Protection for witnesses.**— A witness at an oral or electronic hearing shall be deemed to have objected to answer any question asked him or her upon the ground that the answer may tend to criminate him or her or may tend to establish his or her liability to civil proceedings at the instance of the Crown, or of any person, and no answer given by a witness at a hearing shall be used or be receivable in evidence against the witness in any trial or other proceeding against him or her thereafter taking place, other than a prosecution for perjury in giving such evidence. 1994, c. 27, s. 56(28).

(2) [Repealed 1994, c. 27, s. 56(29)]

15. (1) **What is admissible in evidence at a hearing.**— Subject to subsections (2) and (3), a tribunal may admit as evidence at a hearing, whether or not given or proven under oath or affirmation or admissible as evidence in a court,

(a) any oral testimony; and

(b) any document or other thing,

relevant to the subject-matter of the proceeding and may act on such evidence, but the tribunal may exclude anything unduly repetitious.

(2) **What is inadmissible in evidence at a hearing.**— Nothing is admissible in evidence at a hearing,

   (a) that would be inadmissible in a court by reason of any privilege under the law of evidence; or

   (b) that is inadmissible by the statute under which the proceeding arises or any other statute.

(3) **Conflicts.**— Nothing in subsection (1) overrides the provisions of any Act expressly limiting the extent to or purposes for which any oral testimony, documents or things may be admitted or used in evidence in any proceeding.

(4) **Copies.**— Where a tribunal is satisfied as to its authenticity, a copy of a document or other thing may be admitted as evidence at a hearing.

(5) **Photocopies.**— Where a document has been filed in evidence at a hearing, the tribunal may, or the person producing it or entitled to it may with the leave of the tribunal, cause the document to be photocopied and the tribunal may authorize the photocopy to be filed in evidence in the place of the document filed and release the document filed, or may furnish to the person producing it or the person entitled to it a photocopy of the document filed certified by a member of the tribunal.

(6) **Certified copy admissible in evidence.**— A document purporting to be a copy of a document filed in evidence at a hearing, certified to be a copy thereof by a member of the tribunal, is admissible in evidence in proceedings in which the document is admissible as evidence of the document.

15.1 (1) **Use of previously admitted evidence.**— The tribunal may treat previously admitted evidence as if it had been admitted in a proceeding before the tribunal, if the parties to the proceeding consent. 1994, c. 27, s. 56(30, part).

(2) **Definition.**— In subsection (1),
"previously admitted evidence" means evidence that was admitted, before the hearing of the proceeding referred to in that subsection, in any other proceeding before a court or tribunal, whether in or outside Ontario. 1994, c. 27, s. 56(30, part; 1997, c. 23, s. 13(18), part.

(3) **Additional power.**— This power conferred by this section is in addition to the tribunal's power to admit evidence under section 15. 1997, c. 23, s. 13(18), part.

15.2 Witness panels.— A tribunal may receive evidence from panels of witnesses composed of two or more persons, if the parties have first had an opportunity to make submissions in that regard. 1994, c. 27, s. 56(31).

16. Notice of facts and opinions.— A tribunal may, in making its decision in any proceeding,

   (a) take notice of facts that may be judicially noticed; and

(b) take notice of any generally recognized scientific or technical facts, information or opinions within its scientific or specialized knowledge.

16.1 (1) **Interim decisions and orders.**— A tribunal may make interim decisions and orders.

(2) **Conditions.**— A tribunal may impose conditions on an interim decision or order.

(3) **Reasons.**— An interim decision or order need not be accompanied by reasons. 1994, c. 27, s. 56(32).

16.2 Time frames.— A tribunal shall establish guidelines setting out the usual time frame for completing proceedings that come before the tribunal and for completing the procedural steps within those proceedings. 1999, c. 12, Sch. B, s. 16(6).

17. (1) **Decision.**— A tribunal shall give its final decision and order, if any in any proceeding in writing and shall give reasons in writing therefor if requested by a party. 1993, c. 27, Sch.

(2) **Interest.**— A tribunal that makes an order for the payment of money shall set out in the order the principal sum, and if interest is payable, the rate of interest and the date from which it is to be calculated. 1994, c. 27, s. 56(33).

17.1 (1) **Costs.**— Subject to subsection (2), a tribunal may, in the circumstances set out in a rule made under section 25.1, order a party to pay all or part of another party's costs in a proceeding.

(2) **Exception.**— A tribunal shall not make an order to pay costs under this section unless,
   (a) the conduct or course of conduct of a party has been unreasonable, frivolous or vexatious or a party has acted in bad faith; and
   (b) the tribunal has made rules under section 25.1 with respect to the ordering of costs which include the circumstances in which costs may be ordered and the amount of the costs or the manner in which the amount of the costs is to be determined.

(3) **Amount of costs.**— The amount of the costs ordered under this section shall be determined in accordance with the rules made under section 25.1.

(4) **Continuance of provisions in other statutes.**— Despite section 32, nothing in this section shall prevent a tribunal from ordering a party to pay all or part of another party's costs in a proceeding in circumstances other than those set out in, and without complying with, subsections (1) to (3) if the tribunal makes the order in accordance with the provisions of an Act that are in force on the day this section comes into force. 1999, c. 12, Sch. B, s. 16(7).

18. (1) **Notice of decision.**— The tribunal shall send each party who partici-pated in the proceeding, or the party's counsel or agent, a copy of its final deci-sion or order, including the reasons if any have been given,

(*a*) by regular lettermail;

(*b*) by electronic transmission;

(*c*) by telephone transmission of a facsimile; or

(*d*) by some other method that allows proof of receipt, if the tribunal's rules made under section 25.1 deal with the matter. 1994, c. 27, s. 56(34), part; 1997, c. 23, s. 13(19).

(2) **Use of mail.**— If the copy is sent by regular lettermail, it shall be sent to the most recent addresses known to the tribunal and shall be deemed to be received by the party on the fifth day after the day it is mailed.

(3) **Use of electronic or telephone transmission.**— If the copy is sent by electronic transmission or by telephone transmission of a facsimile, it shall be deemed to be received on the day after it was sent, unless that day is a holiday, in which case the copy shall be deemed to be received on the next day that is not a holiday.

(4) **Use of other method.**— If the copy is sent by a method referred to in clause (1)(d), the tribunal's rules made under section 25.1 govern its deemed day of receipt.

(5) **Failure to receive copy.**— If a party that acts in good faith does not, through absence, accident, illness or other cause beyond the party's control, receive the copy until a later date than the deemed day of receipt, subsection (2), (3) or (4), as the case may be, does not apply. 1994, c. 27, s. 56(34), part.

19. (1) **Enforcement of orders.**— A certified copy of a tribunal's decision or order in a proceeding may be filed in the Ontario Court (General Division) [Superior Court of Justice] by the tribunal or by a party and on filing shall be deemed to be an order of that court and is enforceable as such.

(2) **Notice of filing.**— A party who files an order under subsection (1) shall notify the tribunal within 10 days after the filing.

(3) **Order for payment of money.**— On receiving a certified copy of a tri-bunal's order for the payment of money, the sheriff shall enforce the order as if it were an execution issued by the Ontario Court (General Division) [Superior Court of Justice]. 1994, c. 27, s. 56(35).

20. Record of proceeding.— A tribunal shall compile a record of any pro-ceeding in which a hearing has been held which shall include,

(a) any application, complaint, reference or other document, if any, by which the proceeding was commenced;

(b) the notice of any hearing;

(c) any interlocutory orders made by the tribunal;

(d) all documentary evidence filed with the tribunal, subject to any limitation expressly imposed by any other Act on the extent to or the purposes for which any such documents may be used in evidence in any proceeding;

(e) the transcript, if any, of the oral evidence given at the hearing; and

(f) the decision of the tribunal and the reasons therefor, where reasons have been given.

21. Adjournments.— A hearing may be adjourned from time to time by a tribunal of its own motion or where it is shown to the satisfaction of the tribunal that the adjournment is required to permit an adequate hearing to be held.

21.1 Correction of errors.— A tribunal may at any time correct a typographical error, error of calculation or similar error made in its decision or order. 1994, c. 27, s. 56(36), part.

21.2 (1) Power to review.— A tribunal may, if it considers it advisable and if its rules made under section 25. 1 deal with the matter, review all or part of its own decision or order, and may confirm, vary, suspend or cancel the decision or order. 1994, c. 27, s. 56(36), part; 1997, c. 23, s. 13(20).

(2) **Time for review.**— The review shall take place within a reasonable time after the decision or order is made.

(3) **Conflict.**— In the event of a conflict between this section and any other Act, the other Act prevails. 1994, c. 27, s. 56(36), part.

22. Administration of oaths.— A member of a tribunal has power to administer oaths and affirmations for the purpose of any of its proceedings and the tribunal may require evidence before it to be given under oath or affirmation. R.S.O. 1980, c. 484, s. 22.

23. (1) **Abuse of processes.**— A tribunal may make such orders or give such directions in proceedings before it as it considers proper to prevent abuse of its processes.

(2) **Limitation on examination.**— A tribunal may reasonably limit further examination or cross-examination of a witness where it is satisfied that the examination or cross-examination has been sufficient to disclose fully and fairly all matters relevant to the issues in the proceeding. 1994, c. 27, s. 56(37).

(3) **Exclusion of agents.**— A tribunal may exclude from a hearing anyone, other than a barrister and solicitor qualified to practise in Ontario, appearing as an agent on behalf of a party or as an adviser to a witness if it finds that such person is not competent properly to represent or to advise the party or witness or does not understand and comply at the hearing with the duties and responsibilities of an advocate or adviser.

24. (1) **Notice, etc.**— Where a tribunal is of opinion that because the parties to any proceeding before it are so numerous or for any other reason, it is impracticable,

    (a) to give notice of the hearing; or

    (b) to send its decision and the material mentioned in section 18,

to all or any of the parties individually, the tribunal may, instead of doing so, cause reasonable notice of the hearing or of its decision to be given to such parties by public advertisement or otherwise as the tribunal may direct.

(2) **Contents of notice.**— A notice of a decision given by a tribunal under clause (1)(b) shall inform the parties of the place where copies of the decision and the reasons therefor, if reasons were given, may be obtained.

25. (1) **Appeal operates as stay, exception.**— An appeal from a decision of a tribunal to a court or other appellate body operates as a stay in the matter unless,

    (a) another Act or a regulation that applies to the proceeding expressly provides to the contrary; or

    (b) the tribunal or the court or other appellate body orders otherwise. 1997, c. 23, s. 13(21).

(2) **Idem.**— An application for judicial review under the *Judicial Review Procedure Act*, or the bringing of proceedings specified in subsection 2(1) of that Act is not an appeal within the meaning of subsection (1).

25.0.1 Control of process.— A tribunal has the power to determine its own procedures and practices and may for that purpose,

    (a) make orders with respect to the procedures and practices that apply in any particular proceeding; and

    (b) establish rules under section 25.1. 1999, c. 12, Sch. B, s. 16(8).

25.1 (1) **Rules.**— A tribunal may make rules governing the practice and procedure before it.

(2) **Application.**— The rules may be of general or particular application.

(3) **Consistency with Acts.**— The rules shall be consistent with this Act and with the other Acts to which they relate.

(4) **Public access.**— The tribunal shall make the rules available to the public in English and in French.

(5) **Regulations Act.**— Rules adopted under this section are not regulations as defined in the *Regulations Act*.

(6) **Additional power.**— The power conferred by this section is in addition to any power to adopt rules that the tribunal may have under another Act. 1994, c. 27, s. 56(38).

26. Regulations.— The Lieutenant Governor in Council may make regulations prescribing forms for the purpose of section 12. 1994, c. 27, s. 56(40, 41).

27. Rules, etc., available to public.— A tribunal shall make any rules or guidelines established under this or any other Act available for examination by the public. 1999, c. 12, Sch. B, s. 16(9), part.

28. Substantial compliance.— Substantial compliance with requirements respecting the content of forms, notices or documents under this Act or any rule made under this or any other Act is sufficient. 1999, c. 12, Sch. B, s. 16(9), part.

29. [Repealed 1994, c. 27, s. 56(40)]

30. Additional powers of tribunals to make rules.— [Repealed 1994, c. 27, s. 56(40)]

31. [Repealed 1994, c. 27, s. 56(40)]

32. Conflict.— Unless it is expressly provided in any other Act that its provisions and regulations, rules or by-laws made under it apply despite anything in this Act, the provisions of this Act prevail over the provisions of such other Act and over regulations, rules or by-laws made under such other Act which conflict therewith. 1994, c. 27, s. 56(42).

33. [Repealed 1994, c. 27, s. 56(43)]

34. [Repealed 1994, c. 27, s. 56(43)]

Appendix C

Alberta
Administrative Procedures Act[1]
R.S.A. 1980, c. A-2

HER MAJESTY, by and with the advice and consent of the Legislative Assembly of Alberta, enacts as follows:

1 Definitions.— In this Act,

   (a) "authority" means a person authorized to exercise a statutory power;

   (b) "party" means a person whose rights will be varied or affected by the exercise of a statutory power or by an act or thing done pursuant to that power;

   (c) "statutory power" means an administrative, quasi-judicial or judicial power conferred by statute, other than a power conferred on a court of record of civil or criminal jurisdiction or a power to make regulations, and for greater certainty, but without restricting the generality of the foregoing, includes a power

      (i) to grant, suspend or revoke a charter or letters patent,

      (ii) to grant, renew, refuse, suspend or revoke a permission to do an act or thing which, but for the permission, would be unlawful, whether the permission is called a licence or permit or certificate or is in any other form,

      (iii) to declare or establish a status provided for under a statute for a person and to suspend or revoke that status,

---

[1] In December 1999, the Alberta Law Reform Institute released a report which recommended that the current *Administrative Procedures Act* be repealed and replaced with a new Act, the *Administrative Powers and Procedures Act*. This recommendation was made because the current Act has not been changed to reflect the developments in administrative law and to include new procedures to ensure that administrative tribunals are run more effectively and efficiently. Also, the current Act only applied to a small number of administrative tribunals in Alberta. This new Act will contain a Model Code of powers and procedures for all administrative tribunals in Alberta and an administrative tribunal will be able to apply to the Minister of Justice for an order that all or parts of the Model Code apply to that particular administrative tribunal.

   (iv) to approve or authorize the doing or omission by a person of an act or thing that, but for the approval or authorization, would be unlawful or unauthorized,

   (v) to declare or establish a right or duty of a person under a statute, whether in a dispute with another person or otherwise, or

   (vi) to make an order, decision, direction or finding prohibiting a person from doing an act or thing that, but for the order, decision, direction or finding, it would be lawful for him to do,

or any combination of those powers.

2 Application of Act.— The Lieutenant Governor in Council may, by order,

(a) designate any authority as an authority to which this Act applies in whole or in part,

(b) designate the statutory power of the authority in respect of which this Act applies in whole or in part, and

(c) designate the provisions of this Act which are applicable to the authority in the exercise of that statutory power, and the extent to which they apply,

and this Act only applies to an authority to the extent ordered under this section.

3 Notice to parties.— When

(a) an application is made to an authority, or

(b) an authority on its own initiative proposes

to exercise a statutory power, the authority shall give to all parties adequate notice of the application which it has before it or of the power which it intends to exercise.

4 Evidence and representations.— Before an authority, in the exercise of a statutory power, refuses the application of or makes a decision or order adversely affecting the rights of a party, the authority

(a) shall give the party a reasonable opportunity of furnishing relevant evidence to the authority,

(b) shall inform the party of the facts in its possession or the allegations made to it contrary to the interests of the party in sufficient detail

   (i) to permit him to understand the facts or allegations, and

   (ii) to afford him a reasonable opportunity to furnish relevant evidence to contradict or explain the facts or allegations,

   and

(c) shall give the party an adequate opportunity of making representations by way of argument to the authority.

5 Cross examination.— When an authority has informed a party of facts or allegations and that party

(a) is entitled under section 4 to contradict or explain them, but

(b) will not have a fair opportunity of doing so without cross-examination of the person making the statements that constitute the facts or allegations, the authority shall afford the party an opportunity of cross-examination in the presence of the authority or of a person authorized to hear or take evidence for the authority.

6 When certain representations not permitted.— Where by this Act a party is entitled to make representations to an authority with respect to the exercise of a statutory power, the authority is not by this Act required to afford an opportunity to the party

(a) to make oral representations, or

(b) to be represented by counsel,

if the authority affords the party an opportunity to make representations adequately in writing, but nothing in this Act deprives a party of a right conferred by any other Act to make oral representations or to be represented by counsel.

7 Written decision with reasons.— When an authority exercises a statutory power so as to adversely affect the rights of a party, the authority shall furnish to each party a written statement of its decision setting out

(a) the findings of fact on which it based its decision, and

(b) the reasons for the decision.

8 Requirements of other Acts.— Nothing in this Act relieves an authority from complying with any procedure to be followed by it under any other Act relating to the exercise of its statutory power.

9 Rules of evidence.— Nothing in this Act

(a) requires that any evidence or allegations of fact made to an authority be made under oath, or

(b) requires any authority to adhere to the rules of evidence applicable to courts of civil or criminal jurisdiction.

10 Regulations.— The Lieutenant Governor in Council may make regulations

(a) to prescribe the length of time that is reasonable for the giving of a notice in accordance with this Act, with respect to authorities generally or with respect to a specified authority;

(b) to prescribe forms of notices for the purposes of this Act;

(c) to carry into effect the purposes of this Act.

Appendix D

Ontario
Judicial Review Procedure Act
R.S.O. 1990, c. J.1

1. Definitions.— In this Act,

"application for judicial review" means an application under subsection 2(1);

"court" means the Ontario Court (General Division) [Superior Court of Justice];

"licence" includes any permit, certificate, approval, registration or similar form of permission required by law;

"municipality" has the same meaning as in the *Municipal Affairs Act*, and includes a district, metropolitan and regional municipality and their local boards;

"party" includes a municipality, association of employers, a trade union or council of trade unions which may be a party to any of the proceedings mentioned in subsection 2(1);

"statutory power" means a power or right conferred by or under a statute,

    (a) to make any regulation, rule, by-law or order, or to give any other direction having force as subordinate legislation,

    (b) to exercise a statutory power of decision,

    (c) to require any person or party to do or to refrain from doing any act or thing that, but for such requirement, such person or party would not be required by law to do or to refrain from doing,

    (d) to do any act or thing that would, but for such power or right, be a breach of the legal rights of any person or party;

"statutory power of decision" means a power or right conferred by or under a statute to make a decision deciding or prescribing,

    (a) the legal rights, powers, privileges, immunities, duties or liabilities of any person or party, or

    (b) the eligibility of any person or party to receive, or to the continuation of, a benefit or licence, whether the person or party is legally entitled thereto or not,

and includes the powers of an inferior court.

2. (1) Applications for judicial review.— On an application by way of originating notice, which may be styled "Notice of Application for Judicial Review", the court may, despite any right of appeal, by order grant any relief that the applicant would be entitled to in any one or more of the following:

1. Proceedings by way of application for an order in the nature of mandamus, prohibition or certiorari.
2. Proceedings by way of an action for a declaration or for an injunction, or both, in relation to the exercise, refusal to exercise or proposed or purported exercise of a statutory power.

(2) **Error of law.**— The power of the court to set aside a decision for error of law on the face of the record on an application for an order in the nature of certiorari is extended so as to apply on an application for judicial review in relation to any decision made in the exercise of any statutory power of decision to the extent it is not limited or precluded by the Act conferring such power of decision.

(3) **Lack of evidence.**— Where the findings of fact of a tribunal made in the exercise of a statutory power of decision are required by any statute or law to be based exclusively on evidence admissible before it and on facts of which it may take notice and there is no such evidence and there are no such facts to support findings of fact made by the tribunal in making a decision in the exercise of such power, the court may set aside the decision on an application for judicial review.

(4) **Power to set aside.**— Where the applicant on an application for judicial review is entitled to a judgment declaring that a decision made in the exercise of a statutory power of decision is unauthorized or otherwise invalid, the court may, in the place of such declaration, set aside the decision.

(5) **Power to refuse relief.**— Where, in any of the proceedings enumerated in subsection (1), the court had before the 17th day of April, 1972 a discretion to refuse to grant relief on any grounds, the court has a like discretion on like grounds to refuse to grant any relief on an application for judicial review.

(6) **Where subs. (5) does not apply.**— Subsection (5) does not apply to the discretion of the court before the 17th day of April, 1972 to refuse to grant relief in any of the proceedings enumerated in subsection (1) on the ground that the relief should have been sought in other proceedings enumerated in subsection (1).

3. Defects in form, technical irregularities.— On an application for judicial review in relation to a statutory power of decision, where the sole ground for relief established is a defect in form or a technical irregularity, if the court finds that no substantial wrong or miscarriage of justice has occurred, the court may refuse relief and, where the decision has already been made, may make an order validating the decision, despite such defect, to have effect from such time and on such terms as the court considers proper.

4. Interim order.— On an application for judicial review, the court may make such interim order as it considers proper pending the final determination of the application.

5. Extension of time for bringing application.— Despite any limitation of time for the bringing of an application for judicial review fixed by or under any Act, the court may extend the time for making the application, either before or after expiration of the time so limited, on such terms as it considers proper, where it is satisfied that there are apparent grounds for relief and that no substantial prejudice or hardship will result to any person affected by reason of the delay.

6. (1) **Application to Divisional Court.**— Subject to subsection (2), an application for judicial review shall be made to the Divisional Court.

(2) **Application to judge of Ontario Court (General Division) [Superior Court of Justice].**— An application for judicial review may be made to the Ontario Court (General Division) [Superior Court of Justice] with leave of a judge thereof, which may be granted at the hearing of the application, where it is made to appear to the judge that the case is one of urgency and that the delay required for an application to the Divisional Court is likely to involve a failure of justice.

(3) **Transfer to Divisional Court.**— Where a judge refuses leave for an application under subsection (2), he or she may order that the application be transferred to the Divisional Court.

(4) **Appeal to Court of Appeal.**— An appeal lies to the Court of Appeal, with leave of the Court of Appeal, from a final order of the Ontario Court (General Division) [Superior Court of Justice] disposing of an application for judicial review pursuant to leave granted under subsection (2).

7. Summary disposition of mandamus, etc.— An application for an order in the nature of mandamus, prohibition or certiorari shall be deemed to be an application for judicial review and shall be made, treated and disposed of as if it were an application for judicial review.

8. Summary disposition of actions.— Where an action for a declaration or injunction, or both, whether with or without a claim for other relief, is brought and the exercise, refusal to exercise or proposed or purported exercise of a statutory power is an issue in the action, a judge of the Ontario Court (General Division) [Superior Court of Justice] may on the application of any party to the action, if he or she considers it appropriate, direct that the action be treated and disposed of summarily, in so far as it relates to the exercise, refusal to exercise or proposed or purported exercise of such power, as if it were an application for judicial review and may order that the hearing on such issue be transferred to the Divisional Court or may grant leave for it to be disposed of in accordance with subsection 6(2).

9. (1) **Sufficiency of application.**— It is sufficient in an application for judicial review if an applicant sets out in the notice the grounds upon which he is seeking relief and the nature of the relief that he seeks without specifying the proceedings enumerated in subsection 2(1) in which the claim would have been made before the 17th day of April, 1972.

(2) **Exerciser of power may be a party.**— For the purposes of an application for judicial review in relation to the exercise, refusal to exercise or proposed or purported exercise of a statutory power, the person who is authorized to exercise the power may be a party to the application.

(3) **Idem.**— or the purposes of subsection (2), any two or more persons who, acting together, may exercise a statutory power, whether styled a board or commission or by any other collective title, shall be deemed to be a person under such collective title.

(4) **Notice to Attorney General.**—Notice of an application for judicial review shall be served upon the Attorney General who is entitled as of right to be heard in person or by counsel on the application.

10. Record to be filed in Ontario Court (General Division) [Superior Court of Justice].—When notice of an application for judicial review of a decision made in the exercise or purported exercise of a statutory power of decision has been served on the person making the decision, such person shall forthwith file in the court for use on the application the record of the proceedings in which the decision was made.

11. (1) References in other Acts, etc.— Subject to subsection (2), where reference is made in any other Act or in any regulation, rule or by-law to any of the proceedings enumerated in subsection 2(1), such reference shall be read and construed to include a reference to an application for judicial review.

(2) **Proceedings under *Habeas Corpus Act*.**— Nothing in this Act affects proceedings under the *Habeas Corpus Act* or the issue of a writ of certiorari thereunder or proceedings pursuant thereto, but an application for judicial review may be brought in aid of an application for a writ of habeas corpus.

Appendix E

British Columbia
Judicial Review Procedure Act
R.S.B.C. 1996, c. 241

1. Definitions.— In this Act:

"application for judicial review" means an application under section 2;

"court" means the Supreme Court;

"decision" includes a determination or order;

"licence" includes a permit, certificate, approval, order, registration or similar form of permission required by law;

"record of the proceeding" includes the following:

    (a) a document by which the proceeding is commenced;

    (b) a notice of a hearing in the proceeding;

    (c) an intermediate order made by the tribunal;

    (d) a document produced in evidence at a hearing before the tribunal, subject to any limitation expressly imposed by any other enactment on the extent to which or the purpose for which a document may be used in evidence in a proceeding;

    (e) a transcript, if any, of the oral evidence given at a hearing;

    (f) the decision of the tribunal and any reasons given by it;

"statutory power of decision" means a power or right conferred by an enactment to make a decision deciding or prescribing

    (a) the legal rights, powers, privileges, immunities, duties or liabilities of a person, or

    (b) the eligibility of a person to receive, or to continue to receive, a benefit or licence, whether or not the person is legally entitled to it,

    and includes the powers of the Provincial Court;

"statutory power" means a power or right conferred by an enactment

    (a) to make a regulation, rule, bylaw or order,

    (b) to exercise a statutory power of decision,

    (c) to require a person to do or to refrain from doing an act or thing that, but for that requirement, the person would not be required by law to do or to refrain from doing,

    (d) to do an act or thing that would, but for that power or right, be a breach of a legal right of any person, or

(e) to make an investigation or inquiry into a person's legal right, power, privilege, immunity, duty or liability;

"tribunal" means one or more persons, whether or not incorporated and however described, on whom a statutory power of decision is conferred.

2. (1) Application for judicial review.— An application for judicial review is an originating application and must be brought by petition.

(2) On an application for judicial review, the court may grant any relief that the applicant would be entitled to in any one or more of the proceedings for:

(a) relief in the nature of mandamus, prohibition or certiorari;

(b) a declaration or injunction, or both, in relation to the exercise, refusal to exercise, or proposed or purported exercise, of a statutory power.

3. Error of law.— The court's power to set aside a decision because of error of law on the face of the record on an application for relief in the nature of certiorari is extended so that it applies to an application for judicial review in relation to a decision made in the exercise of a statutory power of decision to the extent it is not limited or precluded by the enactment conferring the power of decision.

4. Existing provision limiting judicial review not affected.— Subject to section 3, nothing in this Act permits a person to bring a proceeding referred to in section 2 if the person is otherwise limited or prohibited by law from bringing the proceeding.

5. (1) Powers to direct tribunal to reconsider.— On an application for judicial review in relation to the exercise, refusal to exercise, or purported exercise of a statutory power of decision, the court may direct the tribunal whose act or omission is the subject matter of the application to reconsider and determine, either generally or in respect of a specified matter, the whole or any part of a matter to which the application relates.

(2) In giving a direction under subsection (1), the court must

(a) advise the tribunal of its reasons, and

(b) give it any directions that the court thinks appropriate for the reconsideration or otherwise of the whole or any part of the matter that is referred back for reconsideration.

6. Effect of direction.— In reconsidering a matter referred back to it under section 5, the tribunal must have regard to the court's reasons for giving the direction and to the court's directions.

7. Power to set aside decision.— If an applicant is entitled to a declaration that a decision made in the exercise of a statutory power of decision is unauthorized or otherwise invalid, the court may set aside the decision instead of making a declaration.

8. (1) **Power to refuse relief.**— If, in a proceeding referred to in section 2, the court had, before February 1, 1977, a discretion to refuse to grant relief on any ground, the court has the same discretion to refuse to grant relief on the same ground.

(2) Despite subsection (1), the court may not refuse to grant relief in a proceeding referred to in section 2 on the ground that the relief should have been sought in another proceeding referred to in section 2.

9. (1) **Defects in form, technical irregularities.**— On an application for judicial review of a statutory power of decision, the court may refuse relief if

    (a) the sole ground for relief established is a defect in form or a technical irregularity, and

    (b) the court finds that no substantial wrong or miscarriage of justice has occurred.

(2) If the decision has already been made, the court may make an order validating the decision despite the defect, to have effect from a time and on terms the court considers appropriate.

10. Interim order.— On an application for judicial review, the court may make an interim order it considers appropriate until the final determination of the application.

11. No time limit for applications.— An application for judicial review is not barred by passage of time unless

    (a) an enactment otherwise provides, and

    (b) the court considers that substantial prejudice or hardship will result to any other person affected by reason of delay.

12. (1) **No writ to issue.**— No writ of mandamus, prohibition or certiorari may be issued.

(2) An application for relief in the nature of mandamus, prohibition or certiorari, must be treated as an application for judicial review under section 2.

13. (1) **Summary disposition of proceedings.**— On the application of a party to a proceeding for a declaration or injunction, the court may direct that any issue about the exercise, refusal to exercise or proposed or purported exercise of a statutory power be disposed of summarily, as if it were an application for judicial review.

(2) Subsection (1) applies whether or not the proceeding for a declaration or injunction includes a claim for other relief.

14. Sufficiency of application.— An application for judicial review is sufficient if it sets out the ground on which relief is sought and the nature of the relief sought, without specifying by which proceeding referred to in section 2 the claim would have been made before February 1, 1977.

15. (1) **Notice to decision maker and right to be a party.**— For an application for judicial review in relation to the exercise, refusal to exercise, or proposed or purported exercise of a statutory power, the person who is authorized to exercise the power

    (a) must be served with notice of the application and a copy of the petition, and

    (b) may be a party to the application, at the person's option.

(2) If 2 or more persons, whether styled a board or commission or any other collective title, act together to exercise a statutory power, they are deemed for the purpose of subsection (1) to be one person under the collective title, and service, if required, is effectively made on any one of those persons.

16. (1) **Notice to Attorney General.**—The Attorney General must be served with notice of an application for judicial review and notice of an appeal from a decision of the court with respect to the application.

(2) The Attorney General is entitled to be heard in person or by counsel at the hearing of the application or appeal.

17. Court may order record filed.— On an application for judicial review of a decision made in the exercise or purported exercise of a statutory power of decision, the court may direct that the record of the proceeding, or any part of it, be filed in the court.

18. (1) **Informations in the nature of quo warranto.**— Informations in the nature of quo warranto are abolished.

(2) If a person acts in an office in which the person is not entitled to act and an information in the nature of quo warranto would, but for subsection (1), have been available against the person the court may, under an application for judicial review, grant an injunction restraining the person from acting and may declare the office to be vacant.

(3) A proceeding for an injunction under this section may not be taken by a person who would not immediately before February 1, 1977, have been entitled to apply for an information in the nature of quo warranto.

19. Relationship between this Act and Crown Proceeding Act.—This Act is subject to the *Crown Proceeding Act*.

20. References in other enactments.— If reference is made in any other enactment to a proceeding referred to in section 2 or 18, the reference is deemed to be a reference to an application for judicial review.

Appendix F

Prince Edward Island Judicial Review Act R.S.P.E.I. 1988, c. J-3

Amendments

Amended 1990, c. 26; in force April 26, 1990
Amended 1993, c. 29, s. 4; in force August 11, 1993
Amended 1997, c. 20, s. 3; in force May 29, 1997
Amended 2000, c. 5, s. 3; in force June 14, 2000

1. Definitions.— In this Act
  (a) "act" includes an omission or failure to act;
  (b) "application for judicial review" means an application to determine whether or not authority conferred on a tribunal by an enactment has been exercised in accordance with the enactment in respect to a decision of the tribunal in relation to the legal rights, powers, privileges, immunities, duties or liabilities of a person or the eligibility of a person to receive, or to continue to receive, a benefit or license;
  (c) "enactment" includes an Act or a regulation;
  (d) "exercise of authority" includes a failure to exercise authority;
  (e) "existing proceedings" means the proceedings referred to in clauses 2(a) and (b);
  (f) "judge" means a judge of the Trial Division of the Supreme Court;
  (g) "record" includes
    (i) a document by which the proceeding is commenced,
    (ii) a notice of a hearing in the proceeding,
    (iii) an intermediate order made by the tribunal,
    (iv) a document produced in evidence at a hearing before the tribunal, subject to any limitation expressly imposed by any other enactment on the extent to or the purpose for which a document may be used in evidence in a proceeding,
    (v) a transcript, if any, of the oral evidence given at a hearing, and
    (vi) the decision of the tribunal and any reasons given by it;

(h) "tribunal" means a person or group of persons upon whom an enactment confers authority to make a decision, whether styled a board or a commission or by any other title, but does not include

    (i) the Provincial Court of Prince Edward Island or a judge thereof,

    (ii) the Supreme Court of Prince Edward Island or a judge thereof, or

    (iii) the Lieutenant Governor in Council when not making a decision pursuant to authority conferred by an enactment.

2. (1) **Purpose.**— The purpose of this Act is to substitute an application for judicial review for the following existing proceedings:

(a) proceedings by way of application for an order in the nature of mandamus, prohibition or certiorari;

(b) proceedings by way of an action for a declaration or for an injunction, or both, in relation to the exercise, refusal to exercise or proposed or purported exercise of a statutory power.

(2) **Treatment of application for prerogative remedies.**— An application in the nature of mandamus, prohibition or certiorari shall be deemed to be an application for judicial review and shall be made, treated and disposed of as if it were an application for judicial review. 1990, c. 26, s. 1.

3. (1) **Application.**— An application for judicial review may be made to a judge or, with the consent of all parties and of the Appeal Division or a judge thereof, to the Appeal Division. 1990, c. 26, s. 2.

(1.1) **Time for bringing application.**— An application for judicial review shall be brought within thirty days of the date of the exercise of authority complained of but a judge may extend the time for making the application, either before or after the expiration of the time so limited, on such terms as he considers proper, where he is satisfied that there are grounds for relief and that no substantial prejudice or hardship will result to any person by reason of the delay. 1990, c. 26, s. 2.

(2) **Sufficiency of application.**— In an application for judicial review the applicant shall set out

(a) the grounds upon which he is seeking relief; and

(b) the nature of the relief he seeks,

but need not specify which of the existing proceedings governs his claim.

(3) **Powers of judge.**— Subject to this Act, a judge, on an application for judicial review, may by order

(a) nullify an act of a tribunal not done pursuant to authority conferred by an enactment;

(b) prohibit an act of a tribunal that would not be an act done pursuant to authority conferred by an enactment;

(c) direct an act by a tribunal in accordance with authority conferred by an enactment if a duty to act is not performed;

(d) declare a right of a person in respect to the exercise of authority conferred by an enactment on a tribunal;

(e) refer a matter back to a tribunal for further consideration either generally or in accordance with specific findings of the judge.

(4) **Interim order.**— On an application for judicial review, a judge may make such interim order as he considers proper pending the final determination of the application including a stay of proceedings before a tribunal.

(5) **Act of a tribunal.**— For the purpose of subsection (3) "an act of a tribunal" includes a decision or order of the tribunal.

(6) **References to judge.**— Where an application is made to the Appeal Division pursuant to subsection (1), any reference in this Act to a judge shall be construed as a reference to the Appeal Division or a judge thereof. 1990, c. 26, s. 2.

4. (1) **Grounds.**— Without limiting the generality of section 3, a judge, on an application for judicial review, may make an order pursuant to section 3 where

(a) there is a breach of the rules of natural justice;

(b) there is a failure to adhere to procedures prescribed by an enactment;

(c) there is an act that is not an act pursuant to authority conferred by an enactment;

(d) there is error in law, whether or not a record of the tribunal discloses the error;

(e) there is a failure to perform a duty in respect to the exercise of authority conferred by an enactment;

(f) there is no evidence to support an exercise of authority conferred by an enactment;

(g) there is unreasonable delay in respect to the exercise of authority conferred by an enactment;

(h) the exercise of authority conferred by an enactment is induced or affected by fraud.

(2) **Order notwithstanding right of appeal.**— A judge may make an order pursuant to section 3 notwithstanding that the authority of a tribunal could have been the subject of an appeal by the applicant if the order is conditional on the applicant filing with the prothonotary a written waiver of any right of appeal from the tribunal in respect to the matter that forms the basis of his application for judicial review.

(3) **Condition precedent to exercise of authority by tribunal.**— A judge may make an order pursuant to section 3 in respect to a report or recommendation where an enactment requires that the report or recommendation precede a decision of a tribunal pursuant to an enactment.

5. Dismissal of application, limitation and interest of applicant.— Without limiting the generality of section 3, a judge may dismiss an application for judicial review at any time on the ground that

(a) the applicant has not brought his application within such time as is specified in subsection 3(1.1) or the order of a judge, whichever is the greater time; or

(b) the applicant is not a person who is, or would be, adversely affected by the exercise of, or failure to exercise, the authority conferred on a tribunal. 1990, c. 26, s. 3.

6. (1) Defect in form, technical irregularity.— An application for judicial review may be dismissed where

(a) the sole ground for an order established is a defect in form or a technical irregularity; and

(b) the judge is of the opinion that no substantial wrong or miscarriage of justice has occurred.

(2) Validation of decision of tribunal.— Where an application is dismissed pursuant to subsection (1), the judge may by order validate the decision of the tribunal notwithstanding the defect on such terms and with effect at such time as the judge considers appropriate.

7. (1) Description of tribunal as a party.— No application for judicial review shall be dismissed or stayed by reason only that the application describes as a party a tribunal.

(2) *Idem.*— A tribunal is properly described for the purpose of an application for judicial review if it is described in the same manner as it is described in an enactment that confers authority on the tribunal.

(3) Amendment.— No application for judicial review shall be dismissed by reason only that the application does not properly describe a tribunal but the judge may order that the application shall be amended on such terms as to costs or extension of time as the judge considers is reasonable.

(4) Service.— Where two or more persons collectively comprise a tribunal, an application for judicial review that relates to that tribunal is sufficiently served on the tribunal if it is served on any of those persons.

8. (1) Record of tribunal.— Unless a judge otherwise orders, a tribunal to which an application for judicial review relates shall file with the prothonotary within ten days of the service of the application on the tribunal a true copy of a record of any hearing in respect to the decision that is the subject of the application.

(2) *Idem.*— The applicant or the tribunal may apply to a judge for an order to settle the content of the record.

(3) **Application does not stay proceeding.**— Unless a judge otherwise orders, an application for judicial review does not stay a proceeding before a tribunal or any act that may be done if an exercise of authority by the tribunal were upheld.

9. Intervention by Minister.— Notice of an application for judicial review shall be served on the Attorney General and the Attorney General is entitled to intervene and to be heard on the application. 1993, c. 29, s. 4; 1997, c. 20, s. 3; 2000, c. 5, s. 3.

10. Amendment of other enactments.— A reference in any other enactment to a writ or order in the nature of certiorari, prohibition or mandamus is deemed also to refer to an application for judicial review.

11. (1) **Abolition of *quo warranto*.**— Writs of *quo warranto* and informations in the nature of *quo warranto* are abolished.

(2) **Judicial review of entitlement to office.**— Where a person assumes a public office to which he is not entitled, a judge on an application for judicial review of the entitlement to the office may enjoin and restrain the person from assuming or acting as if he were entitled to the office and may declare the office vacant.

(3) **Saving.**— The *Controverted Elections (Provincial) Act*, R.S.P.E.I. 1988, c. C-22 applies notwithstanding subsection (2).

12. Notice, Crown proceedings.— Subsection 12(3) of the *Crown Proceedings Act*, R.S.P.E.I. 1988, c. C-32 does not apply to an application for judicial review.

Appendix G

Federal Court Act
R.S.C. 1985, c. F-7

Amendments

Amended R.S.C. 1985, c. 41 (1st Supp.), s. 11

Amended R.S.C. 1985, c. 30 (2nd Supp.), s. 61

Amended R.S.C. 1985, c. 16 (3rd Supp.), s. 7

Amended R.S.C. 1985, c. 51 (4th Supp.), ss. 10 to 12

Amended 1990, c. 8, ss. 1 to 19 and 78 (1), brought into force February 1, 1992 by SI/92-6

Amended 1990, c. 37, s. 34; brought into force April 29, 1993

Amended 1992, c. 1. s. 68; in force February 28, 1992

Amended 1992, c. 26, s. 17; brought into force August 28, 1992 by SI/92-157

Amended 1992, c. 33, s. 69; brought into force May 9, 1995 by SI/95-61

Amended 1992, c. 49, ss. 127 and 128; brought into force February 1, 1993

Amended 1993, c. 27, s. 214; in force June 10, 1993

Amended 1993, c. 34, s. 70; in force May 9, 1995

Amended 1996, c. 10, s. 229; brought into force July 1, 1996 by SI/96-53

Amended 1996, c. 22, s. 1; deemed in force November 28, 1995

Amended 1996, c. 23, s. 187(c); in force June 30, 1996

Amended 1996, c. 31, ss. 82 to 84; brought into force January 31, 1997 by SI/97-21

Amended 1998, c. 26, s. 73; brought into force January 31, 1999 by SI/99-2

Amended 1999, c. 31, s. 92 in force June 17, 1999

Amended 2001, c. 6., s. 115; in force August 8, 2001

SHORT TITLE

1. Short title.— This Act may be cited as the *Federal Court Act*.

INTERPRETATION

2. (1) **Definitions.—** In this Act,

"action for collision" includes an action for damage caused by one or more ships to another ship or ships or to property or persons on board another ship or ships as a result of carrying out or omitting to carry out a manoeuvre, or as a result of non-compliance with law, even though there has been no actual collision;

"Associate Chief Justice" means the Associate Chief Justice of the Court;

"Canadian maritime law" means the law that was administered by the Exchequer Court of Canada on its Admiralty side by virtue of the *Admiralty Act*, chapter A-1 of the Revised Statutes of Canada, 1970, or any other statute, or that would have been so administered if that Court had had, on its Admiralty side, unlimited jurisdiction in relation to maritime and admiralty matters, as that law has been altered by this Act or any other Act of Parliament;

"Chief Justice" means the Chief Justice of the Court;

"Court" means the Federal Court of Canada continued by section 3;

"Court of Appeal" means that division of the Court referred to in section 4 as the Federal Court—Appeal Division;

"Crown" means Her Majesty in right of Canada;

"federal board, commission or other tribunal" means any body or any person or persons having, exercising or purporting to exercise jurisdiction or powers conferred by or under an Act of Parliament or by or under an order made pursuant to a prerogative of the Crown, other than any such body constituted or established by or under a law of a province or any such person or persons appointed under or in accordance with a law of a province or under section 96 of the *Constitution Act, 1867*;

"Federal Court of Appeal" has the meaning given in this section to "Court of Appeal";

"final judgment" means any judgment or other decision that determines in whole or in part any substantive right of any of the parties in controversy in any judicial proceeding;

"judge" means a judge of the Court and includes the Chief Justice and Associate Chief Justice;

"laws of Canada" has the same meaning as those words have in section 101 of the *Constitution Act*, 1867;

"practice and procedure" includes evidence relating to matters of practice and procedure;

"property" means property of any kind, whether real or personal or corporeal or incorporeal, and, without restricting the generality of the foregoing, includes a right of any kind, a share or a chose in action;

"relief" includes every species of relief, whether by way of damages, payment of money, injunction, declaration, restitution of an incorporeal right, return of land or chattels or otherwise;

"Rules" means provisions of law and rules and orders made under section 46;

"ship" means any vessel or craft designed, used or capable of being used solely or partly for navigation, without regard to method or lack of propulsion, and includes (*a*) a ship in the process of construction from the time that it is capable of floating, and

(*b*) a ship that has been stranded, wrecked or sunk and any part of a ship that has broken up;

"Supreme Court" means the Supreme Court of Canada;

"Trial Division" means that division of the Court referred to in section 4 as the Federal Court—Trial Division.

(2) **Senate and House of Commons.**— For greater certainty, the expression "federal board, commission or other tribunal", as defined in subsection (1), does not include the Senate, the House of Commons or any committee or member of either House. 1990, c. 8, s. 1; 2001, c. 6, s. 115.

THE COURT

3. Original Court continued.— The court of law, equity and admiralty in and for Canada now existing under the name of the Federal Court of Canada is hereby continued as an additional court for the better administration of the laws of Canada and shall continue to be a superior court of record having civil and criminal jurisdiction.

4. Court to consist of two divisions.— The Court shall consist of two divisions, called the Federal Court—Appeal Division (which may be referred to as the Court of Appeal or Federal Court of Appeal) and the Federal Court-Trial Division.

THE JUDGES

5. (1) **Constitution of Court.**— The Court shall consist of the following judges:

(*a*) a chief justice called the Chief Justice of the Federal Court of Canada, who shall be the president of the Court, shall be the president of and a member of the Court of Appeal and shall be ex officio a member of the Trial Division;

(*b*) an associate chief justice called the Associate Chief Justice of the Federal Court of Canada, who shall be the president of and a member of the Trial Division and shall be ex officio a member of the Court of Appeal; and

(*c*) not more than twenty-nine other judges, ten of whom shall be appointed to the Court of Appeal and shall be ex officio members of the Trial Division, and the remainder of whom shall be appointed to the Trial Division and shall be ex officio members of the Court of Appeal.

(2) **Supernumerary judges.**— For each office of judge of the Court of Appeal and of the Trial Division, there shall be the additional office of supernumerary judge that a judge of that Division may elect under the *Judges Act* to hold.

(3) **Additional office of judge.**— For each of the offices of Chief Justice and Associate Chief Justice, there shall be the additional office of judge that the Chief Justice or Associate Chief Justice, as the case may be, may elect under the *Judges Act* to hold.

(4) **Appointment of judges.**— The judges shall be appointed by the Governor in Council by letters patent under the Great Seal.

(5) **Who may be appointed judge.**— Any person may be appointed a judge of the Court who

    (*a*) is or has been a judge of a superior, county or district court in Canada,

    (*b*) is or has been a barrister or advocate of at least ten years standing at the bar of any province, or

    (*c*) has, for an aggregate of at least ten years,

        (i) been a barrister or advocate at the bar of any province, and

        (ii) after becoming a barrister or advocate at the bar of any province, exercised powers and performed duties and functions of a judicial nature on a full-time basis in respect of a position held pursuant to a law of Canada or a province.

(6) **Eight judges from Province of Quebec.**— Ten at least of the judges shall be persons who have been judges of the Court of Appeal or of the Superior Court of the Province of Quebec, or have been members of the bar of that Province. R.S.C. 1985, c. 41 (1st Supp.), s. 11; 1992, c. 49, s. 127; 1996, c. 22, s. 1.

6. (1) **Chief Justice and Associate Chief Justice, rank and precedence.**— The Chief Justice has rank and precedence over all the other judges, and the Associate Chief Justice has rank and precedence after the Chief Justice over all the other judges.

(2) **Rank and precedence among other judges.**— The other judges have rank and precedence after the Chief Justice and the Associate Chief Justice and among themselves according to seniority determined by reference to the respective times when they became judges of the Exchequer Court of Canada or of the Court.

(3) **Absence or incapacity of Chief Justice or Associate Chief Justice.**— Where the office of Chief Justice or of Associate Chief Justice is vacant, or the Chief Justice or the Associate Chief Justice is absent from Canada or is for any reason unable or unwilling to act, the powers and duties of the Chief Justice or the Associate Chief Justice shall be exercised and performed by the senior judge who is in Canada and is able and willing to act.

7. (1) **Residence of judges.**— The judges shall reside in the National Capital Region described in the schedule to the *National Capital Act* or within forty kilometres thereof.

(2) **Rota of judges.**— Notwithstanding subsection (1), the Rules may provide for a rota of judges in order to insure a continuity of judicial availability in any centre where the volume of work or other circumstances make such an arrangement expedient.

(3) **No judge to be away for more than one month.**— No judge shall be required under rules made under subsection (2) to remain in any centre other than the National Capital Region for a period longer than one month, unless it becomes necessary to do so to complete the hearing of a cause or matter.

8. (1) **Tenure of office.**—Subject to subsection (2), the judges hold office during good behaviour, but are removable by the Governor General on address of the Senate and House of Commons.

(2) **Cessation of office.**— A judge shall cease to hold office on attaining the age of seventy-five years.

(3) **Transitional.**— A judge who holds office on March 1, 1987 may retire at the age of seventy years. R.S.C. 1985, c. 16 (3rd Supp.), s. 7.

9. (1) **Oath of office.**—Every judge shall, before entering on the duties of the office of judge, take an oath that he will duly and faithfully, and to the best of his skill and knowledge, execute the powers and trusts reposed in him as a judge of the Court.

(2) **How administered.**— The oath referred to in subsection (1) shall be administered to the Chief Justice before the Governor General, and to the other judges by the Chief Justice or, in the case of absence or incapacity of the Chief Justice, by any other judge.

10. (1) **Deputy judges of the Court.**— Subject to subsection (3), any judge of a superior, county or district court in Canada, and any person who has held office as a judge of a superior, county or district court in Canada, may, at the request of the Chief Justice made with the approval of the Governor in Council, act as a judge of the Federal Court and while so acting has all the powers of a judge of the Court and shall be referred to as a deputy judge of the Court.

(2) **Consent required.**— No request may be made under subsection (1) to a judge of a superior, county or district court in a province without the consent of the chief justice or chief judge of the court of which he is a member, or of the attorney general of the province.

(3) **Approval of Governor in Council.**— The Governor in Council may approve the making of requests pursuant to subsection (1) in general terms or for particular periods or purposes, and may limit the number of persons who may act under this section.

(4) **Salary.**— A person who acts as a judge pursuant to subsection (1) shall be paid a salary for the period he acts at the rate fixed by the *Judges Act* for a judge

of the Court, other than the Chief Justice or the Associate Chief Justice, less any amount otherwise payable to him under that Act in respect of that period, and shall also be paid the travel allowances that a judge is entitled to be paid under the *Judges Act*.

BARRISTERS, ADVOCATES, ATTORNEYS AND SOLICITORS

11. (1) **Barrister or advocate.**— Every person who is a barrister or advocate in a province may practise as a barrister or advocate in the Court.

(2) **Attorney or solicitor.**— Every person who is an attorney or solicitor in a superior court of a province may practise as an attorney or solicitor in the Court.

(3) **To be officers of the Court.**— Every person who may practise as a barrister, advocate, attorney or solicitor in the Court is an officer of the Court.

PROTHONOTARIES

12. (1) **Prothonotaries.**— The Governor in Council may appoint as prothonotaries of the Court such fit and proper persons who are barristers or advocates in a province as are, in his opinion, necessary for the efficient performance of the work of the Court that, under the Rules, is to be performed by them.

(2) **Senior Prothonotary and Associate Senior Prothonotary.**— The Governor in Council shall designate one of the prothonotaries to be Senior Prothonotary and one of the prothonotaries to be Associate Senior Prothonotary.

(3) **Powers and duties.**— The powers, duties and functions of the prothonotaries shall be determined by the Rules.

(4) **Salary.**— Each prothonotary shall be paid a salary to be fixed by the Governor in Council.

(5) **Superannuation.**— For the purposes of the *Public Service Superannuation Act*, a prothonotary shall be deemed to be employed in the Public Service.

SHERIFFS AND MARSHALS

13. (1) **Sheriff.**— The Governor in Council may appoint a sheriff of the Court for any geographical area.

(2) **Ex officio sheriffs.**— Where no sheriff is appointed under subsection (1) for a geographical area, the sheriff and deputy sheriffs of the county or other judicial division or part thereof within that geographical area who are appointed under provincial law are ex officio sheriff and deputy sheriffs of the Court.

(3) **Deputy sheriff.**— The Rules may provide for the appointment of deputy sheriffs.

(4) **Marshal.**— Every sheriff of the Court is ex officio a marshal of the Court and every deputy sheriff of the Court is ex officio a deputy marshal of the Court.

ADMINISTRATION OF COURT

14. (1) **Registry of Court.**— There is hereby established a Registry of the Court consisting of a principal office of the Court in Ottawa and such other offices of the Court as may be established by the Rules.

(2) **Staff of Court.**— Such officers, clerks and employees as are required for the purposes of the Court shall be appointed under the *Public Service Employment Act.*

(3) **Organization.**— The employees of the Court shall be organized and the offices shall be operated in such manner as may be provided by the Rules.

ORGANIZATION OF WORK

15. (1) **Sittings of Trial Division.**— Subject to the Rules, any judge of the Trial Division may sit and act at any time and at any place in Canada for the transaction of the business of the Court or any part thereof and, when he so sits or acts, he constitutes the Court.

(2) **Arrangements to be made by Associate Chief Justice.**— Subject to the Rules, all such arrangements as may be necessary or proper for the holding of courts, or otherwise for the transaction of business of the Trial Division, and the arrangements from time to time of judges to hold such courts or to transact such business, shall be made by the Associate Chief Justice.

(3) **Hearings in different places.**— The trial of any matter in the Trial Division may, by order of the Court, take place partly at one place and partly at another.

16. (1) **Sittings of Court of Appeal.**— Except as otherwise provided in this Act or any other Act of Parliament, every appeal and every application for leave to appeal to the Court of Appeal, and every application for judicial review or reference to the Court of Appeal, shall be heard in the Court of Appeal before not fewer than three judges sitting together and always before an uneven number of judges, and, otherwise, the business of that Court shall be dealt with by such judge or judges as the Chief Justice may arrange.

(2) **Arrangements to be made by Chief Justice.**— The Chief Justice shall designate the judges to sit from time to time and the appeals or matters to be heard by them.

(3) **Place of sittings.**— The place of each sitting of the Court of Appeal shall be arranged by the Chief Justice to suit, as nearly as may be, the convenience of the parties.

(4) **No judge to hear appeal from own judgment.**— A judge shall not sit on the hearing of an appeal from a judgment he has pronounced.

(5) **Chief Justice to preside.**— The Chief Justice when present at any sittings of the Court of Appeal shall preside and, in the absence of the Chief Justice, the senior judge who is present shall preside.1990, c. 8, s. 2.

JURISDICTION OF TRIAL DIVISION

17. (1) **Relief against the Crown.**— Except as otherwise provided in this Act or any other Act of Parliament, the Trial Division has concurrent original jurisdiction in all cases where relief is claimed against the Crown.

(2) **Cases.**— Without restricting the generality of subsection (1), the Trial Division has concurrent original jurisdiction, except as otherwise provided, in all cases in which

(*a*) the land, goods or money of any person is in the possession of the Crown;

(*b*) the claim arises out of a contract entered into by or on behalf of the Crown;

(*c*) there is a claim against the Crown for injurious affection; or

(*d*) the claim is for damages under the *Crown Liability and Proceedings Act.*

(3) **Crown and subject: consent to jurisdiction.**— The Trial Division has exclusive original jurisdiction to hear and determine the following matters:

(*a*) the amount to be paid where the Crown and any person have agreed in writing that the Crown or that person shall pay an amount to be determined by the Federal Court, the Trial Division or the Exchequer Court of Canada; and

(*b*) any question of law, fact or mixed law and fact that the Crown and any person have agreed in writing shall be determined by the Federal Court, the Trial Division or the Exchequer Court of Canada.

(4) **Conflicting claims against Crown.**— The Trial Division has concurrent original jurisdiction to hear and determine proceedings to determine disputes where the Crown is or may be under an obligation, in respect of which there are or may be conflicting claims.

(5) **Relief in favour of Crown or against officer.**— The Trial Division has concurrent original jurisdiction

(*a*) in proceedings of a civil nature in which the Crown or the Attorney General of Canada claims relief; and

(*b*) in proceedings in which relief is sought against any person for anything done or omitted to be done in the performance of the duties of that person as an officer, servant or agent of the Crown.

(6) **Trial Division has no jurisdiction.**— Where an Act of Parliament confers jurisdiction in respect of a matter on a court constituted or established by or

under a law of a province, the Trial Division has no jurisdiction to entertain any proceeding in respect of the same matter unless the Act expressly confers that jurisdiction on the Court.1990, c. 8, s. 3.

18. (1) **Extraordinary remedies, federal tribunals.**— Subject to section 28, the Trial Division has exclusive original jurisdiction

   (*a*) to issue an injunction, writ of certiorari, writ of prohibition, writ of mandamus or writ of quo warranto, or grant declaratory relief, against any federal board, commission or other tribunal; and

   (*b*) to hear and determine any application or other proceeding for relief in the nature of relief contemplated by paragraph (*a*), including any proceeding brought against the Attorney General of Canada, to obtain relief against a federal board, commission or other tribunal.

(2) **Extraordinary remedies, members of Canadian Forces.**— The Trial Division has exclusive original jurisdiction to hear and determine every application for a writ of habeas corpus ad subjiciendum, writ of certiorari, writ of prohibition or writ of mandamus in relation to any member of the Canadian Forces serving outside Canada.

(3) **Remedies to be obtained on application.**— The remedies provided for in subsections (1) and (2) may be obtained only on an application for judicial review made under section 18.1. 1990, c. 8, s. 4.

18.1 (1) **Application for judicial review.**— An application for judicial review may be made by the Attorney General of Canada or by anyone directly affected by the matter in respect of which relief is sought.

(2) **Time limitation.**— An application for judicial review in respect of a decision or order of a federal board, commission or other tribunal shall be made within thirty days after the time the decision or order was first communicated by the federal board, commission or other tribunal to the office of the Deputy Attorney General of Canada or to the party directly affected thereby, or within such further time as a judge of the Trial Division may, either before or after the expiration of those thirty days, fix or allow.

(3) **Powers of Trial Division.**— On an application for judicial review, the Trial Division may

   (*a*) order a federal board, commission or other tribunal to do any act or thing it has unlawfully failed or refused to do or has unreasonably delayed in doing; or

   (*b*) declare invalid or unlawful, or quash, set aside or set aside and refer back for determination in accordance with such directions as it considers to be appropriate, prohibit or restrain, a decision, order, act or proceeding of a federal board, commission or other tribunal.

(4) **Grounds of review.**— The Trial Division may grant relief under subsection (3) if it is satisfied that the federal board, commission or other tribunal

(a) acted without jurisdiction, acted beyond its jurisdiction or refused to exercise its jurisdiction;

(b) failed to observe a principle of natural justice, procedural fairness or other procedure that it was required by law to observe;

(c) erred in law in making a decision or an order, whether or not the error appears on the face of the record;

(d) based its decision or order on an erroneous finding of fact that it made in a perverse or capricious manner or without regard for the material before it;

(e) acted, or failed to act, by reason of fraud or perjured evidence; or

(f) acted in any other way that was contrary to law.

(5) **Defect in form or technical irregularity.**— Where the sole ground for relief established on an application for judicial review is a defect in form or a technical irregularity, the Trial Division may

(a) refuse the relief if it finds that no substantial wrong or miscarriage of justice has occurred; and

(b) in the case of a defect in form or a technical irregularity in a decision or order, make an order validating the decision or order, to have effect from such time and on such terms as it considers appropriate. 1990, c. 8, s. 5.

18.2 Interim orders.— On an application for judicial review, the Trial Division may make such interim orders as it considers appropriate pending the final disposition of the application. 1990, c. 8, s. 5.

18.3 (1) Reference by federal tribunal.— A federal board, commission or other tribunal may at any stage of its proceedings refer any question or issue of law, of jurisdiction or of practice and procedure to the Trial Division for hearing and determination.

(2) **Reference by Attorney General of Canada.**— The Attorney General of Canada may, at any stage of the proceedings of a federal board, commission or other tribunal, other than a service tribunal within the meaning of the *National Defence Act*, refer any question or issue of the constitutional validity, applicability or operability of an Act of Parliament or of regulations thereunder, to the Trial Division for hearing and determination. 1990, c. 8, s. 5.

18.4 (1) Hearings in summary way.— Subject to subsection (2), an application or reference to the Trial Division under any of sections 18.1 to 18.3 shall be heard and determined without delay and in a summary way.

(2) **Exception.**— The Trial Division may, if it considers it appropriate, direct that an application for judicial review be treated and proceeded with as an action. 1990, c. 8, s. 5.

18.5 Exception to sections 18 and 18.1.— Notwithstanding sections 18 and 18.1, where provision is expressly made by an Act of Parliament for an appeal as such to the Court, to the Supreme Court of Canada, to the Court Martial Appeal Court, to the Tax Court of Canada, to the Governor in Council or to the Treasury Board from a decision or order of a federal board, commission or other tribunal made by or in the course of proceedings before that board, commission or tribunal, that decision or order is not, to the extent that it may be so appealed, subject to review or to be restrained, prohibited, removed, set aside or otherwise dealt with, except in accordance with that Act. 1990, c. 8, s. 5.

19. Inter-governmental disputes.— Where the legislature of a province has passed an Act agreeing that the Court, whether referred to in that Act by its present name or by its former name of the Exchequer Court of Canada, has jurisdiction in cases of controversies

(*a*) between Canada and that province, or

(*b*) between that province and any other province or provinces that have passed a like Act,

the Court has jurisdiction to determine the controversies and the Trial Division shall deal with any such matter in the first instance.

20. (1) Industrial property, exclusive jurisdiction.— The Trial Division has exclusive original jurisdiction, between subject and subject as well as otherwise,

(*a*) in all cases of conflicting applications for any patent of invention, or for the registration of any copyright, trade-mark, industrial design or topography within the meaning of the *Integrated Circuit Topography Act*; and

(*b*) in all cases in which it is sought to impeach or annul any patent of invention or to have any entry in any register of copyrights, trade-marks, industrial designs or topographies referred to in paragraph (*a*) made, expunged, varied or rectified."

(2) Industrial property, concurrent jurisdiction.— The Trial Division has concurrent jurisdiction in all cases, other than those mentioned in subsection (1), in which a remedy is sought under the authority of any Act of Parliament or at law or in equity respecting any patent of invention, copyright, trade-mark, industrial design or topography referred to in paragraph (1)(*a*). 1990, c. 37, s. 34.

21. Citizenship appeals.— The Trial Division has exclusive jurisdiction to hear and determine all appeals that may be brought pursuant to subsection 14(5) of the *Citizenship Act*.

22. (1) Navigation and shipping.— The Trial Division has concurrent original jurisdiction, between subject and subject as well as otherwise, in all cases in which a claim for relief is made or a remedy is sought under or by virtue of Canadian maritime law or any other law of Canada relating to any matter coming within the class of subject of navigation and shipping, except to the extent that jurisdiction has been otherwise specially assigned.

(2) **Maritime jurisdiction.**— Without limiting the generality of subsection (1), it is hereby declared for greater certainty that the Trial Division has jurisdiction with respect to any one or more of the following:

  (*a*) any claim with respect to title, possession or ownership of a ship or any part interest therein or with respect to the proceeds of sale of a ship or any part interest therein;

  (*b*) any question arising between co-owners of a ship with respect to possession, employment or earnings of a ship;

  (*c*) any claim in respect of a mortgage or hypothecation of, or charge on, a ship or any part interest therein or any charge in the nature of bottomry or respondentia for which a ship or part interest therein or cargo was made security;

  (*d*) any claim for damage or for loss of life or personal injury caused by a ship either in collision or otherwise;

  (*e*) any claim for damage sustained by, or for loss of, a ship including, without restricting the generality of the foregoing, damage to or loss of the cargo or equipment of, or any property in or on or being loaded on or off, a ship;

  (*f*) any claim arising out of an agreement relating to the carriage of goods on a ship under a through bill of lading, or in respect of which a through bill of lading is intended to be issued, for loss or damage to goods occurring at any time or place during transit;

  (*g*) any claim for loss of life or personal injury occurring in connection with the operation of a ship including, without restricting the generality of the foregoing, any claim for loss of life or personal injury sustained in consequence of any defect in a ship or in her apparel or equipment, or of the wrongful act, neglect or default of the owners, charterers or persons in possession or control of a ship or of the master or crew thereof or of any other person for whose wrongful acts, neglects or defaults the owners, charterers or persons in possession or control of the ship are responsible, being an act, neglect or default in the management of the ship, in the loading, carriage or discharge of goods on, in or from the ship or in the embarkation, carriage or disembarkation of persons on, in or from the ship;

  (*h*) any claim for loss of or damage to goods carried in or on a ship including, without restricting the generality of the foregoing, loss of or damage to passengers' baggage or personal effects;

  (*i*) any claim arising out of any agreement relating to the carriage of goods in or on a ship or to the use or hire of a ship whether by charter party or otherwise;

  (*j*) any claim for salvage including, without restricting the generality of the foregoing, claims for salvage of life, cargo, equipment or other property of, from or by an aircraft to the same extent and in the same manner as if the aircraft were a ship;

(*k*) any claim for towage in respect of a ship or of an aircraft while the aircraft is water-borne;

(*l*) any claim for pilotage in respect of a ship or of an aircraft while the aircraft is water-borne;

(*m*) any claim in respect of goods, materials or services wherever supplied to a ship for the operation or maintenance of the ship, including, without restricting the generality of the foregoing, claims in respect of stevedoring and lighterage;

(*n*) any claim arising out of a contract relating to the construction, repair or equipping of a ship;

(*o*) any claim by a master, officer or member of the crew of a ship for wages, money, property or other remuneration or benefits arising out of his employment;

(*p*) any claim by a master, charterer or agent of a ship or shipowner in respect of disbursements, or by a shipper in respect of advances, made on account of a ship;

(*q*) any claim in respect of general average contribution;

(*r*) any claim arising out of or in connection with a contract of marine insurance; and

(*s*) any claim for dock charges, harbour dues or canal tolls including, without restricting the generality of the foregoing, charges for the use of facilities supplied in connection therewith.

(3) **Jurisdiction applicable.**— For greater certainty, it is hereby declared that the jurisdiction conferred on the Court by this section is applicable

(*a*) in relation to all ships, whether Canadian or not and wherever the residence or domicile of the owners may be;

(*b*) in relation to all aircraft where the cause of action arises out of paragraphs (2)(*j*) to (*l*), whether those aircraft are Canadian or not and wherever the residence or domicile of the owners may be;

(*c*) in relation to all claims, whether arising on the high seas, in Canadian waters or elsewhere and whether those waters are naturally navigable or artificially made so, including, without restricting the generality of the foregoing, in the case of salvage, claims in respect of cargo or wreck found on the shores of those waters; and

(*d*) in relation to all mortgages or hypothecations of, or charges by way of security on, a ship, whether registered or not, or whether legal or equitable, and whether created under foreign law or not. 1996, c. 31, s. 82.

23. Bills of exchange and promissory notes, aeronautics and interprovincial works and undertakings.— Except to the extent that jurisdiction has been otherwise specially assigned, the Trial Division has concurrent original jurisdiction, between subject and subject as well as otherwise, in all cases in which a claim for relief is made or a remedy is sought under an Act of Parliament or otherwise in relation to any matter coming within any of the following classes of subjects, namely,

(*a*) bills of exchange and promissory notes, where the Crown is a party to the proceedings;

(*b*) aeronautics; and

(*c*) works and undertakings connecting a province with any other province or extending beyond the limits of a province.

24. (1) **Appeals under other Acts.**— Except as otherwise provided in this Act or any other Act of Parliament, the Trial Division has exclusive original jurisdiction to hear and determine all appeals that under any Act of Parliament may be taken to the Court.

(2) **Transfer of jurisdiction to Court of Appeal.**— The Rules may transfer original jurisdiction to hear and determine a particular class of appeal from the Trial Division to the Court of Appeal. R.S.C. 1985, c. 51 (4th Supp.), s. 10; 1990, c. 8, s. 6.

25. Extraprovincial jurisdiction.— The Trial Division has original jurisdiction, between subject and subject as well as otherwise, in any case in which a claim for relief is made or a remedy is sought under or by virtue of the laws of Canada if no other court constituted, established or continued under any of the Constitution Acts, 1867 to 1982 has jurisdiction in respect of that claim or remedy.

26. (1) **General original jurisdiction.**— The Trial Division has original jurisdiction in respect of any matter, not allocated specifically to the Court of Appeal, in respect of which jurisdiction has been conferred by any Act of Parliament on the Federal Court, whether referred to as such or as the Exchequer Court of Canada.

(2) **Transfer of original jurisdiction to Court of Appeal.**— Notwithstanding subsection (1), the Rules may transfer to the Court of Appeal original jurisdiction to hear and determine a specified class of matter to which that subsection applies.

JURISDICTION OF FEDERAL COURT OF APPEAL

27. (1) **Appeals from Trial Division.**— An appeal lies to the Federal Court of Appeal from any

(*a*) final judgment,

(*b*) judgment on a question of law determined before trial,

(*c*) interlocutory judgment, or

(*d*) determination on a reference made by a federal board, commission or other tribunal or the Attorney General of Canada,

of the Trial Division.

(1.1) **Appeals from Tax Court of Canada.**— An appeal lies to the Federal Court of Appeal from

(*a*) a final judgment,

(*b*) a judgment on a question of law determined before trial, or

(*c*) an interlocutory judgment or order of the Tax Court of Canada,

other than one in respect of which section 18, 18.29 or 18.3 of the *Tax Court of Canada Act* applies.

(2) **Notice of appeal.**— An appeal under this section shall be brought by filing a notice of appeal in the Registry of the Court

(*a*) in the case of an interlocutory judgment, within ten days, and

(*b*) in any other case, within thirty days, in the calculation of which July and August shall be excluded,

after the pronouncement of the judgment or determination appealed from or within such further time as the Trial Division or the Tax Court of Canada, as the case may be, may, either before or after the expiration of those ten or thirty days, as the case may be, fix or allow.

(3) **Service.**— All parties directly affected by an appeal under this section shall be served forthwith with a true copy of the notice of appeal and evidence of service thereof shall be filed in the Registry of the Court.

(4) **Final judgment.**— For the purposes of this section, a final judgment includes a judgment that determines a substantive right except as to any question to be determined by a referee pursuant to the judgment. R.S.C. 1985, c. 51 (4th Supp.), s. 11; 1990, c. 8, s. 7; 1990, c. 8, s. 78.

28. (1) **Judicial review.**— The Court of Appeal has jurisdiction to hear and determine applications for judicial review made in respect of any of the following federal boards, commissions or other tribunals:

(*a*) the Board of Arbitration established by the *Canada Agricultural Products Act*;

(*b*) the Review Tribunal established by the *Canada Agricultural Products Act*;

(*c*) the Canadian Radio-television and Telecommunications Commission established by the *Canadian Radio-television and Telecommunications Commission Act*;

(*d*) the Pension Appeals Board established by the *Canada Pension Plan*;

(*e*) the Canadian International Trade Tribunal established by the *Canadian International Trade Tribunal Act*;

(*f*) the National Energy Board established by the *National Energy Board Act*;

(*g*) [Repealed, 1992, c. 49, s. 128.]

(*h*) the Canada Industrial Relations Board established by the *Canada Labour Code*;

(*i*) the Public Service Staff Relations Board established by the *Public Service Staff Relations Act*;

(*j*) the Copyright Board established by the *Copyright Act*;

(*k*) the Canadian Transportation Agency established by the *Canada Transportation Act*;

(*l*) the Tax Court of Canada established by the *Tax Court of Canada Act*;

(*m*) umpires appointed under the *Employment Insurance Act*;

(*n*) the Competition Tribunal established by the *Competition Tribunal Act*;

(*o*) assessors appointed under the *Canada Deposit Insurance Corporation Act*; and

(*p*) the Canadian Artists and Producers Professional Relations Tribunal by subsection 10(1) of the *Status of the Artist Act*.

(2) **Sections apply.**— Sections 18 to 18.5, except subsection 18.4(2), apply, with such modifications as the circumstances require, in respect of any matter within the jurisdiction of the Court of Appeal under subsection (1) and, where they so apply, a reference to the Trial Division shall be read as a reference to the Court of Appeal.

(3) **Trial Division deprived of jurisdiction.**— Where the Court of Appeal has jurisdiction to hear and determine any matter, the Trial Division has no jurisdiction to entertain any proceeding in respect of the same matter. 1990, c. 8, s. 8; 1992, c. 26, s. 17; 1992, c. 33, s. 69; 1992, c. 49, s. 128; 1993, c. 34, s. 70; 1996, c. 10, s. 229; 1996, c. 23, s. 187(c); 1998, c. 26, s. 73; 1999, c. 31, s. 92.

29. [Repealed, 1990, c. 8, s. 8.]

30. [Repealed, 1990, c. 8, s. 8.]

31. [Repealed, 1990, c. 8, s. 8.]

32. [Repealed, 1990, c. 8, s. 8.]

33. [Repealed, 1990, c. 8, s. 8.]

34. [Repealed, 1990, c. 8, s. 8.]

35. [Repealed, 1990, c. 8, s. 8.]

SUBSTANTIVE PROVISIONS

36. (1) **Prejudgment interest, cause of action within province.**— Except as otherwise provided in any other Act of Parliament, and subject to subsection (2), the laws relating to prejudgment interest in proceedings between subject and subject that are in force in a province apply to any proceedings in the Court in respect of any cause of action arising in that province.

(2) **Prejudgment interest, cause of action outside province.**— A person who is entitled to an order for the payment of money in respect of a cause of

action arising outside any province or in respect of causes of action arising in more than one province is entitled to claim and have included in the order an award of interest thereon at such rate as the Court considers reasonable in the circumstances, calculated

    (*a*) where the order is made on a liquidated claim, from the date or dates the cause of action or causes of action arose to the date of the order; or

    (*b*) where the order is made on an unliquidated claim, from the date the person entitled gave notice in writing of the claim to the person liable therefor to the date of the order.

(3) **Interest on special damages.**— Where an order referred to in subsection (2) includes an amount for special damages, the interest shall be calculated under that subsection on the balance of special damages incurred as totalled at the end of each six month period following the notice in writing referred to in paragraph (2)(b) and at the date of the order.

(4) **Exceptions.**— Interest shall not be awarded under subsection (2)

    (*a*) on exemplary or punitive damages;

    (*b*) on interest accruing under this section;

    (*c*) on an award of costs in the proceeding;

    (*d*) on that part of the order that represents pecuniary loss arising after the date of the order and that is identified by a finding of the Court;

    (*e*) where the order is made on consent, except by consent of the debtor; or

    (*f*) where interest is payable by a right other than under this section.

(5) **Judicial discretion.**— The Court may, where it considers it just to do so, having regard to changes in market interest rates, the conduct of the proceedings or any other relevant consideration, disallow interest or allow interest for a period other than that provided for in subsection (2) in respect of the whole or any part of the amount on which interest is payable under this section.

(6) **Application.**— This section applies in respect of the payment of money under judgment delivered on or after the day on which this section comes into force, but no interest shall be awarded for a period before that day.

(7) **Canadian maritime law.**— This section does not apply in respect of any case in which a claim for relief is made or a remedy is sought under or by virtue of Canadian maritime law. 1990, c. 8, s. 9.

37. (1) **Judgment interest, causes of action within province.**— Except as otherwise provided in any other Act of Parliament and subject to subsection (2), the laws relating to interest on judgments in causes of action between subject and subject that are in force in a province apply to judgments of the Court in respect of any cause of action arising in that province.

(2) **Judgment interest, causes of action outside or in more than one province.**— A judgment of the Court in respect of a cause of action arising out-

side any province or in respect of causes of action arising in more than one province shall bear interest at such rate as the Court considers reasonable in the circumstances, calculated from the time of the giving of the judgment. 1990, c. 8, s. 9.

38. [Repealed, 1990, c. 8, s. 9.]

39. (1) **Prescription and limitation on proceedings in the Court.**— Except as expressly provided by any other Act, the laws relating to prescription and the limitation of actions in force in any province between subject and subject apply to any proceedings in the Court in respect of any cause of action arising in that province.

(2) **Idem, not in province.**— A proceeding in the Court in respect of a cause of action arising otherwise than in a province shall be taken within six years after the cause of action arose.

(3) [Repealed, 1990, c. 8, s. 10.]

40. (1) **Vexatious proceedings.**— Where the Court is satisfied, on application, that a person has persistently instituted vexatious proceedings or has conducted a proceeding in a vexatious manner, the Court may order that no further proceedings be instituted by the person in the Court or that a proceeding previously instituted by the person in the Court not be continued, except by leave of the Court.

(2) **Attorney General of Canada.**— An application under subsection (1) may be made only with the consent of the Attorney General of Canada, who shall be entitled to be heard on the application and on any application made under subsection (3).

(3) **Application for rescission or leave to proceed.**— A person against whom an order under subsection (1) has been made may apply to the Court for rescission of the order or for leave to institute or continue a proceeding.

(4) **Court may grant leave.**— Where an application is made under subsection (3) for leave to institute or continue a proceeding, the Court may grant leave if it is satisfied that the proceeding is not an abuse of process and that there are reasonable grounds for the proceeding.

(5) **No appeal.**— A decision of the Court under subsection (4) is final and is not subject to appeal. R.S., c. 10 (2nd Supp.), s. 39; 1990, c. 8, s. 11.

42. Maritime law continued.— Canadian maritime law as it was immediately before June 1, 1971 continues subject to such changes therein as may be made by this Act or any other Act of Parliament. R.S., c. 10 (2nd Supp.), s. 42.

43. (1) **Jurisdiction *in personam*.**— Subject to subsection (4), the jurisdiction conferred on the Court by section 22 may in all cases be exercised *in personam*.

(2) **Jurisdiction** *in rem*.— Subject to subsection (3), the jurisdiction conferred on the Court by section 22 may be exercised *in rem* against the ship, aircraft or other property that is the subject of the action, or against any proceeds of sale thereof that have been paid into court.

(3) **Exception.**— Notwithstanding subsection (2), the jurisdiction conferred on the Court by section 22 shall not be exercised in rem with respect to a claim mentioned in paragraph 22(2)(*e*), (*f*), (*g*), (*h*), (*i*), (*k*), (*m*), (*n*), (*p*) or (*r*) unless, at the time of the commencement of the action, the ship, aircraft or other property that is the subject of the action is beneficially owned by the person who was the beneficial owner at the time when the cause of action arose.

(4) **Where action** *in personam* **may be commenced.**— No action *in personam* may be commenced in Canada for a collision between ships unless

(*a*) the defendant is a person who has a residence or place of business in Canada;

(*b*) the cause of action arose in Canadian waters; or

(*c*) the parties have agreed that the Court is to have jurisdiction.

(5) **Exception.**— Subsection (4) does not apply to a counter-claim or an action for a collision, in respect of which another action has already been commenced in the Court.

(6) **Where suit pending outside Canada.**— Where an action for a collision between ships has been commenced outside Canada, an action shall not be commenced in Canada by the same person against the same defendant on the same facts unless the action in the other jurisdiction has been discontinued.

(7) **Ship owned by sovereign power.**— No action in rem may be commenced in Canada against

(*a*) any warship, coast-guard ship or police vessel;

(*b*) any ship owned or operated by Canada or a province, or any cargo laden thereon, where the ship is engaged on government service; or

(*c*) any ship owned or operated by a sovereign power other than Canada, or any cargo laden thereon, with respect to any claim where, at the time the claim arises or the action is commenced, the ship is being used exclusively for non-commercial governmental purposes.

(8) **Arrest.**— The jurisdiction conferred on the Court by section 22 may be exercised in rem against any ship that, at the time the action is brought, is beneficially owned by the person who is the owner of the ship that is the subject of the action.

(9) **Reciprocal security.**— In an action for a collision in which a ship, aircraft or other property of a defendant has been arrested, or security given to answer judgment against the defendant, and in which the defendant has instituted a cross-action or counter-claim in which a ship, aircraft or other property of the

plaintiff is liable to arrest but cannot be arrested, the Court may stay the proceedings in the principal action until security has been given to answer judgment in the cross-action or counter-claim. 1990, c. 8, s. 12; 1996, c. 31, s. 83.

44. Mandamus, injunction, specific performance or appointment of receiver.— In addition to any other relief that the Court may grant or award, a mandamus, injunction or order for specific performance may be granted or a receiver appointed by the Court in all cases in which it appears to the Court to be just or convenient to do so, and any such order may be made either unconditionally or on such terms and conditions as the Court deems just.

PROCEDURE

45. (1) Giving of judgment after judge ceases to hold office.— Where a judge resigns his office or is appointed to any other court or otherwise ceases to hold office, he may, at the request of the Chief Justice, at any time within eight weeks after that event give judgment in any cause, action or matter previously tried by or heard before him as if he had continued in office.

(2) Taking part in giving of judgment after judge ceases to hold office.— Where a person to whom subsection (1) applies has heard a cause, action or matter in the Federal Court of Appeal jointly with other judges of the Court of Appeal, he may, at the request of the Chief Justice, at any time within the period mentioned in subsection (1) take part in the giving of judgment by that Court as if he were still a judge.

(3) Where judge unable to take part in giving of judgment.— Where a person to whom subsection (1) applies or any other judge by whom a matter in the Court of Appeal has been heard is unable to take part in the giving of judgment or has died, the remaining judges may give judgment and, for that purpose, shall be deemed to constitute the Court.

45.1 (1) Rules Committee.— There shall be a rules committee composed of the following members:
  (*a*) the Chief Justice and the Associate Chief Justice;
  (*b*) seven judges designated by the Chief Justice;
  (*c*) five members of the bar of any province designated by the Attorney General of Canada, after consultation with the Chief Justice; and
  (*d*) the Attorney General of Canada or a representative thereof.

(2) Representation.— The persons referred to in paragraph (1)(*c*) should be representative of the different regions of Canada and have experience in fields of law in respect of which the Court has jurisdiction.

(3) Chief Justice shall preside.— The Chief Justice or a member designated by the Chief Justice shall preside over the rules committee.

(4) Term.— The persons referred to in paragraphs (1)(*b*) and (*c*) shall be designated to serve for a period not exceeding three years.

(5) **Expenses.**— Each person referred to in paragraphs (1)(*c*) and (*d*) is entitled to be paid travel and living expenses incurred in carrying out duties as a member of the rules committee while absent from the person's ordinary place of residence but those expenses shall not exceed the maximum limits authorized by Treasury Board directive for employees of the Government of Canada. 1990, c. 8, s. 13.

46. (1) **Rules.**— Subject to the approval of the Governor in Council and subject also to subsection (4), the rules committee may make general rules and orders

(*a*) for regulating the practice and procedure in the Trial Division and in the Court of Appeal, including, without restricting the generality of the foregoing,

(i) rules providing, in a proceeding to which the Crown is a party, for examination for discovery of a departmental or other officer of the Crown,

(ii) rules providing for discovery and production, and supplying of copies, of documents by the Crown in a proceeding to which the Crown is a party,

(iii) rules providing for production of documents by the Crown in a proceeding to which the Crown is not a party,

(iv) rules providing for the medical examination of a person in respect of whose injury a claim is made,

(v) rules governing the taking of evidence before a judge or any other qualified person, within or outside Canada, before or during trial and on commission or otherwise, of any person at a time either before or after the commencement of proceedings in the Court to enforce the claim or possible claim in respect of which the evidence is required,

(vi) rules providing for the reference of any question of fact for inquiry and report by a judge or other person as referee,

(vii) rules respecting the service of documents within Canada and rules authorizing and governing the service of documents outside Canada,

(viii) rules governing the recording of proceedings in the course of a hearing and the transcription of that recording,

(ix) rules governing the appointment of assessors and the trying or hearing of a cause or other matter wholly or partly with the assistance of assessors, and

(x) rules governing the material to be furnished to the Court by any federal board, commission or other tribunal for the purposes of any application or reference;

(*b*) for the effectual execution and working of this Act and the attainment of its intention and objects;

(*c*) for the effectual execution and working of any Act by or under which any jurisdiction is conferred on the Court or any division of it or on any judge of the Court in respect of proceedings in the Court and the attainment of the intention and objects of that Act including, without restricting the generality of the foregoing, a rule deeming any jurisdiction conferred on the Court or a judge to have been conferred on a specified division of the Court;

(*d*) for fixing the fees to be paid by a party to the Registry for payment into the Consolidated Revenue Fund in respect of proceedings in the Court;

(*e*) for regulating the duties of officers of the Court;

(*f*) for fixing the fees that sheriffs, marshals or other persons to whom process may be issued may receive and take, and for regulating their obligation, if any, to account for those fees to the persons or departments by whom they are employed, or their right to retain them for their own use;

(*g*) for awarding and regulating costs in the Court in favour of or against the Crown, as well as the subject;

(*h*) empowering a prothonotary to exercise any authority or jurisdiction, subject to supervision by the Court, even though the authority or jurisdiction may be of a judicial nature; and

(*i*) dealing with any other matter that any provision of this Act contemplates being the subject of a rule or the Rules.

(2) **Extent of rules.**— Rules and orders made under this section may extend to matters arising out of or in the course of proceedings under any Act involving practice and procedure or otherwise, for which no provision is made by that Act or any other Act but for which it is found necessary to provide in order to ensure the proper working of that Act and the better attainment of its objects.

(3) **Uniformity.**— Rules and orders made under this section may provide for a procedure that is uniform in whole or in part in respect of all or any class or classes of matters and for a uniform nomenclature in any such matters.

(4) **Advance publication of rules and amendments.**— Where the rules committee proposes to amend, vary or revoke any rule or order made under this section or to make any rule or order additional to the general rules and orders first made under this section and published together, the committee

(*a*) shall give notice of the proposal by publishing it in the Canada Gazette and shall, in the notice, invite any interested person to make representations to the committee in writing with respect thereto within sixty days after the day of that publication; and

(*b*) may, after the expiration of the sixty days referred to in paragraph (a) and subject to the approval of the Governor in Council, implement the proposal either as originally published or as revised in such manner as the committee deems advisable having regard to any representations so made to it.

(5) Rules and amendments to be laid before Parliament.— A copy of each rule or order and of each amendment, variation or revocation of a rule or order made under this section shall be laid before both Houses of Parliament within ten days after the opening of the session next after the approval by the Governor in Council of the making thereof. 1990, c. 8, s. 14.

47. [Repealed, 1990, c. 8, s. 15.]

48. (1) **How proceeding against Crown instituted.**— A proceeding against the Crown shall be instituted by filing in the Registry of the Court the original and two copies of a document that may be in the form set out in the schedule and by payment of the sum of two dollars as a filing fee.

(2) **Procedure for filing originating document.**— The original and two copies of the originating document may be filed as required by subsection (1) by being forwarded, together with a remittance for the filing fee, by registered mail addressed to "The Registry, The Trial Division, The Federal Court of Canada, Ottawa, Canada".

(3) **Service of originating document.**— When the original and two copies of the originating document have been filed and the filing fee has been paid as required by this section, an officer of the Registry of the Court shall, after verifying the accuracy of the copies, forthwith, on behalf of the claimant, serve the originating document on Her Majesty by transmitting the copies to the office of the Deputy Attorney General of Canada.

(4) **Certificate.**— When the copies have been transmitted to the office of the Deputy Attorney General of Canada under subsection (3), a certificate signed by an officer of the Registry respecting the date of filing and the date of transmission of the copies shall be delivered, or forwarded by registered mail, to the claimant or the claimant's counsel or solicitor at the address appearing on the originating document, or at such other address as may have been communicated to the Registry for the purpose.

(5) **Certificate to be evidence.**— A certificate under subsection (4) is evidence of the date of filing and the date of service of the originating document referred to in the certificate.

49. No juries.— All causes or matters before the Court shall be heard and determined without a jury.

50. (1) **Stay of proceedings.**— The Court may, in its discretion, stay proceedings in any cause or matter,

    (*a*) on the ground that the claim is being proceeded with in another court or jurisdiction; or

    (*b*) where for any other reason it is in the interest of justice that the proceedings be stayed.

(2) **Idem.**— The Court shall, on the application of the Attorney General of Canada, stay proceedings in any cause or matter in respect of a claim against the Crown if it appears that the claimant has an action or proceeding in respect of the same claim pending in any other court against a person who, at the time when the cause of action alleged in the action or proceeding arose, was, in respect thereof, acting so as to engage the liability of the Crown.

(3) **Lifting of stay.**— Any stay ordered under this section may subsequently be lifted in the discretion of the Court.

50.1 (1) **Stay of proceedings.**— The Court shall, on application of the Attorney General of Canada, stay proceedings in any cause or matter in respect of a claim against the Crown where the Crown desires to institute a counter-claim or third-party proceedings in respect of which the Court lacks jurisdiction.

(2) **Recommence in provincial court.**— Where the Court stays proceedings under subsection (1), the party who instituted the proceedings may recommence those proceedings in a court constituted or established by or under a law of a province and otherwise having jurisdiction with respect to the subject-matter of the proceedings.

(3) **Prescription and limitation of actions.**— Where proceedings are recommenced pursuant to subsection (2) within one hundred days after the proceedings are stayed in the Court, the claim against the Crown in the recommenced proceedings shall, for the purposes of any laws relating to prescription and the limitation of actions, be deemed to have been instituted on the day the proceedings in the Court were instituted. 1990, c. 8, s. 16.

51. Reasons for judgment to be filed.— Where a judge gives reasons for a judgment pronounced by him or pronounced by a court of which he was a member, he shall file a copy of the reasons in the Registry of the Court.

JUDGMENTS OF COURT OF APPEAL

52. Powers of Court of Appeal.— The Federal Court of Appeal may
- (a) quash proceedings in cases brought before it in which it has no jurisdiction or whenever those proceedings are not taken in good faith;
- (b) in the case of an appeal from the Trial Division; and
  - (i) dismiss the appeal or give the judgment and award the process or other proceedings that the Trial Division should have given or awarded,
  - (ii) in its discretion, order a new trial, if the ends of justice seem to require it, or
  - (iii) make a declaration as to the conclusions that the Trial Division should have reached on the issues decided by it and refer the matter back for a continuance of the trial on the issues that remain to be determined in the light of that declaration;

(*c*) in the case of an appeal other than an appeal from the Trial Division,

    (i) dismiss the appeal or give the decision that should have been given, or

    (ii) in its discretion, refer the matter back for determination in accordance with such directions as it considers to be appropriate;

(*d*) [Repealed, 1990, c. 8, s. 17]

EVIDENCE

53. (1) **Taking of evidence.**— The evidence of any witness may by order of the Court be taken, subject to any rule or order that may relate to the matter, on commission, on examination or by affidavit.

(2) **Admissibility of evidence.**— Evidence that would not otherwise be admissible shall be admissible, in the discretion of the Court and subject to any rule that may relate to the matter, if it would be admissible in a similar matter in a superior court of a province in accordance with the law in force in any province, notwithstanding that it is not admissible by virtue of section 40 of the *Canada Evidence Act.*

54. (1) **Who may administer oath, affidavit or affirmation.**— All persons authorized to take and receive affidavits to be used in any of the superior courts of a province may administer oaths and take and receive affidavits, declarations and solemn affirmations in that province to be used in the Court.

(2) **Person empowered by commission.**— The Governor in Council may, by commission, empower such person as the Governor in Council thinks necessary, within or outside Canada, to administer oaths and to take and receive affidavits, declarations and solemn affirmations in or concerning any proceeding had or to be had in the Court.

(3) **Oath, affidavit or affirmation as valid as if taken before the Court.**— Every oath, affidavit, declaration or solemn affirmation taken or made pursuant to this section is as valid and of the same effect, to all intents, as if it had been administered, taken, sworn, made or affirmed before the Court.

(4) **Style of commissioner.**— Every commissioner empowered under subsection (2) shall be styled a commissioner for administering oaths in the Federal Court of Canada.

PROCESS

55. (1) **Application of process.**— The process of the Court runs throughout Canada and any other place to which legislation enacted by Parliament has been made applicable.

(2) **Enforcement of order for payment of money.**— An order for payment of money, whether for costs or otherwise, may be enforced in the same manner as a judgment.

(3) **No attachment for non-payment only.**— No attachment as for contempt shall issue for the non-payment of money alone.

(4) **Sheriff to execute process.**— A sheriff or marshal shall execute the process of the Court that is directed to him, whether or not it requires him to act outside his geographical jurisdiction, and shall perform such other duties as may be expressly or impliedly assigned to him by the Rules.

(5) **Absence or incapacity of sheriff.**— In any case where there is no sheriff or marshal or a sheriff or marshal is unable or unwilling to act, the process of the Court shall be directed to a deputy sheriff or deputy marshal, or to such other person as may be provided by the Rules or by a special order of the Court made for a particular case, and any such person is entitled to take and retain for his own use such fees as may be provided by the Rules or the special order. 1996, c. 31, s. 84.

56. (1) **Analogy to provincial process.**— In addition to any writs of execution or other process that are prescribed by the Rules for enforcement of its judgments or orders, the Court may issue process against the person or the property of any party, of the same tenor and effect as those that may be issued out of any of the superior courts of the province in which any judgment or order is to be executed, and where, by the law of that province, an order of a judge is required for the issue of any process, a judge of the Court may make a similar order with respect to like process to issue out of the Court.

(2) **Process against person.**— No person shall be taken into custody under process of execution for debt issued out of the Court.

(3) **Process against property.**— All writs of execution or other process against property, whether prescribed by the Rules or authorized by subsection (1), shall, unless otherwise provided by the Rules, be executed, with respect to the property liable to execution and the mode of seizure and sale, as nearly as possible in the same manner as similar writs or process, issued out of the superior courts of the province in which the property to be seized is situated, are, by the law of that province, required to be executed, and the writs or other process issued by the Court shall bind property in the same manner as similar writs or process issued by the provincial superior courts, and the rights of purchasers thereunder are the same as those of purchasers under those similar writs or process.

(4) **Claim against property seized.**— Every claim made by any person to property seized under a writ of execution or other process issued out of the Court, or to the proceeds of the sale of that property, shall, unless otherwise provided by the Rules, be heard and disposed of as nearly as may be according to the procedure applicable to like claims to property seized under similar writs or process issued out of the courts of the province.

(5) [Repealed, 1990, c. 8, s. 18.]

GENERAL

57. (1) **Constitutional questions.**— Where the constitutional validity, applicability or operability of an Act of Parliament or of the legislature of any province, or of regulations thereunder, is in question before the Court or a federal board, commission or other tribunal, other than a service tribunal within the meaning of the *National Defence Act*, the Act or regulation shall not be adjudged to be invalid, inapplicable or inoperable unless notice has been served on the Attorney General of Canada and the attorney general of each province in accordance with subsection (2).

(2) **Time of notice.**— Except where otherwise ordered by the 'Court or the federal board, commission or other tribunal, the notice referred to in subsection (1) shall be served at least ten days before the day on which the constitutional question described in that subsection is to be argued.

(3) **Notice of appeal or application for judicial review.**— The Attorney General of Canada and the attorney general of each province are entitled to notice of any appeal or application for judicial review made in respect of the constitutional question described in subsection (1).

(4) **Right to be heard.**— The Attorney General of Canada and the attorney general of each province are entitled to adduce evidence and make submissions to the Court or federal board, commission or other tribunal in respect of the constitutional question described in subsection (1).

(5) **Appeal.**— Where the Attorney General of Canada or the attorney general of a province makes submissions under subsection (4), that attorney general shall be deemed to be a party to the proceedings for the purposes of any appeal in respect of the constitutional question described in subsection (1). 1990, c. 8, s. 19.

57.1 Fees to be paid to Receiver General.— All fees payable in respect of proceedings in the Court shall be paid to the Receiver General unless those fees are, in accordance with an arrangement made by the Minister of Justice, to be received and dealt with in the same manner as amounts paid as provincial court fees, in which case they shall be dealt with as so provided. 1990, c. 8, s. 19.

58. (1) **Law reports editor.**— The Minister of Justice shall appoint or designate a fit and proper person to be editor of the official reports of the decisions of the Court and may appoint a committee of not more than five persons to advise the editor.

(2) **Contents.**— Only such of the decisions of the Court or such parts of such decisions as, in the opinion of the editor, are of sufficient significance or importance to warrant publication in the official reports shall be included therein.

(3) **Printing and distribution.**— The official reports shall be printed and shall be distributed with or without charge as the Governor in Council may direct.

(4) **Official languages.**— Each decision reported in the official reports shall be published therein in both official languages.

59. Police force.— Such services or assistance in connection with the conduct of the Court's hearings, the Security of the Court, its premises and staff or the execution of its orders and judgments as may, having regard to the circumstances, be found necessary shall be provided, at the request of the Chief Justice, by the Royal Canadian Mounted Police or such other police force as the Governor in Council may designate.

Appendix H

Constitution Act, 1982

Enacted as Schedule B to the *Canada Act 1982* (U.K.) 1982, c. 11, which came into force on April 17, 1982

PART I

Canadian Charter of Rights and Freedoms

Whereas Canada is founded upon principles that recognize the supremacy of God and the rule of law:

Guarantee of Rights and Freedoms

1. Rights and freedoms in Canada.— The Canadian Charter of Rights and Freedoms guarantees the rights and freedoms set out in it subject only to such reasonable limits prescribed by law as can be demonstrably justified in a free and democratic society.

Fundamental Freedoms

2. Fundamental freedoms.— Everyone has the following fundamental freedoms:
- (*a*) freedom of conscience and religion;
- (*b*) freedom of thought, belief, opinion and expression, including freedom of the press and other media of communication;
- (*c*) freedom of peaceful assembly; and
- (*d*) freedom of association.

Democratic Rights

3. Democratic rights of citizens.— Every citizen of Canada has the right to vote in an election of members of the House of Commons or of a legislative assembly and to be qualified for membership therein.

4. (1) **Maximum duration of legislative bodies.**— No House of Commons and no legislative assembly shall continue for longer than five years from the date fixed for the return of the writs of a general election of its members.

(2) **Continuation in special circumstances.**— In time of real or apprehended war, invasion or insurrection, a House of Commons may be continued by Parliament and a legislative assembly may be continued by the legislature beyond five years if such continuation is not opposed by the votes of more than one-third of the members of the House of Commons or the legislative assembly, as the case may be.

5. Annual sitting of legislative bodies.— There shall be a sitting of Parliament and of each legislature at least once every twelve months.

Mobility Rights

6. (1) **Mobility of citizens.**— Every citizen of Canada has the right to enter, remain in and leave Canada.

(2) **Rights to move and gain livelihood.**— Every citizen of Canada and every person who has the status of a permanent resident of Canada has the right

    (*a*) to move to and take up residence in any province; and

    (*b*) to pursue the gaining of a livelihood in any province.

(3) **Limitation.**— The rights specified in subsection (2) are subject to

    (*a*) any laws or practices of general application in force in a province other than those that discriminate among persons primarily on the basis of province of present or previous residence; and

    (*b*) any laws providing for reasonable residency requirements as a qualification for the receipt of publicly provided social services.

(4) **Affirmative action programs.**— Subsections (2) and (3) do not preclude any law, program or activity that has as its object the amelioration in a province of conditions of individuals in that province who are socially or economically disadvantaged if the rate of employment in that province is below the rate of employment in Canada.

Legal Rights

7. Life, liberty and security of person.— Everyone has the right to life, liberty and security of the person and the right not to be deprived thereof except in accordance with the principles of fundamental justice.

8. Search or seizure.— Everyone has the right to be secure against unreasonable search or seizure.

9. Detention or imprisonment.— Everyone has the right not to be arbitrarily detained or imprisoned.

10. Arrest or detention.— Everyone has the right on arrest or detention
- (*a*) to be informed promptly of the reasons therefor;
- (*b*) to retain and instruct counsel without delay and to be informed of that right; and
- (*c*) to have the validity of the detention determined by way of *habeas corpus* and to be released if the detention is not lawful.

11. Proceedings in criminal and penal matters.— Any person charged with an offence has the right
- (*a*) to be informed without unreasonable delay of the specific offence;
- (*b*) to be tried within a reasonable time;
- (*c*) not to be compelled to be a witness in proceedings against that person in respect of the offence;
- (*d*) to be presumed innocent until proven guilty according to law in a fair and public hearing by an independent and impartial tribunal;
- (*e*) not to be denied reasonable bail without just cause;
- (*f*) except in the case of an offence under military law tried before a military tribunal, to the benefit of trial by jury where the maximum punishment for the offence is imprisonment for five years or a more severe punishment;
- (*g*) not to be found guilty on account of any act or omission unless, at the time of the act or omission, it constituted an offence under Canadian or international law or was criminal according to the general principles of law recognized by the community of nations;
- (*h*) if finally acquitted of the offence, not to be tried for it again and, if finally found guilty and punished for the offence, not to be tried or punished for it again; and
- (*i*) if found guilty of the offence and if the punishment for the offence has been varied between the time of commission and the time of sentencing, to the benefit of the lesser punishment.

12. Treatment or punishment.— Everyone has the right not to be subjected to any cruel and unusual treatment or punishment.

13. Self-crimination.— A witness who testifies in any proceedings has the right not to have any incriminating evidence so given used to incriminate that witness in any other proceedings, except in a prosecution for perjury or for the giving of contradictory evidence.

14. Interpreter.— A party or witness in any proceedings who does not understand or speak the language in which the proceedings are conducted or who is deaf has the right to the assistance of an interpreter.

Equality Rights

15. (1) **Equality before and under law and equal protection and benefit of law.**— Every individual is equal before and under the law and has the right to the equal protection and equal benefit of the law without discrimination and, in particular, without discrimination based on race, national or ethnic origin, colour, religion, sex, age or mental or physical disability.

(2) **Affirmative action programs.**— Subsection (1) does not preclude any law, program or activity that has as its object the amelioration of conditions of disadvantaged individuals or groups including those that are disadvantaged because of race, national or ethnic origin, colour, religion, sex, age or mental or physical disability.

Official Languages of Canada

16. (1) **Official languages of Canada.**— English and French are the official languages of Canada and have equality of status and equal rights and privileges as to their use in all institutions of the Parliament and government of Canada.

(2) **Official languages of New Brunswick.**— English and French are the official languages of New Brunswick and have equality of status and equal rights and privileges as to their use in all institutions of the legislature and government of New Brunswick.

(3) **Advancement of status and use.**— Nothing in this Charter limits the authority of Parliament or a legislature to advance the equality of status or use of English and French.

16.1 (1) **English and French linguistic communities in New Brunswick.**— The English linguistic community and the French linguistic community in New Brunswick have equality of status and equal rights and privileges, including the right to distinct educational institutions and such distinct cultural institutions as are necessary for the preservation and promotion of those communities.

(2) **Role of the legislature and government of New Brunswick.**— The role of the legislature and government of New Brunswick to preserve and promote the status, rights and privileges referred to in subsection (1) is affirmed.

17. (1) **Proceedings of Parliament.**— Everyone has the right to use English or French in any debates and other proceedings of Parliament.

(2) **Proceedings of New Brunswick legislature.**— Everyone has the right to use English or French in any debates and other proceedings of the legislature of New Brunswick.

18. (1) **Parliamentary statutes and records.**— The statutes, records and journals of Parliament shall be printed and published in English and French and both language versions are equally authoritative.

(2) **New Brunswick statutes and records.**— The statutes, records and journals of the legislature of New Brunswick shall be printed and published in English and French and both language versions are equally authoritative.

19. (1) **Proceedings in courts established by Parliament.**— Either English or French may be used by any person in, or in any pleading in or process issuing from, any court established by Parliament.

(2) **Proceedings in New Brunswick courts.**— Either English or French may be used by any person in, or in any pleading in or process issuing from, any court of New Brunswick.

20. (1) **Communications by public with federal institutions.**— Any member of the public in Canada has the right to communicate with, and to receive available services from, any head or central office of an institution of the Parliament or government of Canada in English or French, and has the same right with respect to any other office of any such institution where
- (*a*) there is a significant demand for communications with and services from that office in such language; or
- (*b*) due to the nature of the office, it is reasonable that communications with and services from that office be available in both English and French.

(2) **Communications by public with New Brunswick institutions.**— Any member of the public in New Brunswick has the right to communicate with, and to receive available services from, any office of an institution of the legislature or government of New Brunswick in English or French.

21. Continuation of existing constitutional provisions.— Nothing in sections 16 to 20 abrogates or derogates from any right, privilege or obligation with respect to the English and French languages, or either of them, that exists or is continued by virtue of any other provision of the Constitution of Canada.

22. Rights and privileges preserved.— Nothing in sections 16 to 20 abrogates or derogates from any legal or customary right or privilege acquired or enjoyed either before or after the coming into force of this Charter with respect to any language that is not English or French.

Minority Language Educational Rights

23. (1) **Language of instruction.**— Citizens of Canada
- (*a*) whose first language learned and still understood is that of the English or French linguistic minority population of the province in which they reside, or
- (*b*) who have received their primary school instruction in Canada in English or French and reside in a province where the language in which they received that instruction is the language of the English or French linguistic minority population of the province,

have the right to have their children receive primary and secondary school instruction in that language in that province.

(2) **Continuity of language instruction.**— Citizens of Canada of whom any child has received or is receiving primary or secondary school instruction in English or French in Canada, have the right to have all their children receive primary and secondary school instruction in the same language.

(3) **Application where numbers warrant.**— The right of citizens of Canada under subsections (1) and (2) to have their children receive primary and secondary school instruction in the language of the English or French linguistic minority population of a province

    (*a*) applies wherever in the province the number of children of citizens who have such a right is sufficient to warrant the provision to them out of public funds of minority language instruction; and

    (*b*) includes, where the number of those children so warrants, the right to have them receive that instruction in minority language educational facilities provided out of public funds.

Enforcement

24. (1) **Enforcement of guaranteed rights and freedoms.**— Anyone whose rights or freedoms, as guaranteed by this Charter, have been infringed or denied may apply to a court of competent jurisdiction to obtain such remedy as the court considers appropriate and just in the circumstances.

(2) **Exclusion of evidence bringing administration of justice into disrepute.**— Where, in proceedings under subsection (1), a court concludes that evidence was obtained in a manner that infringed or denied any rights or freedoms guaranteed by this Charter, the evidence shall be excluded if it is established that, having regard to all the circumstances, the admission of it in the proceedings would bring the administration of justice into disrepute.

General

25. Aboriginal rights and freedoms not affected by Charter.— The guarantee in this Charter of certain rights and freedoms shall not be construed so as to abrogate or derogate from any aboriginal, treaty or other rights or freedoms that pertain to the aboriginal peoples of Canada including

    (*a*) any rights or freedoms that have been recognized by the Royal Proclamation of October 7, 1763; and

    (*b*) any rights or freedoms that now exist by way of land claims agreements or may be so acquired.

26. Other rights and freedoms not affected by Charter.— The guarantee in this Charter of certain rights and freedoms shall not be construed as denying the existence of any other rights or freedoms that exist in Canada.

27. Multicultural heritage.— This Charter shall be interpreted in a manner consistent with the preservation and enhancement of the multicultural heritage of Canadians.

28. Rights guaranteed equally to both sexes.— Notwithstanding anything in this Charter, the rights and freedoms referred to in it are guaranteed equally to male and female persons.

29. Rights respecting certain schools preserved.— Nothing in this Charter abrogates or derogates from any rights or privileges guaranteed by or under the Constitution of Canada in respect of denominational, separate or dissentient schools.

30. Application to territories and territorial authorities.— A reference in this Charter to a Province or to the legislative assembly or legislature of a province shall be deemed to include a reference to the Yukon Territory and the Northwest Territories, or to the appropriate legislative authority thereof, as the case may be.

31. Legislative powers not extended.— Nothing in this Charter extends the legislative powers of any body or authority.

Application of Charter

32. (1) **Application of Charter.**— This Charter applies
    (*a*) to the Parliament and government of Canada in respect of all matters within the authority of Parliament including all matters relating to the Yukon Territory and Northwest Territories; and
    (*b*) to the legislature and government of each province in respect of all matters within the authority of the legislature of each province.

(2) **Exception.**— Notwithstanding subsection (1), section 15 shall not have effect until three years after this section comes into force.

33. (1) **Exception where express declaration.**— Parliament or the legislature of a province may expressly declare in an Act of Parliament or of the legislature, as the case may be, that the Act or a provision thereof shall operate notwithstanding a provision included in section 2 or sections 7 to 15 of this Charter.

(2) **Operation of exception.**— An Act or a provision of an Act in respect of which a declaration made under this section is in effect shall have such operation as it would have but for the provision of this Charter referred to in the declaration.

(3) **Five year limitation.**— A declaration made under subsection (1) shall cease to have effect five years after it comes into force or on such earlier date as may be specified in the declaration.

(4) **Re-enactment.**— Parliament or the legislature of a province may re-enact a declaration made under subsection (1).

(5) **Five year limitation.**— Subsection (3) applies in respect of a re-enactment made under subsection (4).

Citation

34. Citation.— This Part may be cited as the *Canadian Charter of Rights and Freedoms.*

Appendix I

Checklist for Decisions and Reasons for Decision of Administrative Tribunals

In preparing decisions, administrative tribunals want to ensure that their decisions and the reasons for decision are adequate. This checklist can be used by administrative tribunals as a guide to ensure that their decisions and reasons for decisions are adequate or to assist administrative tribunals in establishing their own standard format for the contents of their decisions and reasons for decision.

1. The name of the administrative tribunal including the name of the specific committee or body who is responsible for making the decision.
2. The nature of the proceeding and the names of the parties to the proceeding including any agents or lawyers representing them.
3. The relevant section or sections of the governing statute of the administrative tribunal and any other applicable statute including the section or sections which gives the administrative tribunal the authority to initiate the inquiry.
4. The dates of the actual hearing, including the dates of any motions that were decided prior to the beginning of the hearing.
5. The names of the members of the administrative tribunal who are responsible for making the decision.
6. A summary of the relevant or important facts, including identifying the witnesses who gave evidence at the hearing and referring to the exhibits that were introduced at the hearing (unless there is a long list of exhibits).
7. The findings of fact which includes indicating what evidence has been accepted and what evidence has been rejected and explaining why.
8. The issues in the case.
9. The thought process of the members of the administrative tribunal, including conclusions on each issue in the case and the relevant evidence of witnesses and arguments of counsel.
10. The findings of credibility for witnesses including the reasons why it found a particular witness or all or part of the witness's testimony to be credible or not credible and referring to the evidence which supports that finding.

11. The opinions of any expert witnesses and whether their opinion has been accepted or rejected.
12. The determinations of any procedural, legal or constitutional issues.
13. Policies or guidelines that were considered by the members of the administrative tribunal.
14. The names of cases that the parties referred to in their submissions, including prior cases decided by the administrative tribunal, and whether these cases have been followed or distinguished.
15. The decision or ultimate finding of the members of the administrative tribunal.
16. The date and signature of the members of the administrative tribunal.

Appendix J

Guidelines for Review of Draft Decisions[1]

(a) General

1. The Tribunal's decision draft review process is intended to maintain and enhance the general quality, consistency and coherence of the Tribunal's caselaw.[2] The Tribunal has always recognized that this process must respect the independence and autonomy of adjudicators.

2. In *Consolidated Bathurst* and *Tremblay*, the Supreme Court of Canada confirmed that fostering the quality and reasonable consistency and coherence of decisions is a legitimate and important institutional role for tribunals.[3] The Court approved internal consultation processes designed to influence, but not to constrain, adjudicators on general legal and policy issues. It also explicitly recognized the importance of adjudicative coherence as a relevant criterion in decision-making.[4]

3. Draft review is one of the Tribunal's processes for fostering the quality, consistency and coherence of its decisions. The review process is the responsibility of the Counsel to the Chair and the Associate Counsel in the Office of

---

[1] © 2001, Workplace Safety and Insurance Appeals Tribunal, reproduced with permission. The Workers' Compensation Appeals Tribunal, now called the Workplace Safety and Insurance Appeals Tribunal, developed these guidelines for the review of draft decisions and reasons for decision.

[2] See the Tribunal's 1990 Annual Report, p. 6.

[3] *Consolidated Bathurst Ltd. v. International Woodworkers of America Local 2-69* (1990), 68 D.L.R. (4th) 524 at pp. 555, 562-63, 567; and *Tremblay v. Quebec (Commissions des Affaires Sociales)* (1992), 90 D.L.R. (4th) 609 at pp. 621-23, 624-25.

[4] *Consolidated Bathurst, per* Gauthier, at p. 562: "A decision-maker may also be swayed by the opinion of the majority of his colleagues in the interest of adjudicative coherence since this is a relevant criterion to be taken into consideration even when the decision-maker is not bound by any *stare decisis* rule."

the Counsel to the Chair (OCC).[5] Drafts referred for review by adjudicators are reviewed by the Counsel to the Chair and the Associate Counsel against the Tribunal's *Hallmarks of Decision Quality*.[6]

4. Review of a draft decision may be particularly helpful where the draft:
   (a) addresses a new development or issue that is of particular current, Tribunal-wide interest;
   (b) raises issues which may be expected to lead to media attention, a judicial review application, an Ombudsman complaint, or a reconsideration request;
   (c) departs from the approach previously taken in Tribunal decisions;
   (d) may affect Board policy or practice; or
   (e) involves a dissent on a significant issue.

5. As an expert appeal body deciding difficult medical and legal issues, the Tribunal is concerned with providing training to its new members. Draft review during the orientation period is intended to assist new Vice-Chairs in the development of their workplace safety and insurance knowledge, writing skills and understanding of the Tribunal's *Hallmarks of Decision Quality*. As part of their training, new Vice-Chairs are required to write at least one mock decision and submit it to the OCC for draft review. Once assigned to hearings, new Vice-Chairs are asked to consider the following guidelines in deciding whether to request draft review:
   (a) New Vice-Chairs with no previous workplace safety and insurance experience are encouraged to submit their first 20 drafts.
   (b) New Vice-Chairs with previous workplace safety and insurance experience are encouraged to submit their first 10 drafts.

(b) Process

6. In accordance with the fundamental principle that the power to decide rests with Tribunal Members, it is for the Vice-Chair or any Panel Member assigned to a case to request review of a draft decision. Where a Panel Member requests review of a draft minority or majority decision, it is helpful for Counsel to review both drafts. In deciding whether to refer a draft for review, Tribunal Members should consider their responsibility to ensure that their decisions reasonably comply with the Tribunal's *Hallmarks of Decision Quality*. In particular, decisions should be reasonably consistent with previous cases unless Tribunal Members are satisfied that the prior decisions are distinguishable or wrong and reasons are given.

---

[5] In accordance with *Quebec Inc. v. Quebec (Régie des Permis d'alcool)*, [1996] 35 S.C.R. 919, OCC Counsel are independent from the Tribunal Counsel Office and do not make submissions in individual cases.

[6] These *Hallmarks* were adopted by the Tribunal in 1989 in its "Statement of Missions, Goals and Commitments", and updated in 2000. A copy can be found in Appendix K.

7. From time to time, the Tribunal Chair or Counsel to the Chair may identify issues that in their view are of particular, current Tribunal-wide interest for the purpose of draft review.

8. Unless a Tribunal Member requests draft review by a particular Counsel, the review will be done by the first available Counsel. Requests for review of a second draft will be referred to the Counsel who reviewed the first draft, unless the person requesting review specifies otherwise.

9. Drafts referred for review will not be shared by OCC Counsel with the Tribunal Chair or with any Tribunal Member other than the referring Member unless otherwise instructed by that Member. OCC Counsel may, however, discuss drafts amongst themselves.

10. OCC Counsel's comments regarding a draft decision will be forwarded to the Tribunal Member who requested draft review. If the Member is part of a Panel, it is the Member's responsibility to bring significant issues to the attention of the other Panel Members.

11. After reviewing a draft, OCC Counsel may occasionally suggest that it would be helpful to review a second draft of the decision. The decision whether to request review of the second draft rests with the Member who requested the review of the first draft.

12. If, in the course of their work, OCC Counsel encounter a draft that deals with an issue that they expect would be of special interest to the Tribunal Chair, they may advise the adjudicator of this. They shall not, however, mention that advice to the Tribunal Chair nor bring the draft to his or her attention in any other manner.

13. OCC Counsel are available to discuss any legal question with a Tribunal Member, or to provide research assistance, before or after a draft is written. A Tribunal Member is also welcome to consult at any time with any other Member of the Tribunal, including the Tribunal Chair, on any generic issue of law or policy.

14. Where, as a result of OCC draft review (or, indeed, for any reason), Members decide that they must address an issue or an authority that was not in view at the hearing, they should consider whether natural justice requires that the parties to the case be given an opportunity to make further submissions, or to lead further evidence.

15. OCC Counsel may meet with the Tribunal Chair to discuss released decisions and generic issues and problems.

Appendix K

Hallmarks of Decision Quality

The following is the list of hallmarks of good quality relating to adjudicative decisions as adopted by the Workplace Safety and Insurance Appeals Tribunal[1] in its Statement of Missions, Goals and Commitments in 1989 and updated in 2000.

1. The decision does not overlook relevant issues fairly raised by the facts.

2. The decision makes the evidence base clear; if the decision is based on a mediation or agreement, it records the mediation or agreement.

3. The decision conforms with the applicable law and reflects the Tribunal's commitment to the rule of law. Where the decision is based on a mediation or agreement, it records that the adjudicator is satisfied that the decision accords with the law.

4. The decision uses clear language where possible, conforms reasonably with Tribunal decision formats, and uses technical and legal terminology consistently with other decisions.

5. On issues of law or generic medical issues, the decision does not conflict with previous Tribunal decisions, unless reasons for the disagreement are given. Conflicts may occur during periods of development on contentious issues. Conflicting approaches should not be a feature of the Tribunal's body of decisions over the long term.

6. The decision is part of a body of decisions which, overall, is a reasonably coherent, accessible and helpful resource for understanding and preparing to deal with the issues in new cases and for invoking the important principle that like cases should receive like treatment. Thus, decisions which deal with novel issues or take novel approaches will generally be more detailed than those which apply established caselaw.

---

[1] Reproduced with permission. The Workplace Safety and Insurance Appeals Tribunal was previously called the Workers' Compensation Appeals Tribunal.

Appendix L

Table of Simple Word Substitutes[1]

Instead of	Use
abutting	next to
accompany	go with
accordingly	so
accumulate	gather, collect
accurate	correct, exact, right
acquire	get
additional	added, more, other, extra
address	discuss
adequate	enough
adjacent to	next to

---

[1] Many authors have written articles, chapters and even entire books on the basic rules of writing. These authors emphasize the importance of using short, common and definite words, and many of these authors have prepared lists of simple words. This table was developed by reviewing these lists and incorporating the words which are applicable to administrative tribunals: B. Dickson, "Judgment Writing" (1983), 2 *Civil Justice Quarterly* 4, at p. 7; D.H. Layh, "Plain English: Increasing the Power of our Writing" (1992), 56 Sask. L. Rev. 1, at pp. 15-16; L. Mailhot and J.D. Carnwath, *Decisions, Decisions...A Handbook for Judicial Writing* (Cowansville: Les Editions Yvon Blais Inc., 1998), pp. 82, 129-39; J.J. George, *Judicial Opinion Writing Handbook*, 3rd ed. (Buffalo: William S. Hein & Co. Inc., 1993), pp. 288-93; R.C. Wydick, *Plain English for Lawyers* (California: California Law Review Inc., 1978), pp. 731-3, 739; *Foundations of Administrative Justice — A New Course for Administrative Tribunal Members* (Vancouver: British Columbia Council of Administrative Tribunals, 1997), pp. 1-3 of Handout #4-3.

Instead of	Use
adjudicate	decide
advert	refer, mention
advise	tell, recommend, suggest
afford an opportunity	let, allow
along the lines of	like
alteration	change
an adequate number	enough
an excessive number	too many
anticipate	expect
a number of	some, about, approximately
apparent	clear, plain
apprise	inform, tell
as a means of	to
ascertain	find out, identify
assist	help, aid
attempt	try
at that point in time	then
at the present time	now
at the time	when
at this point in time	now
be benefitted by	benefit from
because of the fact that	because
be determinative of	determine
be dispositive of	dispose of
be influential on	influence
be responsible for	handle
by means of	by, with
by reason of	because of

Instead of	Use
by virtue of	by, under
category	class, group, type, section, level
cause it be done	have it done
cognizant	aware
combined	joined, connected
commence	start, begin
communicate	talk, write, tell
compensation	pay, reward, salary
comply with	follow
comprise	form, include, make up
conceal	hide
concerning	about, on
conclude	close, end
concur	agree
consequence	result
consequently	so
constitutes	is, forms, makes up
contains	has
contiguous to	next to
continue	go on, keep on
contribute	give
currently	now
delete	cut, drop, cancel, remove
deleterious	harmful
demonstrate	show
depart	leave, go
designate	appoint, choose
desist	stop

Instead of	Use
despite the fact that	although
determine	decide, find
disburse	pay, spend
disclose	show
discontinue	stop, finish
disseminate	issue, send out
does not operate to	does not
due to the fact that	due to, because, since
during such time as	while
during the course of	during
during the time that	while
elect	choose, pick, take
eliminate	cut, drop, get rid of, cancel, remove
elucidate	explain, show
employ	use
encounter	meet
encourage	urge
endeavour	try
establish	prove
evaluate	check
evident	clear
evidentiary material	evidence
evince	show, make clear, prove
examine	look at, check
expedite	speed up, rush, hurry
expertise	skill, ability
facilitate	help
factor	cause, reason

Instead of	Use
failed to	didn't
feasible	can be done, possible, workable, practical
file a motion	move
final	last
finalize	complete, finish
for a period of	for
forfeit	give up, lose
for the duration of	during
for the purpose of	for, to
for the reason that	because
from the point of view of	from, for
function	role, purpose
have a need of	need
hence	so
he was aware of the fact that	he knew that
however	but
identical	same
immediately	now, at once
implement	carry out, do
in accordance with	by, following, under
in addition	also, besides, too
in all likelihood that	probably
in an effort to	to
in as much as	since, because
in a timely manner	on time, promptly
in cases in which	when, where, if
inception	start, beginning
in conjunction with	with

Instead of	Use
in connection with	with, about
incorporate	blend, join, mix
incumbent upon	must
indicate	show
in favour of	for
initiate	begin, start
in lieu of	instead of
in many cases	often
in order that	so
in order to	to
inquire	ask
in regard to	about
in relation to	with, about
in some instances	sometimes
in so much as	since, because
in terms of	in
in the case of	when
in the course of	during, in
in the event that	if
in the interests of	for
in the majority of cases	usually
in the nature of	like
in the near future	soon
in this case	here
in view of	because, since
is able to	can
is applicable	applies
is binding upon	binds

Instead of	Use
is entitled to	may
is required to	must
is unable to	cannot
it is essential	must
limited number	few
locate	find
location	place, area, site, scene
magnitude	size
maintain	keep, hold
make application	apply
make contact with	see, meet, talk to
make reference to	refer to
maximum	most, longest, greatest, top
methodology	method, way, system, approach, procedure
minimize	decrease, reduce
modify	change
moreover	also, now, next
most of the time	usually
necessitate	cause, require
nevertheless	but, even so
no later than	by
notify	let know, tell
notwithstanding the fact that	although
numerous	many
objective	aim, goal, purpose
observe	see, look at
obtain	get
on a regular basis	regularly

Instead of	Use
on a timely basis	now, at once
on the basis of	by, from, because
on the part of	by
optimum	best
option	choice
parameters	limits
participate	take part
perform	do
period of time	period, time
permit	let, allow
personnel	staff, workers, people
pertaining to	about, on
point in time	point, time, when, now
portion	part, piece, section
possess	have, own
preclude	prevent
previously	before
prior to	before
proceed	do, go on, keep on
proficiency	skill, ability
provide	give
provided that	if
purchase	buy
pursuant to	under, by
reach a resolution	resolve
reason for	why
regarding	about, of, on
relating to	about, on

Instead of	Use
remain	stay
remainder	rest
render	give, make
request	ask
requirement	need
reside	live
retain	keep, hold
review	check, go over, look at
shall	must, will
similar to	like
solicit	ask for
state	say
subsequent	later, next
subsequently	after, then
subsequent to	after
sufficient	enough
take action to	act, do
take into consideration	consider
terminate	end, stop
therefore	so
there is no doubt but that	no doubt
time period	time, period
to the effect that	that
transmit	send
transpire	happen, occur, take place
transport	send, bring, move
under the provisions of	under
until such time as	until

Instead of	Use
utilize	use
viable	practical, possible, workable
whenever	when
whereas	since, because
with a view to	to
with reference to	about
with regard to	about
with respect to	on, about
with the exception of	except for
with the object of	to
witnessed	saw

Appendix M

Table of Transitional Words[1]

To introduce an idea	to begin with, basically, primarily, initially, originally, first, generally, in general, as a general rule, traditionally
To add to an idea	also, furthermore, moreover, in addition, additionally
To define an idea	for example, for instance, in particular, namely, specifically, that is, to illustrate, in fact
To emphasize an idea	actually, really, finally, more important, interestingly, impressively, in other words, indeed, normally, usually, clearly, naturally, surely
To summarize an idea	in short, in conclusion, in summary, all in all, on the whole
To show a relationship between two ideas	thus, therefore, hence, then, consequently, as a result, in effect, accordingly
To show similarity between two ideas	similarly, comparably, correspondingly, analogously, equally, likewise

[1] In addition to emphasizing the importance of using short, common and definite words, the authors of articles and books on basic rules of writing emphasize the importance of using transition words to connect paragraphs and many of these authors have prepared lists of transitional words. This table was developed by reviewing these lists and incorporating the words which are applicable to administrative tribunals: D.H. Layh, "Plain English: Increasing the Power of our Writing" (1992), 56 Sask. L. Rev. 1, at p. 20; L. Mailhot and J.D. Carnwath, *Decisions, Decisions...A Handbook for Judicial Writing* (Cowansville: Les Editions Yvon Blais Inc., 1998), pp. 25, 141-2; J.J. George, *Judicial Opinion Writing Handbook*, 3rd. ed. (Buffalo: William S. Hein & Co. Inc., 1993), pp. 271, 304-6.

To show contrast between two ideas	on the contrary, in contrast, conversely, but, however, yet, on the other hand, instead, despite that, in comparison, even so, regardless, still, nevertheless, nonetheless, notwithstanding, otherwise

Bibliography

Administrative Law (Vancouver: Continuing Legal Education Society of British Columbia, 1988)

Administrative Law for the Non-specialist: Taking a Walk Along the Boardwalk (Toronto: Canadian Bar Association — Ontario, 1991)

Aitken, M., R. Cohen, and M. Silva, "Curial Deference to Administrative Tribunals: To Southam and Beyond" in *Law Society of Upper Canada Special Lectures 2000 — Constitutional and Administrative Law* (Toronto: Law Society of Upper Canada, 2000)

Alberta, *Administrative Procedures Model Code* (Edmonton: Alberta Law Reform Institute, 1999)

Alberta, *Powers and Procedures for Administrative Tribunals in Alberta — Report No. 79* (Edmonton: Alberta Law Reform Institute, 1999)

Anisman, P., and R.F. Reid, eds., *Administrative Law Issues and Practice* (Scarborough: Carswell Thomson Professional Publishing, 1995)

Barnhorst, S., and J. Mather, *Introduction to Canadian Law* (Scarborough: Prentice-Hall Canada Inc., 1985)

Barnhorst, S., and J. Mather-Zetzl, *The Law in Canada* (Scarborough: Prentice-Hall Canada Inc., 1990)

Bilson, B., "Part and Parcel of a Member's Job: A Report on the 1998 CCAT Training Survey" (1999), 12 C.J.A.L.P. 213

Blake, S., *Administrative Law in Canada*, 2nd ed. (Toronto: Butterworths, 1997)

Bourgeois, D., *Public Law in Canada* (Scarborough: Nelson Canada, 1990)

Boyd, N., *Canadian Law — An Introduction*, 2nd ed. (Toronto: Harcourt Brace & Co., 1998)

Bredt, C.D., "Administrative Law Basics — Outline for Argument on Behalf of the Department" in *Everything You Always Wanted to Know About . . .* (Ottawa: Canadian Bar Association, 1997)

Brown, D.J.M., and J.M. Evans, *Judicial Review of Administrative Action in Canada* (Toronto: Canvasback Publishing, 1998)

Buckingham, D.E. *et al.*, *Learning About Law* (Toronto: McGraw-Hill Ryerson Ltd., 1997)

213

Canada, *A Guide to the Making of Federal Acts and Regulations* (Ottawa: Department of Justice, 1995)

Canada, *Canada's System of Justice* (Ottawa: Department of Justice, 1993)

Canadian Encyclopedic Digest (Ontario), vol. 1, 3rd ed. (Scarborough: Carswell Thomson Professional Publishing, 1996) "Administrative Law"

Case, R., and D.J. Baum, *Thinking About Law: An Issues Approach*, 2nd ed. (Toronto: IPI Publishing Ltd., 1995)

Casey, J.T., *The Regulation of Professions in Canada* (Scarborough: Carswell Thomson Professional Publishing, 1994)

Cavalluzzo, P., "Jurisdiction of Administrative Tribunals under the *Canadian Charter of Rights and Freedoms*" in *Law Society of Upper Canada Special Lectures 2000 — Constitutional and Administrative Law* (Toronto: Law Society of Upper Canada, 2000)

Chaplin, M.A., "Abracadabra — Deference!" (1997), 3 *Administrative Agency Practice* 5

Cockfield, A., ed., *The Clinical Law Manual*, 10th ed. (Kingston: Queen's Law Students Legal Aid Society, 1993)

Crane, B.A., "Identifying the Forms of Bias" (1996), 1 *Administrative Agency Practice* 139

Dickinson, G. *et al.*, *Understanding the Law*, 2nd ed. (Toronto: McGraw-Hill Ryerson Ltd., 1996)

Dickson, B., "Judgment Writing" (1983), 2 *Civil Justice Quarterly* 4

Douglas, C.G., "How to Write a Concise Opinion" (1983), 22 Judges' J. 4

Dussault, R., and L. Borgeat, *Administrative Law — A Treatise*, 2nd ed. (Toronto: Carswell, 1985)

Elliott, D.W., and R.E. Warskett, eds., *Introduction to Public Law - Readings on the State, the Administrative Process, and Basic Values*, 4th ed. (North York: Captus Press, 1999)

Ellis, S.R , C. Trethewey, and F. Rotter, "Tribunals — Reasons, and Reasons for Reasons" (1990-1991), 4 C.J.A.L.P. 105

Evans, J.M., "Administrative Tribunals and Charter Challenges: Jurisdiction, Discretion and Relief" (1996-1997), 10 C.J.A.L.P. 355

Evans, J.M., H. N. Janisch, and D.J. Mullan, *Administrative Law - Cases, Text, and Materials*, 4th ed. (Toronto: Emond Montgomery Publications Ltd., 1995)

Forsyth, G., "Administrative Tribunals and their Duty to Give Reasons" (1999), 24 N.S.L. News 81

Foundations of Administrative Justice — A New Course for Administrative Tribunal Members (Vancouver: British Columbia Council of Administrative Tribunals, 1997)

Gall, G.L., *The Canadian Legal System*, 4th ed. (Scarborough: Carswell Thomson Professional Publishing, 1995)

Gauk, C., "The Annotated Alberta *Administrative Procedures Act* — Section 7: The Duty to Give Reasons" (1995), 1 *Administrative Agency Practice* 49

George, J.J., *Judicial Opinion Writing Handbook*, 3rd ed. (Buffalo: William S. Hein & Co. Inc., 1993)

Gibson, D.L. *et al.*, *All About Law — Exploring the Canadian Legal System*, 4th ed. (Toronto: Nelson Canada, 1996)

Hogg, P.W., *Constitutional Law of Canada*, 4th ed. (Scarborough: Carswell Thomson Professional Publishing, 1997)

Holloway, I., "The Transformation of Canadian Administrative Law" (1993), 6 C.J.A.L.P. 295

Janisch, H., "What is Administrative Law?" (1995), 1 *Administrative Agency Practice* 3

Jennings, W.H. *et al.*, *Canadian Law*, 5th ed. (Toronto: McGraw-Hill Ryerson Ltd., 1991)

Jones, D.P., and A.S. de Villars, *Principles of Administrative Law*, 3rd ed. (Scarborough: Carswell Thomson Professional Publishing, 1999)

Komar, R.N., *Reasons for Judgment — A Handbook for Judges and Other Judicial Officers* (Toronto: Butterworths, 1980)

Krever, H., *New Federally Appointed Judges Seminar 1999 — Judicial Review* (Ottawa: Canadian Institute for the Administration of Justice, 1999)

Kwaw, E.M.A., *The Guide to Legal Analysis, Legal Methodology and Legal Writing* (Toronto: Emond Montgomery Publications Limited, 1992)

Labelle, D., "Report on the Study on Training for Administrative Tribunal Members in Canada" (1992-1993), 6 C.J.A.L.P. 251

Laskin, J.B. *et al.*, eds., *The Canadian Charter of Rights Annotated* (Aurora: Canada Law Book Inc., 1982)

Layh, D.H., "Plain English: Increasing the Power of our Writing" (1992), 56 Sask. L. Rev. 1

Lester, G.S., "Bias: How and When to Raise the Objection" (1997), 3 *Administrative Agency Practice* 49

Liepner, M., and B. Griffith, *Applying the Law*, 3rd ed. (Toronto: McGraw-Hill Ryerson Ltd., 1990)

Macaulay, R.W., and J.L.H. Sprague, *Practice and Procedure Before Administrative Tribunals* (Scarborough: Carswell Thomson Professional Publishing, 1997)

Macdonald, R.A., and D. Lametti, "Reasons for Decision in Administrative Law" (1990), 3 C.J.A.L.P. 123

Maciura, J., and R. Steinecke, *The Annotated Statutory Powers Procedure Act* (Aurora: Canada Law Book Inc., 1998)

Mailhot, L., and J.D. Carnwath, *Decisions, Decisions . . . A Handbook for Judicial Writing* (Cowansville: Les Editions Yvon Blais Inc., 1998)

Manitoba, *Report on Administrative Law; Part I: Procedures of Provincial Government Agencies* (Winnipeg: Law Reform Commission, 1984)

Manitoba, *Report on Administrative Law; Part II: Judicial Review of Administrative Action* (Winnipeg: Law Reform Commission, 1987)

Manuel, W.J., and C. Donszelmann, *Law of Administrative Investigations and Prosecutions* (Aurora: Canada Law Book Inc., 1999)

McCallum, S.K., *Multi-Media Training Guide for Members of Administrative Agencies* (Victoria: University of Victoria, 1995)

McMillan, J., "Tribunals and the Charter: The Search for Implied Jurisdiction — A Case Comment on *Cooper v. Canada (Human Rights Commission)*" (1998), 32 U.B.C. L. Rev. 365

Morris, M.H., "Administrative Decision-makers and the Duty to Give Reasons: An Emerging Debate" (1998), 11 C.J.A.L.P. 155

Mullan, D.J., "Administrative Tribunals: Their Evolution in Canada from 1945 to 1984" in *Regulations, Crown Corporations and Administrative Tribunals*, I. Bernier, and A. Lajoie, eds. (Toronto: University of Toronto Press, 1985)

Mullan, D.J., *Essentials of Canadian Law — Administrative Law* (Toronto: Irwin Law, 2001)

Mullan, D., "Recent Developments in Administrative Law — The Apparent Triumph of Deference!" (1999), 12 C.J.A.L.P. 191

Nova Scotia, *Agencies, Boards and Commissions: The Administrative Justice System in Nova Scotia — Discussion Paper* (Halifax: Law Reform Commission of Nova Scotia, 1996)

Nova Scotia, *Agencies, Boards and Commissions: The Administrative Justice System in Nova Scotia — Final Report* (Halifax: Law Reform Commission of Nova Scotia, 1997)

Olivo, L.M., *Introduction to Law in Canada* (North York: Captus Press Inc., 1999)

Ontario, *Directions — Review of Ontario's Regulatory Agencies Report* (Toronto: Queen's Printer for Ontario, 1989)

Ontario, *Everyday Justice — Report of the Agency Reform Commission on Ontario's Regulatory and Adjudicative Agencies* (Toronto: Queen's Printer for Ontario, 1998)

Ontario, *Excellence in Administrative Justice: Delivering Better Service* (Toronto: Agency Reform Commission, 1997)

Ontario, "Parliamentary Process" in *Parliament: People and Places. Your Guide to the Legislative Assembly of Ontario* (Toronto: Office of the Legislative Assembly of Ontario, 1998)

Ontario, *Report on Restructuring Regulatory and Adjudicative Agencies* (Toronto: Government Task Force on Agencies, Boards and Commissions, 1997)

Priest, M., "*Charter* Procedure in Administrative Cases: The Tribunal's Perspective" (1994), 7 C.J.A.L.P. 151

Public Law — Reference Materials (Toronto: Law Society of Upper Canada, 2000)

Richards, R.G., "Charter Procedure in Administrative Cases — General Principles and Concerns" in *Current and Emerging Issues — Administrative and Constitutional Law* (Ottawa: Canadian Bar Association, 1993)

Roman, A.J., *Effective Advocacy Before Administrative Tribunals* (Toronto: Carswell, 1989)

Rooke, C., *A Grammar Booklet for Lawyers* (Toronto: The Law Society of Upper Canada, 1992)

Saunders, R.P., ed., *Introduction to Legal Processes*, 2nd ed. (North York: Captus Press, 1994).

Sopinka, J., Lederman, S.N., and Bryant, A.W., *The Law of Evidence in Canada*, 2nd ed. (Toronto: Butterworths, 1999)

Special Lectures of the Law Society of Upper Canada 1992 — Administrative Law: Principles, Practice and Pluralism (Scarborough: Carswell Thomson Professional Publishing, 1993)

Spetz, S.N. and G.S. Spetz

Canadian Law Fundamentals (Mississauga: Copp Clark Pitman Ltd., 1989)

>*Take Notice — An Introduction to Canadian Law*, 3rd ed. (Mississauga: Copp Clark Pitman Ltd., 1989)

Sprague, J.L.H.

>"In My Opinion: Discretion in a Nutshell" (1997), 3 *Administrative Agency Practice* 43

>"Natural Justice and Fairness in a Nutshell" (1997), 3 *Administrative Agency Practice* 15

>"Open Sesame!: Public Access to Agency Proceedings" (1999), 13 C.J.A.L.P. 1

>"Remedies for the Failure to Provide Reasons" (2000), 13 C.J.A.L.P. 209

>"The Role of Agency Staff in Post-hearing Deliberations and Reasons Writing" (1995), 1 *Administrative Agency Practice* 41

>"White Knight Watching Over You: Judicial Review in a Nutshell" (1997), 3 *Administrative Agency Practice* 69

Steele, G., "Reflections on Writing a Reasoned Decision" (1996), 2 *Administrative Agency Practice* 108

Steinecke, R.

>*A Complete Guide to the Regulated Health Professions Act* (Aurora: Canada Law Book Inc., 1995)

>*How to Write Reasons* (Toronto: Steinecke Maciura LeBlanc, 2001)

Strayer, B.L.

>"Good Agency Decisions: A Judge's Perspective" (1995), 1 *Administrative Agency Practice* 55

>"The Application of the *Charter* in Administrative Law: Getting Your Foot in the Door" in *Public Interest v. Private Rights: Striking the Balance in Administrative Law* (Winnipeg: Law Society of Manitoba, 1990)

Swaigen, J., *A Manual for Ontario Adjudicators* (Courtice: Society of Ontario Adjudicators and Regulators, 2000)

Taking the Tribunal to Court: A Practical Guide for Administrative Law Practitioners (Toronto: Canadian Bar Association-Ontario, 2000)

Theberge, J., *Administrative Law — When Government Agencies Affect You* (Saskatoon: Public Legal Education Association of Saskatchewan, 1995)

Turner, D., and M. R. Uhlemann, eds., *A Legal Handbook for the Helping Professional* (Victoria: Sedgewick Society for Consumer and Public Education, 1991)

Ungar, S., *Introduction to Law*, 2nd ed. (Toronto: IPI Publishing Limited, 1989)

Vayda, E.J., and M. T. Satterfield, *Law for Social Workers — A Canadian Guide*, 3rd ed. (Scarborough: Carswell Thomson Professional Publishing, 1997)

Veiga-Minhinnett, A.C., *Ontario Civil Practice Handbook — A Guide for Law Clerks and Legal Professionals* (Toronto: Butterworths, 1996)

Waddams, S.M., *Introduction to the Study of Law*, 5th ed. (Scarborough: Carswell Thomson Professional Publishing, 1997)

Williams, B., and V.A. Pylypchuk, "What's so Different About Administrative Advocacy" in *Current and Emerging Issues — Administrative and Constitutional Law* (Ottawa: Canadian Bar Association, 1993)

Wydick, R.C., *Plain English for Lawyers* (California: California Law Review Inc., 1978)

Yates, R.A., and R.W. Yates, *Canada's Legal Environment — It's History, Institutions and Principles* (Scarborough: Prentice Hall Canada Inc., 1993)

Yates, R.A., R.W. Yates, and P. Bain, *Introduction to Law in Canada*, 2nd ed. (Scarborough: Prentice Hall Allyn and Bacon Canada, 2000)

Yee, G., "Procedures in Dealing with Bias — The Adjudicator's Perspective" (1997), 3 *Administrative Agency Practice* 54

Index

Subordinate Legislation
comparison to policies and guidelines, 11-12
comparison to primary legislation, 11
defined, 11
examples of, 11, 19, 23
validity, 11